# PAGODA
# BUSINESS
# BIBLE

## Advanced

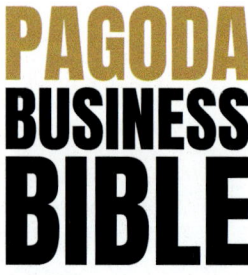

**Copyright** © 2024 by PAGODA SCS

All rights reserved. No part of this publication may be reproduced, stored in a retrieval system, or transmitted, in any form, or by any means, electronic, mechanical, photocopying, recording or otherwise, without the prior written permission of the copyright holder and the publisher.

**Published by PAGODA Books**
PAGODA Books is the professional language publishing company of the PAGODA Education Group.
19F, PAGODA Tower, 419, Gangnam-daero,
Seocho-gu, Seoul, 06614, Rep. of KOREA
www.pagodabook.com

**First published 2024
Second impression 2025
Printed in the Republic of Korea**

**ISBN   978-89-6281-920-5 (13730)**

**Publisher** | Kyung-Sil Park
**Writer**      | PAGODA Language Education Center

A defective book may be exchanged at the store where you purchased it.

# PAGODA

**Advanced**
▲ MEETING | WRITING | PRESENTATION ▲

This is
BUSINESS ENGLISH

# BUSINESS BIBLE

PAGODA Books

# 목차

## MEETING ............ 7

### Icebreaking
**1** I don't think we've met. — 008

### A Project Management Meeting
**2** Would that work for you? — 016

### Talking about Time
**3** We should be able to wrap it up in an hour. — 024

### Rescheduling
**4** Would you mind pushing back the meeting to a later time? — 032

### Small Talk
**5** What are you guys up to this weekend? — 040

### Bargaining
**6** Can you meet us halfway? — 048

### Making Suggestions
**7** Let me play the devil's advocate. — 056

### Action Plans
**8** We need to set up a timeline for completing the next phase of the project. — 064

### Delays
**9** We're behind schedule. — 072

### Progress Report
**10** How's the project coming along? — 080

### Zoom/WebEX Meeting Expressions
**11** Are we all on the same page? — 088

### Zoom/WebEX Troubleshooting
**12** I'm experiencing some major connectivity issues. — 096

**Advanced**

## WRITING ... 105

| | | |
|---|---|---|
| 1 | Requesting Progress Updates | 106 |
| 2 | Disagreeing with Someone | 114 |
| 3 | Making Urgent Requests | 122 |
| 4 | Expressing Gratitude to Someone | 130 |
| 5 | Sending a Contract and Requesting Confirmation | 138 |
| 6 | Sending a Request to Sign an NDA | 146 |
| 7 | Addressing Claims and Complaints | 154 |
| 8 | Contract Termination Notice | 162 |
| 9 | Declining Invitations | 170 |
| 10 | Responding to a Job Application | 178 |
| 11 | Sharing Policy Updates | 186 |
| 12 | Offering Condolences | 194 |

## PRESENTATION ... 203

| | | |
|---|---|---|
| 1 | Hooking Your Audience | 204 |
| 2 | Telling a Story | 212 |
| 3 | Building Anticipation | 220 |
| 4 | Describing a User Experience | 228 |
| 5 | Comparing and Contrasting | 236 |
| 6 | Indicating Importance and Priority | 244 |
| 7 | Describing a Process or Sequence | 252 |
| 8 | Talking about Finances | 260 |
| 9 | Using Analogies | 268 |
| 10 | Making a Proposal | 276 |
| 11 | Concluding a Presentation | 284 |
| 12 | Q&A Sessions | 292 |

# PAGODA
# BUSINESS
# BIBLE

Advanced

# MEETING

**Icebreaking**

# 1　I don't think we've met.

## Learning Objectives

- Learners can introduce themselves.
- Learners can ask where the other person works.
- Learners can talk about how long they've been with the company.

## Warm Up

**Work with a partner or In a group. Discuss the following questions.**

1. Do you meet people often in business situations?
2. How do you normally break the ice when you meet someone for the first time?
3. Do you feel comfortable talking about yourself?

 **Dialogue**

**Practice the dialogue with a partner.**

A: Hi! **I don't think we've met.** My name is Hanna Kim.

B: Hi, Hanna. Nice to meet you. I'm Joe Cruz. I just joined the company. I started last week, in fact.

A: Well, nice to meet you, too. And welcome to the company, Joe.

B: Thank you. It's great to be here. This is a really nice office building.

A: It sure is! **So, what department are you in?**

B: I'm in Accounting. And yourself, Hanna?

A: I'm with the Overseas Sales Team.

B: I see. **Have you been working here long?**

A: It'll be five years come December. Time flies.

B: Yeah, that's what they say. Five years? Nice.

A: How are you settling in? Is Josh over there showing you the ropes?

B: Yes, Josh is great. I'm really learning a lot.

A: Oh, I think the meeting is about to start. **Let's catch up later.**

B: Yes, let's do that.

A: 안녕하세요! **전에 뵌 적 없는 것 같은데요.** 제 이름은 Hanna Kim입니다.

B: 안녕하세요, Hanna. 만나서 반가워요. 전 Joe Cruz입니다. 막 입사했습니다. 실은 지난주부터 출근했어요.

A: 네, 저도 만나서 반가워요. 그리고 입사 환영합니다, Joe.

B: 감사합니다. 이곳에 오게 되어서 정말 기뻐요. 사옥이 참 좋아요.

A: 맞아요! **그럼 어느 부서에 계세요?**

B: 회계부에 있습니다. 그럼, 그쪽은요 Hanna?

A: 전 해외영업팀에 있어요.

B: 그렇군요. **회사에 근무한 지 오래되셨나요?**

A: 12월에 5년이 됩니다. 세월이 쏜살같아요.

B: 네, 그렇다고 하죠. 5년이요? 좋네요.

A: 잘 적응하고 계시죠? 그쪽 Josh가 요령은 잘 알려주고 있고요?

B: 네, Josh는 참 좋아요. 전 정말 많이 배우고 있어요.

A: 아, 회의가 시작될 것 같네요. **나중에 또 봬요.**

B: 네, 그렇게 하죠.

> **Comprehension Check**

**Answer the questions.**

1. What department does Joe Cruz work in?
2. How long has Hanna Kim been with the company?

## Vocabulary

**Match the words or expressions with the correct definitions.**

1. join _____
2. in fact _____
3. Overseas Sales Team _____
4. it'll be _____
5. come _____
6. settle in _____
7. show someone the ropes _____
8. be about to _____
9. catch up later _____

a. 곧 ~하려던 참이다
b. 나중에 계속 얘기하다
c. (시점이) 오면/되면
d. 입사하다
e. ~이 된다
f. ~에게 일을/업무를 가르쳐주다
g. (직장 등에) 적응하다
h. 해외영업팀
i. 사실은

### ⊕ Bonus Resources

### How do you find ~ 어때요? ~ 어떻게 생각하세요?

A: **How do you find** living in Daejeon? 대전에서의 생활 어떠세요?
B: I don't think I've been here long enough to really know.
여기 그리 오래 살지 않아서 잘 모르겠어요.

How do you find ~?는 직역하면 '~을 어떻게 찾아요?'가 되지만 일상에서는 무엇에 대한 상대방의 생각을 물을 때 쓰는 표현이다. What do you think of ~?와 유사하다.

**Grammar Points**

**Read the following and practice making sentences.**

**1. I don't think ~**

> I don't think ~ 뒤에 주어+동사가 붙을 때는 '~가 아닌 것 같네요'를 의미한다. 앞에 이미 don't라는 부정이 나온 만큼, 주어+동사는 부정형으로 쓰지 않는다는 것을 기억한다.
> 
> 📖 *I don't think* that's it. 그건 아닌 것 같은데요.

a) I don't think I _____ what that is. 그게 뭔지 모르겠는데요.

b) I don't think I _____ to know. 전 알고 싶지 않은 것 같은데요.

c) I don't think we _____ enough money. 우린 돈이 충분하지 않은 것 같아요.

**2. Let's ~ later.**

> Let's ~ later는 짧은 표현이지만 두 가지 뜻이 동시에 존재한다. 우선 '뭔가를 함께 하자', 그리고 '그걸 나중에 하자'는 뜻이 담겨 있어 회의하거나 잠깐 얘기를 나눌 때도 유용하게 사용할 수 있다.
>
> 📖 *Let's* look at that *later*. 그건 나중에 보죠.

a) Let's _____ later. 그거에 대해 나중에 얘기하죠.

b) Let's_____ for dinner later. 나중에 저녁 같이 하죠.

c) Let's _____ this later. 이건 나중에 계속 논의하죠.

---

### ✏ Write

**Make your own dialogue using the expressions from Grammar Points.**

A: _____

B: _____

A: _____

B: _____

 **Practice**

**Shadowing**

**Listen and repeat.**

1. **I don't think** we're there yet.
   **I don't think** I like the way this is going.

2. **So, what** ideas do you have?
   **So, what** projects are you working on?

3. **Have you been** going to the gym?
   **Have you been** sleeping well?

4. **Let's** come back to it **later**.
   **Let's** go grab something to eat **later**.

5. **How do you find** working for a multinational company?

**Making Sentences**

**Practice making sentences. Use the words in the parentheses or use your own. Then, read your sentences to your partner or group. After sharing your sentences, practice saying someone else's sentences.**

1. I don't think _____. (we, that, client)

2. So, what _____? (year, choice, items)

3. Have you been _____? (write, call, tell)

4. Let's _____ later. (get, go, have)

## Roleplay

**Roleplay the following scenarios with a partner. Practice and change roles.**

Scenario 1

> **Two people are meeting each other for the first time at a meeting.**
> 
> **Person 1:** say hi to Person 2 / say you don't think you've met Person 2 and introduce yourself
> 
> **Person 2:** say hi / introduce yourself

Scenario 2

> **Two people are meeting each other for the first time at a meeting.**
> 
> **Person 1:** say hi / ask what team Person 2 is in
> 
> **Person 2:** say you're in the procurement team / do some ice breaking

## Homework

**Write a short dialogue of two people meeting for the first time.**

_____

_____

**Warm Up Sample Answers**
1. (Yes, I / No, I don't) meet people often in business situations.
2. I (ask about their job / talk about the company).
3. (Yes, I / No, I don't) feel comfortable talking about myself.

**Comprehension Check Answer**
1. He works in the Accounting Department.
2. She's been with the company for almost 5 years.

**Vocabulary Answers**
1. d, 2. i, 3. h, 4. e, 5. c, 6. g, 7. f, 8. a, 9. b

**Grammar Points Answers**
1. a) know  b) want  c) have
2. a) talk about that  b) get together  c) continue discussing

**Write Sample Answer**
A: I don't think that's a good idea, Frank. I mean, we've tried that already.
B: We did. And it almost worked.
A: We spent a lot of money, though.
B: Let's talk more about this later.

**Making Sentences Sample Answers**
1. I don't think (we could finish on time / that's an issue / the client liked that).
2. So, what (year is that in / choice do we have / items can we ship)?
3. Have you been (writing it all down / calling him / telling the truth)?
4. Let's (get together / go for a walk / have a chat) later.

**Roleplay Sample Answer**
Scenario 1
Person 1: Hi. I don't think we've met. I'm Kevin Kim.
Person 2: Hi. Nice to meet you. I'm Janice Johnson.
Person 1: What department are you in?
Person 2: I'm in Consumer Products. Yourself?
Person 1: I'm in Purchasing. Let's catch up later.
Person 2: Sure!

**Homework Sample Answer**
Person 1: You're Patty? Your first day, right? I don't think we've met. I'm Seth.
Person 2: Hi, Seth. Nice to meet you.
Person 1: Nice to meet you, too.
Person 2: So, what department are you in?
Person 1: I'm in Marketing. How do you find working here so far?
Person 2: I love it so far. Have you been with the company long?
Person 1: Three years now. It looks like the meeting is starting soon. Let's catch up later.

**Meeting Tip**

# How to Break the Ice
어색한 분위기를 깨는 방법

**① Go for it.** 일단 해본다.

Be the first one to break the ice. Approach people and start talking.
먼저 나서서 어색한 분위기를 깨 본다. 사람들에게 다가가서 말을 걸어 본다.

**② Find a mutual interest.** 공통 관심사를 찾는다.

Try to find an interest that both of you share. It can be sports, movies, TV shows, music, books, travel, etc. Make sure it's a light subject.
둘 다 공통으로 관심이 있는 무언가를 찾는다. 스포츠나 영화, TV 프로그램, 음악, 책, 여행 등이 될 수 있다. 가벼운 주제여야 한다는 것을 잊지 않는다.

**③ Compliment, but be careful.** 칭찬하되 조심한다.

Find something about the person to compliment, such as what they're wearing. Of course, you should avoid anything that involves the body.
상대방이 입고 있는 옷과 같이 칭찬할 만한 것을 찾아본다. 물론 신체에 관한 것은 피해야 한다.

**④ Don't be distracted.** 산만해지지 않는다.

Give that person your full focus. If you look distracted, the other person will see you as insincere.
상대방에게 집중한다. 산만해 보이면 상대방은 나를 무성의한 사람으로 간주한다.

**⑤ Ask them questions.** 질문한다.

People like talking about themselves. So, ask questions.
사람들은 자신들에 관해 얘기하는 걸 좋아한다. 그러니 질문한다.

## 2 — A Project Management Meeting
# Would that work for you?

## Learning Objectives

- Learners can discuss managing a project.
- Learners can get participants to volunteer to take the lead on tasks or deliverables.
- Learners can offer to take the lead on tasks or deliverables.

## Warm Up

**Work with a partner or in a group. Discuss the following questions.**
1. Do you attend many project progress meetings?
2. Have you ever volunteered to take on a task or a deliverable?
3. Why might it be better to have people volunteer rather than be assigned to tasks?

## Dialogue

**Practice the dialogue with a partner.**

A: **We have a number of key deliverables.** I'll need volunteers to take the lead on each of them. Okay, first, we need someone to work with the designers on the packaging.

B: Are you talking about giving them the design ideas we have?

A: Yes, and that person should also come up with some new design ideas. Do you want to take it on?

B: Sure. **I'd be happy to take it on.**

A: That's great, Will. I was thinking you're the right person for the job. Second, I need someone to fly to San Diego and interview the subs.

C: I'll take the lead on that.

A: Fantastic, Linda. **I believe you've been to San Diego a few times before.**

C: Yes, I have. I'll need an engineer to go with me, though.

A: Fred is all geared up to go. He's already familiar with the project. **Would that work for you?**

C: That'll work.

A: 완성해야 할 핵심 결과물 몇 가지가 있습니다. 각각 담당할 지원자가 필요합니다. 자, 먼저, 디자이너들과 포장지 작업을 함께 할 사람이 필요해요.
B: 우리가 가진 아이디어들을 주는 걸 말씀하시는 건가요?
A: 맞아요. 그리고 그분은 새로운 디자인 아이디어들도 제시해야 합니다. 하시겠어요?
B: 좋습니다. **제가 하겠습니다.**
A: 잘됐네요, Will. 당신이 그 일의 적임자라고 생각하고 있었어요. 두 번째는 San Diego로 가서 하청업체들을 인터뷰할 사람이 필요해요.
C: 그건 제가 맡겠습니다.
A: 아주 좋아요, Linda. **San Diego에 몇 번 갔던 걸로 알고 있어요.**
C: 네, 갔었습니다. 근데 저와 함께 갈 엔지니어가 필요해요.
A: Fred가 만반의 준비를 갖추었어요. 이미 이 프로젝트에 대해 잘 알고 있고요. **괜찮겠어요?**
C: 좋습니다.

### ✓ Comprehension Check

**Answer the questions.**

1. How is the leader getting people to take on each deliverable?
2. What kind of specialist does Linda need to go with her to San Diego?

## Vocabulary

**Match the words or expressions with the correct definitions.**

1. key _____
2. deliverable _____
3. take the lead _____
4. packaging _____
5. come up with _____
6. the right person _____
7. though _____
8. gear up _____
9. be familiar with _____

a. 그렇지만
b. (완성해야 할) 결과물
c. 리드하다, 이끌다
d. 포장
e. 적임자
f. 핵심
g. ~을 제시하다
h. ~을 잘 알다, ~에 익숙하다
i. 준비를 갖추다

### ⊕ Bonus Resources

**right up one's alley** 딱 ~의 전문

A: I'll take care of that. 제가 처리할게요.
B: Yes, it's **right up your alley**. 그래요, 딱 당신의 전문 분야입니다.

one's alley는 '~의 골목'으로 직역되는데, 아무래도 자기가 사는 골목이면 그곳을 아주 잘 알 수밖에 없다. right up one's alley는 어떤 것이 '~의 전문 분야'라는 뜻이다.

# Grammar Points

**Read the following and practice making sentences.**

1. I believe you've ~

> I believe you've ~는 '당신이 ~을 했다고 알고 있다'라는 패턴이다. I believe는 원래 '나는 ~을 믿는다'라는 뜻으로 많이 쓰이지만 여기서는 '나는 ~라고 알고 있다'로, '확신한다'가 아니라 '사실일 거라고 여기다'에 가깝다.
>
> 📖 *I believe you've had a meeting with them.* 당신이 그들과 회의를 한 걸로 알고 있어요.

a) I believe you've _____. 당신이 보고서를 끝낸 걸로 알고 있어요.

b) I believe you've _____ for a while. 당신이 이것에 대해 한동안 알고 있던 걸로 알고 있어요.

c) I believe you've _____ the supplier. 당신이 납품업체와 이미 얘기한 걸로 알고 있어요.

2. Would that ~?

> Would that ~?은 '그게 ~할까요?'를 물을 때 쓰는 패턴이다. 뒤에 동사원형이 붙는다.
>
> 📖 *Would that be all right?* 그게 괜찮을까요?

a) Would that _____ a problem? 그게 문제를 일으킬까요?

b) Would that _____ rude? 그게 무례할까요?

c) Would that _____ the requirement? 그게 요구 사항을 충족시킬까요?

---

### ✍ Write

**Make your own dialogue using the expressions from Grammar Points.**

A: _____

B: _____

A: _____

B: _____

 **Practice**

**Shadowing**

**Listen and repeat.**

1. **We have** some issues to address.
   **We have** no way of knowing.

2. **I'd be happy to** take a look.
   **I'd be happy to** speak at the event.

3. **I believe you've** seen this before.
   **I believe you've** been to China before.

4. **Would that** take care of the cost?
   **Would that** save the account?

5. That's **right up your alley**, isn't it?

**Making Sentences**

Practice making sentences. Use the words in the parentheses or use your own. Then, read your sentences to your partner or group. After sharing your sentences, practice saying someone else's sentences.

1. We have _____. (no, some, two)

2. I'd be happy to _____. (wait, go, write)

3. I believe you've _____. (tried, seen, met)

4. Would that _____? (work, create, be)

## Roleplay

**Roleplay the following scenarios with a partner. Practice and change roles.**

Scenario 1

**Two people are discussing a problem at a meeting.**

**Person 1:** say you have some problems with a company regarding delivery / ask if Person 2 could talk to the CEO of the company and if that would be all right

**Person 2:** say you'd be happy to talk to the CEO

Scenario 2

**Two people are talking about product samples at a meeting.**

**Person 1:** tell Person 2 you will need samples

**Person 2:** say Bill will send the samples / ask if that works

## Homework

**Write a short dialogue of people discussing some key deliverables at a meeting.**

_____
_____

### Warm Up Sample Answers
1. (Yes, I / No, I don't) attend many project progress meetings. / No, I've never attended one.
2. (Yes, I have / No, I haven't) volunteered. / Yes, I often volunteer to take on tasks or deliverables.
3. It might be better because people can (have more ownership / choose ones they like).

### Comprehension Check Answers
1. The leader is asking for volunteers to lead them.
2. She needs an engineer to go with her.

### Vocabulary Answers
1. f, 2. b, 3. c, 4. d, 5. g, 6. e, 7. a, 8. i, 9. h

### Grammar Points Answers
1. a) finished the report  b) known about this  c) already talked to
2. a) create/cause  b) be  c) meet

### Write Sample Answer
A: I believe you've seen the drawings already.
B: I have, but I'd like to take a look at them again. Would that be all right?
A: Of course. Here you go.
B: Thanks. I have to say I really like these drawings.

### Making Sentences Sample Answers
1. We have (no idea who that is / some resources / two volunteers for this job).
2. I'd be happy to (wait for you / go now / write the report).
3. I believe you've (tried bulgogi before / all seen this / already met John).
4. Would that (work / create problems / be enough)?

### Roleplay Sample Answer
Scenario 1
Person 1: We have some problems with Acme Inc. regarding delivery.
Person 2: I believe you've had problems with them before.
Person 1: Yes, I have. You know the CEO, don't you?
Person 2: Yeah. I know him really well.
Person 1: Maybe you could talk to him? Would that be all right?
Person 2: Sure. I'd be happy to do that for you.

### Homework Sample Answer
Person 1: We have a number of key deliverables. Who can take care of Item 1?
Person 2: I'll take the lead on that. It's right up my alley.
Person 1: Great. How about Item 2?
Person 3: I'd be happy to take it on. I'll also take Item 3. Would that work for you?
Person 1: That'll be great. I believe you've done something similar to Item 3 before.

**Meeting Tip**

# Get Going on These Effective Project Management Tips
프로젝트 관리 팁 활용하기

There are many tips and strategies for managing projects effectively. Let's take a look at just four tips that start with "Get."
프로젝트를 효율적으로 관리할 수 있는 팁과 전략은 많다. 여기서는 Get으로 시작하는 네 가지 팁만 살펴보자.

① **Get the goal straight.** 목표를 명확하게 한다.

Effective project execution starts with communicating the goals of the project to your team members. Also share the goals with others who have a stake in the success of the project.
효율적인 프로젝트 실행은 팀원들에게 프로젝트 목표를 알리는 것으로 시작된다. 프로젝트 성공에 이해관계가 있는 다른 이들에게도 목표를 공유한다.

② **Get agreement.** 동의를 얻는다.

Agree with the stakeholders on the timing of progress reports, key deliverables, and any milestones.
진행 보고서와 완성해야 할 핵심 결과물, 주요 단계 등에 대해 이해관계자들과 합의한다.

③ **Get the right team together.** 적절한 팀을 구성한다.

Creating a solid team is crucial to the success of the project. The right skills are important but so are people's personalities and attitudes. Teamwork requires collaboration and an environment that is supportive.
프로젝트 성공을 위해 튼튼한 팀을 만드는 건 필수이다. 적합한 기술도 중요하지만, 사람들의 성격과 태도 역시 중요하다. 팀워크는 협력과 서로에게 힘이 되는 환경을 요구한다.

④ **Get good at managing your time.** 시간 관리 능력을 갖춘다.

Control your day. Manage your time in a productive way, both individually and as a team.
나의 하루를 통제한다. 나의 개인적인 시간은 물론, 팀의 시간 역시 생산적으로 관리한다.

## 3 Talking about Time
# We should be able to wrap it up in an hour.

### Learning Objectives

- Learners can talk about specific durations.
- Learners can ask how long a meeting will take.
- Learners can explain why they might need to leave earlier.

### Warm Up

**Work with a partner or in a group. Discuss the following questions.**

1. On average, how long do your meetings last?
2. In your opinion, how long should most meetings take?
3. If you need to leave early, what do you do?

 ## Dialogue

**Practice the dialogue with a partner.**

A: Let's take a look at the agenda. Jeff is taking the minutes today.

B: Sorry, May. How long do you think this meeting will last?

A: **This won't take long.** We just have two items to discuss. **We should be able to wrap it up in an hour.**

B: Oh, an hour?

A: Is there some place you need to be?

B: **I'm running late for another meeting.**

A: Oh, you have that meeting with the consultant. You're supposed to discuss the new project in London.

B: Yeah, that's the one. My manager can start without me, but I should probably be there.

A: Why don't you go now, Ian? I'll send you the minutes.

B: That'll be great. Thanks.

A: **Could I have a quick word with you around 3?** I just need a few minutes. It's about another project.

B: Sure. That'd be fine. I'll drop by your office at 3.

---

A: 의제를 봅시다. 오늘 회의록은 Jeff가 작성합니다.

B: 죄송해요, May. 이 회의가 얼마나 걸릴 것 같나요?

A: 오래 안 걸릴 겁니다. 논의할 건 두 안건뿐이에요. 1시간 안에 끝낼 수 있을 거예요.

B: 아, 1시간이요?

A: 어디 가야 할 곳이 있나요?

B: 다른 회의에 늦을 것 같아서요.

A: 아, 그 컨설턴트와 회의가 있죠. London에 있는 새 프로젝트에 대해 논의하기로 되어 있죠.

B: 네, 그거 맞아요. 제 매니저가 저 없이 시작할 수는 있지만, 그래도 제가 있어야 할 듯해서요.

A: 지금 가시죠, Ian? 회의록을 보내 드릴게요.

B: 그러면 정말 좋죠. 고마워요.

A: 3시 정도에 잠깐 얘기 좀 할 수 있을까요? 몇 분이면 돼요. 다른 프로젝트 관련입니다.

B: 물론이죠. 좋습니다. 3시에 그쪽 사무실에 들를게요.

### ✓ Comprehension Check

**Answer the questions.**

1. Does May think the meeting will last more than an hour?
2. Why does Ian have to leave early?

# Vocabulary

**Match the words or expressions with the correct definitions.**

1. agenda _____
2. take the minutes _____
3. take long _____
4. items to discuss _____
5. wrap up _____
6. run late _____
7. that's the one _____
8. have a quick word _____
9. drop by _____

a. 의제
b. 늦다
c. 회의록을 작성하다
d. 잠깐 들르다
e. 그거 맞다
f. 오래 걸리다
g. 잠깐 얘기하다
h. 논의할 안건들
i. 마무리하다, 끝내다

### ⊕ Bonus Resources

**get a move on** 빨리하다, 서두르다

A: Let's **get a move on**. I'm running late.  우리 서두릅시다. 제가 늦을 것 같아요.
B: Don't worry. This won't take very long.  걱정하지 마세요. 오래 안 걸릴 겁니다.

get a move on은 어떤 일을 진행하기 위해 다른 사람들을 재촉할 때 쓰며, '빨리하다, 서두르다'를 의미한다. 유사한 표현인 get rolling을 쓰는 경우도 많다.

# Grammar Points

**Read the following and practice making sentences.**

1. We should be able to ~

> We should be able to ~는 '~을 할 수 있을 것이다'인데, '~을 할 수 있다'를 뜻하는 be able to 앞에 should를 붙이면서 상황이 달라질 수 있는 여지를 남겨 놓는 것이다.
> 
> *We should be able to manage that.* 그건 해낼 수 있을 겁니다.

a) We should be able to _____. 우리 목표에 도달할 수 있을 겁니다.

b) We should be able to _____ by 6. 6시까지는 집에 도착할 수 있을 겁니다.

c) We should be able to _____. 그건 할 수 있을 겁니다.


2. I'm running late for ~

> I'm running late for ~는 '~에 늦을 것 같다'를 뜻한다. 시계가 작동하는 것도 run이라고 하는데, 시계가 '늦게 가고 있다'를 의미하는 running late를 비유해서 나온 표현이다.
> 
> *I'm running late for a meeting with a client.* 고객과의 회의에 늦을 것 같은데요.

a) I'm running late for an _____. 중요한 세미나에 늦을 것 같은데요.

b) I'm running late for my _____. 제 치과 진료 약속에 늦을 것 같은데요.

c) I'm running late for my _____. 이사님과의 저녁 식사에 늦을 것 같은데요.


### ⊘ Write

**Make your own dialogue using the expressions from Grammar Points.**

A: _____

B: _____

A: _____

B: _____

 **Practice**

**Shadowing**

**Listen and repeat.**

1. **This won't** look good.
   **This won't** be easy.

2. **We should be able to** make that happen.
   **We should be able to** convince them.

3. **I'm running late for** work.
   **I'm running late for** a meeting with a vendor.

4. **Could I** take that?
   **Could I** ask you not to do that?

5. We need to **get a move on**.

**Making Sentences**

**Practice making sentences. Use the words in the parentheses or use your own. Then, read your sentences to your partner or group. After sharing your sentences, practice saying someone else's sentences.**

1. This won't _____. (take, be, make)

2. We should be able to _____. (get, start)

3. I'm running late for _____. (meeting, lunch)

4. Could I _____? (tell, ask, sit)

 ## Roleplay

**Roleplay the following scenarios with a partner. Practice and change roles.**

Scenario 1

> **Some people are in a meeting that is about to start.**
> **Person 1:** say the meeting will wrap up in two hours
> **Person 2:** say you're running late for a meeting with the director / ask if you can leave early

Scenario 2

> **Some people are in a meeting that is about to start.**
> **Person 1:** say you're running late for another meeting in an hour / ask how long this meeting will take
> **Person 2:** say it'll wrap up in an hour / say Person 1 can leave early

 ## Homework

**Write a short dialogue of two people talking about time during a meeting.**

_____

_____

### Warm Up Sample Answers
1. Most meetings I attend last (an hour / 2 hours / more than 2 hours). / It depends on the meeting.
2. I think most meetings should take (an hour / 2 hours / less than an hour).
3. I tell the leader beforehand. / I just leave quietly.

### Comprehension Check Answers
1. No, May thinks the meeting will finish in an hour.
2. Because he is running late for another meeting.

### Vocabulary Answers
1. a, 2. c, 3. f, 4. h, 5. i, 6. b, 7. e, 8. g, 9. d

### Grammar Points Answers
1. a) reach our (target/goal)  b) get home  c) do that
2. a) important seminar  b) dental appointment  c) dinner with the director

### Write Sample Answer
A: Could I ask you to finish by 2?
B: We should be able to finish by then. Do you have to go somewhere?
A: I'm running late for another meeting.
B: I see. Let's start then.

### Making Sentences Sample Answers
1. This won't (take 2 hours / be a long meeting / make it right).
2. We should be able to (get an approval / start next week).
3. I'm running late for (the project meeting / my lunch with the team).
4. Could I (tell you later / ask him directly / sit in the back)?

### Roleplay Sample Answer
Scenario 1
Person 1: Let's get started.
Person 2: I'm running late for a meeting with a director.
Person 1: We should be able to wrap it up in 2 hours.
Person 2: Could I leave early?
Person 1: That's fine. I'll send you the minutes.
Person 2: That'll be great. Thank you.

### Homework Sample Answer
Person 1: This won't take long. We should be able to wrap it up in an hour. Sam, could I have a quick word with you after the meeting?
Person 2: I'm running late for another meeting. I need to get a move on. Can we talk later?
Person 1: Sure. I'll call you.

**Meeting Tip**

# Time Management Questions and Tips
시간 관리 질문과 팁

### ① Are my goals achievable? 목표는 달성 가능한가?

Goals should be achievable. They should also be measurable.
목표는 달성할 수 있어야 한다. 더불어 측정할 수 있어야 한다.

### ② Which tasks are important? 어떤 업무가 중요한가?

All tasks are not equal. Decide which are urgent and which are important.
모든 업무는 동등하지 않다. 어떤 것이 시급하고 어떤 것이 중요한지 정한다.

### ③ How long will each task take? 각 업무는 얼마나 걸리는가?

Don't just work on a task without considering how long it will take. Setting a time for each task will help you focus better.
시간이 얼마나 걸릴지 고려하지 않고 무작정 일을 하지 않는다. 업무마다 소요 시간을 정하면 집중력을 높일 수 있다.

### ④ What should I do each day? 매일 어떤 업무를 해야 하는가?

Decide on what tasks you will work on each day. At the end of the day, review what was done and what should be done the following day.
매일 어떤 업무를 진행할지 정한다. 하루 일이 끝날 때 무엇을 했는지, 그리고 다음 날 무엇을 할지 검토한다.

## 4 Rescheduling

# Would you mind pushing back the meeting to a later time?

##  Learning Objectives

- Learners can talk about rescheduling meetings.
- Learners can ask to move up or push back meetings.
- Learners can thank or apologize to others for a schedule change.

##  Warm Up

**Work with a partner or in a group. Discuss the following questions.**

1. How often do your meetings get rescheduled?
2. What are some reasons for people to reschedule meetings?
3. In your opinion, what days are best for meetings?

## Dialogue

**Practice the dialogue with a partner.**

A: Ben! Wait up! I'm glad I caught you before you left.
B: Hi, Anna. What's up?
A: You know the meeting with your team on Wednesday?
B: We're meeting at 4 P.M., right?
A: Yes, but the CEO wants to see me at 4.
B: Okay. **Thanks for letting me know in advance. Let's move up the meeting to 1 P.M.**
A: **Would you mind pushing back the meeting to a later time?**
B: Sure. What time?
A: How about 5 P.M.? Would that be too late?
B: No, no. That'll be fine. 5 P.M. it is. I'll let everyone know.
A: Thank you so much, Ben. **I'm sorry for the inconvenience.**
B: Not a problem. I'll see you at 5.
A: Yes, see you then.

A: Ben! 기다려요! 나가시기 전에 만날 수 있어서 다행이네요.
B: 안녕하세요, Anna. 무슨 일이죠?
A: 수요일 그쪽 팀과 할 회의 아시죠?
B: 오후 4시에 만나는 거 맞죠?
A: 네, 그런데 CEO께서 저를 4시에 보자고 하시네요.
B: 그래요. 미리 알려주셔서 고마워요. 오후 1시로 회의를 앞당기죠.
A: 회의를 나중으로 늦출 수 있을까요?
B: 그러죠. 몇 시로요?
A: 오후 5시 어때요? 너무 늦나요?
B: 아뇨, 아뇨. 괜찮습니다. 오후 5시로 하죠. 모두에게 알릴게요.
A: 정말 고마워요, Ben. **번거롭게 해드려서 죄송하네요.**
B: 괜찮습니다. 5시에 봬요.
A: 네, 그때 봬요.

### ✓ Comprehension Check

**Answer the questions.**

1. Why did they reschedule the meeting?
2. What time do Ben and Anna agree to meet?

 **Vocabulary**

**Match the words or expressions with the correct definitions.**

1. wait up _____
2. catch (someone) _____
3. What's up? _____
4. let (someone) know _____
5. in advance _____
6. move up _____
7. push back _____
8. a later time _____
9. inconvenience _____

a. 기다리다
b. 늦추다, 미루다
c. ~에게 알리다
d. 번거로움, 불편
e. 무슨 일이죠?
f. ~를 만나다
g. 앞당기다
h. 미리
i. 나중, 더 늦은

⊕ **Bonus Resources**

### heads-up 미리 알림

A: The meeting is going to be postponed. 회의가 미루어질 겁니다.
B: Okay. Thanks for the **heads-up**. 알았어요. 미리 알려 주셔서 감사합니다.

heads-up은 '미리 알림'으로, '~에게 (뭔가를 준비할 수 있도록) 미리 알리다'를 의미하는 give ~ heads-up 패턴도 쓰기도 한다. 야구 같은 스포츠에서 정신을 똑바로 차리고 머리를 들어 공을 주시하는 것에서 유래되었다.

**Grammar Points**

**Read the following and practice making sentences.**

1. **Would you mind + ~ing?**

> Would you mind + ~ing?는 '~하시겠어요?'라고 정중하게 물을 때 쓰는 패턴이다. Would you mind 대신 Do you mind를 사용할 수도 있다.
> 
> *Would you mind taking this?* 이거 가져가시겠어요?

   a) Would you mind _____? Mindy와 얘기하시겠어요?
   b) Would you mind _____? 조용히 좀 해주시겠어요?
   c) Would you mind _____? John과 일할 수 있으세요?

2. **I'm sorry for ~**

> I'm sorry for ~는 '~에 대해 죄송합니다'라고 가볍게 사과할 때 쓰기 좋은 패턴이다. 격식 없는 상황에서는 I'm 없이 그저 Sorry for ~를 사용해도 무방하다.
> 
> *I'm sorry for the mix-up.* 혼란스럽게 해드려 죄송합니다.

   a) I'm sorry for _____. 착오가 있어 죄송합니다.
   b) I'm sorry for _____. 기다리게 해드려서 죄송합니다.
   c) I'm sorry for _____. 너무 늦게 답변드려서 죄송합니다.

---

### ✏ Write

**Make your own dialogue using the expressions from Grammar Points.**

A: _____
B: _____
A: _____
B: _____

 **Practice**

**Shadowing**

**Listen and repeat.**

1. **Thanks for** gett**ing** that done.
   **Thanks for** allow**ing** me to attend the seminar.

2. **Let's** take it slow.
   **Let's** delay the launch.

3. **Would you mind** do**ing** something about this?
   **Would you mind** contact**ing** their supervisor?

4. **I'm sorry for** the error on the bill.
   **I'm sorry for** the delay.

5. I'll give you a **heads-up** when I hear something.

**Making Sentences**

**Practice making sentences. Use the words in the parentheses or use your own. Then, read your sentences to your partner or group. After sharing your sentences, practice saying someone else's sentences.**

1. Thanks for _____. (work, offer)

2. Let's _____. (do, move, get)

3. Would you mind _____? (start, move, wait)

4. I'm sorry for _____. (mistake, not telling, texting)

## Roleplay

**Roleplay the following scenarios with a partner. Practice and change roles.**

Scenario 1

> **Two people are talking about pushing back a meeting.**
> **Person 1:** ask Person 2 to push back the meeting to Friday / say you're sorry for the inconvenience
> **Person 2:** offer to push it back to Friday 3 P.M.

Scenario 2

> **Two people are talking about rescheduling a meeting.**
> **Person 1:** ask if Person 2 can reschedule the meeting / say you're sorry for the short notice
> **Person 2:** offer to move back the meeting to Friday

## Homework

**Write a short dialogue of two people talking about rescheduling a meeting.**

_____
_____

### Warm Up Sample Answers
1. My meetings (often / don't) get rescheduled.
2. They (have another meeting / have to attend to an urgent task).
3. I think the best days for meetings are Mondays and Wednesdays.

### Comprehension Check Answers
1. Anna has a meeting with the CEO at 4.
2. They agree to meet at 5 P.M.

### Vocabulary Answers
1. a, 2. f, 3. e, 4. c, 5. h, 6. g, 7. b, 8. i, 9. d

### Grammar Points Answers
1. a) talking to Mindy  b) keeping it down  c) working with John
2. a) the error  b) making you wait  c) replying so late

### Write Sample Answer
A: You know our meeting tomorrow? Would you mind meeting earlier?
B: Sure. Let's meet at 11.
A: 11 sounds good. I'm sorry for the short notice.
B: No worries.

### Making Sentences Sample Answers
1. Thanks for (working with us / offering us the project).
2. Let's (do that some other time / move on to the next item / get it done).
3. Would you mind (starting now / moving the chairs / waiting a few weeks)?
4. I'm sorry for (the mistake / not telling you sooner / texting you so late).

### Roleplay Sample Answer
Scenario 1
Person 1: Can we push back the meeting to Friday?
Person 2: Sure. Let's push it back to Friday 3 P.M.
Person 1: Would you mind pushing it back to 5 P.M.?
Person 2: Yes, that's fine.
Person 1: I'm sorry for the inconvenience.
Person 2: Not a problem.

### Homework Sample Answer
Person 1: I don't think I can attend our meeting tomorrow morning. I have to meet a client at 11 A.M.
Person 2: Thanks for letting me know in advance. Let's move up the meeting to 9 A.M.
Person 1: Would you mind pushing back the meeting to a later time? Late afternoon would be better. I'm sorry for the inconvenience.
Person 2: Okay. How about 4 P.M.?
Person 1: That would be perfect.
Person 2: Okay. Again, thanks for the heads-up.

**Meeting Tip**

## Pros and Cons of Most Popular Calendar Apps You Can Use to Schedule Meetings
회의 일정을 위해 쓸 수 있는 가장 인기 많은 캘린더 앱의 장단점

### ① MS Outlook Calendar MS 아웃룩 캘린더

**PROS:** It's free and works with other MS products. For existing MS users, it's easy to use.
**CONS:** It's doesn't work well with other calendar services.

장점: 무료이며 다른 MS 제품들과 연결이 가능하다. 기존 MS 제품 사용자에게는 사용하기 편리하다.
단점: 다른 캘린더 서비스와의 연결이 쉽지 않다.

### ② Google Calendar 구글 캘린더

**PROS:** It's free and works with other Google products. It also works well with other calendar services.
**CONS:** If you use another e-mail service, it's not compatible with Google Calendar.

장점: 무료이며 다른 구글 제품들과 연결이 가능하다. 다른 캘린더 서비스와도 연결이 잘 된다.
단점: 다른 이메일 서비스를 쓰면 구글 캘린더와 호환이 되지 않는다.

### ③ Calendar 캘린더

**PROS:** It has many features, including scheduling and calendar features.
**CONS:** The free plan is very limited, and it can be fairly expensive to use the paid plan.

장점: 스케줄링과 캘린더를 포함한 기능이 다양하다.
단점: 무료 플랜은 매우 제한적이며 유료 플랜은 꽤 비쌀 수 있다.

### ④ Fantastical 판타스티컬

**PROS:** It has a very nice design with many features and options.
**CONS:** It only works with Apple products. While it has a free version, you need the paid version to get the premium features.

장점: 많은 기능과 옵션이 있으며 디자인이 세련됐다.
단점: 애플 제품과만 호환된다. 무료 버전이 있지만 유료 버전을 써야만 프리미엄 기능들을 얻을 수 있다.

### ⑤ Apple Calendar 애플 캘린더

**PROS:** It's free and integrates well with other Apple products. It has a clean, easy-to-use design.
**CONS:** It does not work with Android and Windows systems.

장점: 무료이며 다른 애플 제품과 호환이 좋다. 깔끔하고 사용하기 쉬운 디자인을 지니고 있다.
단점: 안드로이드나 윈도우 시스템과 연결이 되지 않는다.

**Small Talk**

# 5 What are you guys up to this weekend?

## Learning Objectives

- **Learners can greet people they already know.**
- **Learners can make small talk.**
- **Learners can talk about their plans for the weekend.**

## Warm Up

**Work with a partner or in a group. Discuss the following questions.**

1. Are you good at making small talk?
2. What do you usually talk about when you meet some business associates?
3. What are some things you do on the weekend?

 **Dialogue**

**Practice the dialogue with a partner.**

A: Jeff. Alan. It's really good to see you guys.
B: Yeah, it's good to see you, too, Matt.
C: Hey, Matt. It's been a while.
A: It sure has. **I didn't expect to run into you guys at this meeting.**
B: We might be supplying some materials for the new project. You've been working out? You look really fit.
A: Thanks. Yeah, I've been going to the gym lately. How's business going for you guys?
B: **There's always a lot to do.** The work never seems to end.
A: I know what you mean. There's always so much work, right? You finish one task, and then there's another one waiting just around the corner.
B: Well, at least the weekend's coming up.
A: Right. **What are you guys up to this weekend?**
B: **I'm planning on taking my kids to the beach.**
C: I'm helping a friend move. You?
A: Unfortunately, I have to catch up on some work.

A: Jeff, Alan. 정말 반갑네요.
B: 그래요, Matt. 저도 반가워요.
C: 안녕하세요, Matt. 오랜만이네요.
A: 그러네요. **이 회의에서 우연히 만날 거라고는 예상 못 했네요.**
B: 새 프로젝트에 자재를 납품할 수도 있어서요. 운동하시나요? 건강해 보이세요.
A: 고마워요. 네, 요즘 헬스장을 다니고 있어요. 하는 일들은 잘 되고 있어요?
B: **늘 할 일은 많죠.** 일은 결코 끝이 없는 것 같아요.
A: 무슨 말인지 알아요. 늘 할 일이 많죠, 그렇죠? 업무를 하나 끝내면 하나 더 코앞에서 기다리고 있잖아요.
B: 뭐, 그래도 금방 주말입니다.
A: 그러게요. **이번 주말에 뭐 하세요?**
B: **저는 아이들 데리고 바닷가에 갈 계획입니다.**
C: 저는 친구 이사하는 거 돕습니다. 당신은요?
A: 안타깝게도 밀린 일을 해야 해요.

### ✓ Comprehension Check

**Answer the questions.**

1. What didn't Matt expect?
2. What are Jeff and Alan doing this weekend?

##  Vocabulary

**Match the words or expressions with the correct definitions.**

1. a while _____
2. run into _____
3. work out _____
4. a lot _____
5. never _____
6. just around the corner _____
7. be coming up _____
8. be planning on _____
9. catch up on _____

a. ~이 다가오다
b. ~을 계획하고 있다
c. 운동하다
d. 꽤 됨
e. 코 앞에 있는, 임박한
f. 절대 ~아니다, 절대 ~없다
g. 많은
h. ~와 우연히 만나다
i. ~를 따라잡다

### ⊕ Bonus Resources

**be into**  ~을 매우 좋아하다, ~에 빠지다

A: What are you doing on Saturday? 토요일에 뭐 하세요?
B: I'm going cycling. **I'm** really **into** it these days.
자전거 타러 가요. 요즘 그거에 푹 빠졌어요.

'~에 빠지다'로 직역되는 be into는 취미나 관심사, 특정 사람을 매우 좋아한다고 말할 때 광범위하게 쓸 수 있는 표현이다.

**Grammar Points**

**Read the following and practice making sentences.**

**1. I didn't expect to ~**

> I didn't expect to ~는 '~할 거라고는 생각 못 했다'를 뜻한다. 나에게 벌어진 예상치 못한 일에 하소연할 때, 기분 좋게 놀랐을 때도 간단하게 쓸 수 있는 표현이다.
> 
> 📖 *I didn't expect to see Angela there.* 거기서 Angela를 볼 거라고는 생각 못 했어요.

a) I didn't expect to _____ from you so soon.
   당신으로부터 이렇게 빨리 회답이 올 거라고는 예상 못 했습니다.

b) I didn't expect to _____ the party. 파티에 초대받을 거라고는 예상 못 했습니다.

c) I didn't expect to _____ this. 이걸 듣고 있게 될 거라고는 예상 못 했습니다.

**2. I'm planning on + ~ing**

> I'm planning on + ~ing는 '~을 할 계획이다'를 뜻한다. 유사한 표현인 I plan to ~를 사용할 수도 있다.
> 
> 📖 *I'm planning on working from home.* 집에서 일할 계획입니다.

a) I'm planning on _____ tomorrow. 내일 그녀에게 얘기할 계획입니다.

b) I'm planning on _____ by next month. 다음 달까지 마칠 계획입니다.

c) I'm planning on _____. 그렇게 할 계획입니다.

---

### ✏ Write

**Make your own dialogue using the expressions from Grammar Points.**

A: _____

B: _____

A: _____

B: _____

 **Practice**

**Shadowing**

**Listen and repeat.**

1. **I didn't expect to** see that.
   **I didn't expect to** have this much fun.

2. **There's** no one there.
   **There's** something I need to tell you.

3. **What are you** up to?
   **What are you** going to do?

4. **I'm planning on** watch**ing** some movies.
   **I'm planning on** go**ing** out to dinner with my family.

5. I've **been into** golf lately.

**Making Sentences**

Practice making sentences. Use the words in the parentheses or use your own. Then, read your sentences to your partner or group. After sharing your sentences, practice saying someone else's sentences.

1. I didn't expect to _____. (be, get, see)

2. There's _____. (time, Joey)

3. What are you _____? (work on, tell, have)

4. I'm planning on _____. (stay, go, do)

 ## Roleplay

**Roleplay the following scenarios with a partner. Practice and change roles.**

Scenario 1

> **Two people are talking about their vacation plans.**
> **Person 1:** ask what Person 2 is doing for vacation
> **Person 2:** say you're planning on going to Bali

Scenario 2

> **Two people are talking about the weekend.**
> **Person 1:** ask what Person 2 is up to this weekend
> **Person 2:** say you're planning to go to Busan / say there's a lot to do there and give examples

 ## Homework

**Write a short dialogue of people talking about work and the weekend.**

_____

_____

### Warm Up Sample Answers
1. (I think / I don't think) I'm good at making small talk.
2. I usually talk about (my company / their company / our company / our past projects together).
3. I (sometimes / usually) (sleep / watch Netflix / catch up on reading / go out with my family / see some friends).

### Comprehension Check Answers
1. He didn't expect to run into Jeff and Alan at the meeting.
2. One is taking his kids to the beach, and the other is helping a friend move.

### Vocabulary Answers
1. d, 2. h, 3. c, 4. g, 5. f, 6. e, 7. a, 8. b, 9. i

### Grammar Points Answers
1. a) hear back  b) be invited to  c) be listening to
2. a) talking to her  b) finishing it  c) doing that

### Write Sample Answer
A: How's work these days?
B: Good. I'm planning on transferring to the Singapore branch next year.
A: Wow. That must be nice.
B: It sure is. I didn't expect to get a chance like that.

### Making Sentences Sample Answers
1. I didn't expect to (be here on time / get a headache / see so many people).
2. There's (no time for that / Joey getting into his car).
3. What are you (working on lately / telling me / having for dinner tonight)?
4. I'm planning on (just staying home this weekend / going to Saipan this summer / doing nothing for a while).

### Roleplay Sample Answer
Scenario 1
Person 1: What are you doing for vacation?
Person 2: I'm planning on going to Bali. I didn't expect to be going there, but my wife insisted.
Person 1: There's a lot of fun things to do there.
Person 2: Really? This'll be my first time.
Person 1: You'll love it. I hope you have fun!
Person 2: I'm sure I will.

### Homework Sample Answer
Person 1: I didn't expect to run into you guys here. How's business going for you guys?
Person 2: Busy, busy, busy. There's always a lot to do.
Person 1: Same here. What are you guys up to this weekend?
Person 2: I'm planning on taking my kids to the beach.
Person 3: I'm going bowling. I've been really into it lately.

**Meeting Tip**

# Be a Small Talk Pro
스몰톡 전문가가 되자

### ① Be fully engaged. 집중한다.

When talking, don't look at your smartphone or tablet. Put them away and give your full attention to the people you're with.

대화할 때는 스마트폰이나 태블릿을 보지 않는다. 그것들을 치우고 함께 있는 사람들에게 집중한다.

### ② Be animate. 활발하게 반응한다.

Show that you're listening with both nonverbal and verbal cues. Make eye contact with the person speaking and nod occasionally. Use responses like, "Yeah?", "Really?", "Uh-huh."

비언어적, 언어적 신호를 둘 다 보내서 내가 듣고 있다는 걸 보여준다. 이야기하는 사람과 눈을 맞추고 가끔 고개를 끄덕인다. '그래요?', '정말요?', '음.' 같은 추임새를 사용한다.

### ③ Repeat back key words. 주요 단어들을 반복한다.

For long conversations, repeat back some simple words. For example, when someone says, "I was there for two days," say, "Two days?" For "I went to Chicago," you might say, "Wow, Chicago."

긴 대화에서는 간단한 단어들을 반복해 준다. 예를 들어, 누가 '거기에 이틀 있었어요.'라고 하면 '이틀이요?'라고 한다. 'Chicago 갔었어요.'라는 말에 '와, Chicago요.'라고 한다.

### ④ Ask open-ended questions. 개방형 질문을 한다.

Avoid asking questions that will get a simple yes or no. Ask open-ended ones. For instance, after lunch, you don't ask, "Did you have a good lunch?" Instead, you might ask, "How was your lunch?"

예/아니요 답변이 나올 질문은 피한다. 개방형 질문을 한다. 예를 들어, 점심 후에 '점심 잘 드셨어요?'라고 묻지 않는다. 대신에 '점심 어떠셨어요?'라고 묻는다.

## 6 Bargaining

# Can you meet us halfway?

### Learning Objectives

- Learners can engage in bargaining.
- Learners can ask for concessions.
- Learners can make concessions.

### Warm Up

**Work with a partner or in a group. Discuss the following questions.**

1. Do you ever have to negotiate with a client or a vendor?
2. What is usually the most important factor when you negotiate?
3. Do you think you're good at bargaining?

## Dialogue

**Practice the dialogue with a partner.**

A: Well, we've made some progress, but we're nowhere near where we need to be.

B: We're open to suggestions, Steve.

A: **We might be able to make concessions on delivery.** Instead of two months, we could possibly accept three. That should help you lower some costs. Wouldn't it?

B: That won't make much of a difference. Delivery costs will be the same.

A: If you have any other ideas, now is the time to talk about it.

B: **What do you say we put all the cards on the table?**

A: Okay, sure. I'm all ears.

B: **We could give you a 10% discount if you increase your order by 10%.**

A: **Can you meet us halfway?** We increase the order by 5%, and you give us a 5% discount.

B: Let me make some phone calls. I need to check with my boss.

A: 자, 어느 정도 진전은 있지만, 우리가 도달해야 할 목표 근처에도 못 갔습니다.

B: 건의 사항이 있으시면 말씀하시죠, Steve.

A: **배송 부분에서 양보할 수 있을 것도 같습니다.** 두 달 대신 석 달을 수용할 수도 있어요. 그러면 비용을 좀 줄이실 수 있을 거예요. 안 그러요?

B: 그래 봤자 별 차이가 안 나요. 배송료는 그대로일 거예요.

A: 다른 아이디어들이 있으시면 지금이 논의하기 좋은 때입니다.

B: **우리 모든 걸 다 오픈하면 어떨까요?**

A: 그래요, 좋습니다. 전 들을 준비가 돼 있어요.

B: **주문을 10% 늘리시면 저희는 10% 할인해 드릴 수 있습니다.**

A: **협의점을 맞춰볼까요?** 우린 주문을 5% 늘리고 그쪽에선 5% 할인해 주시고요.

B: 전화 몇 통 좀 할게요. 제 상사와 확인해 봐야 해요.

### ✓ Comprehension Check

**Answer the questions.**

1. What concession is Steve offering on delivery?
2. When Steve says to meet halfway, what is he asking for?

## Vocabulary

**Match the words or expressions with the correct definitions.**

1. progress _____
2. nowhere near _____
3. open to _____
4. make concessions _____
5. instead of _____
6. should help _____
7. make a difference _____
8. all ears _____
9. halfway _____

a. ~ 대신
b. 차이를 낳다, 변화를 만들다
c. 중간지점
d. 귀를 기울이고 있는
e. ~에 마음이 열려 있다
f. 진전
g. 도움이 될 듯하다
h. 양보하다
i. ~에 근처에도 못 간

### ⊕ Bonus Resources

**sticking point** 걸림돌, 발목 잡는 요소

A: The delivery date is a real **sticking point**. 배송 날짜가 큰 걸림돌이네요.
B: Okay. We might be able to shorten the delivery time.
알았습니다. 배송 시간을 줄일 수 있을 것도 같아요.

무언가 끈적이면 붙은 것을 쉽사리 빼 내기가 어려울 수밖에 없다. sticking point는 말 그대로 '끈적한 요소'라는 뉘앙스로, 논의할 때 어떤 걸림돌이나 발목을 잡는 요소를 뜻한다.

# Grammar Points

**Read the following and practice making sentences.**

1. We might be able to ~

> We might be able to ~는 우리 쪽에서 '~할 수 있을 것도 같다'를 말할 때 쓸 수 있는 패턴이다. might란 단어에서 나타내듯, 확실히 해당 액션을 취하겠다는 게 아니고 사실상 상대방의 반응을 보려는 의도가 담겨 있다.
>
> *We might be able to accommodate your request.* 그쪽 요청을 수용할 수 있을 것도 같습니다.

a) We might be able to _____ a plan. 방안을 마련할 수 있을 것도 같습니다.
b) We might be able to _____. 그렇게 해드릴 수 있을 것도 같습니다.
c) We might be able to _____ earlier. 더 일찍 보낼 수 있을 것도 같습니다.

2. What do you say we ~?

> '우리가 ~하면 당신은 어떻게 말하나요?'로 직역되는 What do you say we ~?는 '우리 ~하면 어떨까요?'라는 뜻으로, 무언가를 공손히 제안할 때 쓴다.
>
> *What do you say we ask them?* 우리 그분들에게 물어보면 어떨까요?

a) What do you say we _____ this over? 우리 한번 잘 생각해 보면 어떨까요?
b) What do you say we _____? 우리 잠깐 쉬면 어떨까요?
c) What do you say we _____? 우리 다시 시작하면 어떨까요?

### Write

**Make your own dialogue using the expressions from Grammar Points.**

A: _____
B: _____
A: _____
B: _____

 **Practice**

**Shadowing**

**Listen and repeat.**

1. **We might be able to** accept your new proposal.
   **We might be able to** take a look at our numbers again.

2. **What do you say we** move to a different room?
   **What do you say we** go with Sam's plan?

3. **We could** do that for now.
   **We could** push the date back.

4. **Can you** give us a minute?
   **Can you** let me know?

5. Is that the main **sticking point**?

**Making Sentences**

**Practice making sentences. Use the words in the parentheses or use your own. Then, read your sentences to your partner or group. After sharing your sentences, practice saying someone else's sentences.**

1. We might be able to _____. (make, do, say)

2. What do you say we _____? (ask, go, let)

3. We could _____. (start, meet, consider)

4. Can you _____? (imagine, see, go back)

052

## Roleplay

**Roleplay the following scenarios with a partner. Practice and change roles.**

Scenario 1

> **Two people are bargaining for a better deal at a meeting.**
>
> **Person 1:** ask if Person 2 can place another order next month
>
> **Person 2:** say you might be able to do that if Person 1 gives you a discount

Scenario 2

> **Two people are bargaining at a meeting.**
>
> **Person 1:** ask for a lower price
>
> **Person 2:** say you could do that if Person 1 increases the order

## Homework

**Write a short dialogue of two people bargaining at a meeting.**

_____

_____

### Warm Up Sample Answers
1 Yes, I (sometimes / frequently) negotiate with clients. / No, I never negotiate with vendors.
2. Usually (the price / delivery time / quality) is the most important factor.
3. (Yes, I think / No, I don't think) I'm good at bargaining.

### Comprehension Check Answers
1. Steve is offering three months instead of two months on delivery.
2. He is asking for a 5% discount for increasing the order by 5%.

### Vocabulary Answers
1. f, 2. i, 3. e, 4. h, 5. a, 6. g, 7. b, 8. d, 9. c

### Grammar Points Answers
1. a) come up with  b) do that  c) send it out
2. a) think  b) take a break  c) start over

### Write Sample Answer
A: What do you say we look at the price again?
B: All right. We might be able to offer you a 5% discount.
A: Can you offer us 10%?
B: We could offer 8%. That's the best we can do.

### Making Sentences Sample Answers
1. We might be able to (make that work / do something about that / say yes).
2. What do you say we (ask the manufacturer about this / go there now / let this go)?
3. We could (start again from scratch / meet at your office / possibly consider that).
4. Can you (imagine that / see the different colors / go back to the first page)?

### Roleplay Sample Answer
Scenario 1
Person 1: Can you place another order next month?
Person 2: We might be able to do that if you give us a discount.
Person 1: We could consider giving you a 2% discount.
Person 2: That's quite low. Would you consider 5% discount if we place a larger order next month?
Person 1: What do you say we take a break so our team can discuss this?
Person 2: Let's do that.

### Homework Sample Answer
Person 1: What do you say we put all the cards on the table? We might be able to make concessions on delivery.
Person 2: Okay. Can you meet us halfway? We could give you a 10% discount if you increase your order by 15%. Plus, you allow us to deliver your order in three months, not two.
Person 1: Increasing the order might be a sticking point. Let me talk to my boss.

**Meeting Tip**

# 5 Negotiating Personality Types
협상할 때의 5가지 성격 유형

### ① Extroverted  외향적 성격

It's easy to think that extroverts are better negotiators, but as the book *Quiet* points out, introverts have good negotiating skills. They rarely make impulsive decisions.

외향적인 사람들이 협상을 더 잘한다고 생각하기 쉽지만, 〈콰이어트〉라는 책이 지적하듯이 내성적인 사람들은 좋은 협상 기술을 갖추고 있다. 충동적인 결정을 거의 하지 않는다.

### ② Agreeable  잘 맞춰주는 성격

If people are too agreeable, their self-esteem is dependent on how others view them. They might be too concerned with relationships to get truly good deals.

너무 잘 맞춰주는 사람이라면, 다른 사람들이 자신을 어떻게 보느냐에 따라 자존감이 좌우된다. 아주 좋은 협상 결과를 얻기에는 관계에 너무 집중할 수도 있다.

### ③ Conscientious  성실한 성격

Conscientious people tend to prepare for negotiations more thoroughly. They are also better organized.

성실한 성격을 지닌 사람들은 협상을 위해 철저하게 준비하는 성향이 있다. 또한 더 체계적이기도 하다.

### ④ Neurotic  신경증적 성격

People who are neurotic are more anxious and insecure than others. They tend to be dissatisfied with the results of negotiations.

신경증적 성격을 지닌 사람들은 타인보다 걱정이 많고 불안함을 더 느낀다. 협상 결과에 대한 만족감이 떨어지는 경향을 보인다.

### ⑤ Open  열린 성격

Being open means being open-minded and imaginative. They find creative ways to make gains.

열린 성격은 마음이 열려 있고 창의적인 것을 뜻한다. 창의적인 방식으로 이득을 챙긴다.

# 7 Making Suggestions

## Let me play the devil's advocate.

 ### Learning Objectives

- Learners can play the devil's advocate during discussions.
- Learners can weigh in with opinions or other suggestions.
- Learners can mention that a participant has made a good point.

 ### Warm Up

**Work with a partner or in a group. Discuss the following questions.**

1. Why is it good to have a variety of suggestions in meetings?
2. In your team, who makes the most suggestions during meetings?
3. Do you feel you need to make more suggestions?

 # Dialogue

**Practice the dialogue with a partner.**

A: The owner is furious about what happened.
B: Who can blame him? No matter how we look at it, it was our fault. It was our own workers that damaged the wall.
A: All right. What do we do?
B: **Here's what I think.** We should just go and apologize to the owner.
A: Okay, Mary says we should apologize. **Does anyone want to weigh in?** Ted?
C: I don't think that's a good idea.
B: What? You mess up. Then you apologize. It's that simple.
C: **Hear me out. Let me play the devil's advocate.**
B: Go ahead.
C: Let's say we apologize. Then the owner wants that in writing. We do that. Then the owner sues us.
A: Ted's got a point.
B: He does. No one wants a lawsuit. Do you have any ideas, Ted?
C: I say we should just fix the wall. After that, we can talk to the owner.

A: 이번 일에 대해서 건물주가 꽤 화가 나 있어요.
B: 누가 그를 탓하겠어요? 어떤 식으로 봐도 우리 잘못입니다. 벽을 훼손한 건 우리 직원들이었으니까요.
A: 좋아요. 어떻게 해야 할까요?
B: **전 이렇게 생각해요.** 그냥 직접 주인을 찾아가서 사과하는 게 좋겠어요.
A: 자, Mary는 사과하자고 해요. **다른 사람 의견 있나요?** Ted?
C: 그건 좋은 생각이 아닌 것 같아요.
B: 예? 자, 당신이 뭔가를 망쳤어요. 그러면 사과하면 되는겁니다. 아주 간단해요.
C: **제 말 좀 들어봐요. 반대쪽 입장에서 이야기해 보겠습니다.**
B: 그러세요.
C: 우리가 사과한다고 치자고요. 그러면 주인은 서면으로 사과를 원합니다. 우린 그렇게 해줘요. 그러면 주인은 우리를 고소할 거예요.
A: Ted의 말이 일리가 있네요.
B: 맞네요. 소송을 원하는 사람은 아무도 없어요. Ted, 아이디어 좀 없어요?
C: 그냥 우리가 벽을 고치는 겁니다. 그런 다음에 건물주와 얘기하면 되죠.

## ✓ Comprehension Check

**Answer the questions.**

1. What does Mary say they should do?
2. What does Ted think will happen when they apologize in writing?

 **Vocabulary**

**Match the words or expressions with the correct definitions.**

| | |
|---|---|
| 1. furious _____ | a. 선의의 비판자, 일부러 반대 입장 쪽에 서는 사람 |
| 2. no matter how _____ | b. 꽤 화가 난 |
| 3. fault _____ | c. 서면으로 |
| 4. damage _____ | d. 잘못 |
| 5. weigh in _____ | e. 어떤 식으로 ~해도 |
| 6. mess up _____ | f. 훼손하다, 피해를 주다 |
| 7. devil's advocate _____ | g. (논의 등에) 끼어들다 |
| 8. in writing _____ | h. 고소하다 |
| 9. sue _____ | i. 실수하다, 망치다 |

⊕ **Bonus Resources**

### get it  이해하다

A: Here's what you should do. Go and ask him.
이렇게 해보세요. 가서 그에게 물어보는 겁니다.

B: I don't **get it**. You want me to go to him? 이해가 안 되네요. 그에게 가라고요?

get it은 직역으로 '그것을 받는다'로, 상대방의 뜻을 받는다는 뉘앙스가 있다. 반대로 don't를 앞에 붙여 흔히 '이해하지 못했다'를 뜻하는 don't get it도 자주 쓴다.

**Grammar Points**

**Read the following and practice making sentences.**

**1. Here's what ~**

> Here's what ~은 '~는 이렇다'를 뜻하며, 상세한 설명으로 들어가기 전에 서두 역할을 하는 표현이다.
> 
> *Here's what happened.* 일은 이렇게 된 겁니다.

a) Here's what my _____. 제 상사는 이렇게 말씀하셨어요.

b) Here's what _____. 우린 이렇게 할 수 있습니다.

c) Here's what _____. 이런 일이 일어날 수 있어요.

**2. Does anyone want to ~?**

> Does anyone want to ~?는 '~하고 싶은 사람 있나요?'라는 뜻으로 대안으로 쓸 수 있는 Is there anyone who wants to ~라는 표현보다 훨씬 깔끔하고 짧은 표현이다.
> 
> *Does anyone want to say something?* 뭐라도 말하고 싶은 사람 있나요?

a) Does anyone want to _____? 뭐라도 덧붙이고 싶은 사람 있나요?

b) Does anyone want to _____? 뭘 건의하고 싶은 사람 있나요?

c) Does anyone want to _____? 다음에 가고 싶은 사람 있나요?

---

### ⓒ Write

**Make your own dialogue using the expressions from Grammar Points.**

A: _____

B: _____

A: _____

B: _____

 **Practice**

**Shadowing**

**Listen and repeat.**

1. **Here's what** it comes down to.
   **Here's what** has to be done.

2. **Does anyone want to** say something?
   **Does anyone want to** offer a theory?

3. **Hear** us **out**.
   **Hear** him **out**.

4. **Let me** go grab my file.
   **Let me** see what I can do.

5. Do you **get it**?

**Making Sentences**

**Practice making sentences. Use the words in the parentheses or use your own. Then, read your sentences to your partner or group. After sharing your sentences, practice saying someone else's sentences.**

1. Here's what _____. (he, they, can)

2. Does anyone want to _____? (take, sit, go)

3. Hear _____ out. (them, her)

4. Let me _____. (see, circle back, know)

 ## Roleplay

**Roleplay the following scenarios with a partner. Practice and change roles.**

Scenario 1

> **People are making suggestions at a meeting.**
> **Person 1:** say we should delay the project
> **Person 2:** ask if anyone wants to weigh in
> **Person 3:** say you want to play the devil's advocate / ask what if some of the materials are already shipped

Scenario 2

> **People are making different suggestions at a meeting.**
> **Person 1:** ask for suggestions
> **Person 2:** say we should consider asking the designer to redo the table design
> **Person 3:** say you want to play the devil's advocate / ask what we would do if the designer demands a large sum of money

 ## Homework

**Write a short dialogue of two people making suggestions at a meeting.**

_____

_____

### Warm Up Sample Answers
1. It's good because (people get a chance to voice their ideas / new ideas emerge).
2. In my team (I make / my boss makes) the most suggestions.
3. (Yes, I / No, I don't) feel I need to make more suggestions.

### Comprehension Check Answers
1. Mary says they should apologize to the owner.
2. Ted thinks the owner will sue them.

### Vocabulary Answers
1. b, 2. e, 3. d, 4. f, 5. g, 6. i, 7. a, 8. c, 9. h

### Grammar Points Answers
1. a) boss said  b) we could do  c) (might/may) happen
2. a) add anything  b) make a suggestion  c) go next

### Write Sample Answer
A: Does anyone want to respond to that suggestion?
B: Yes. Here's what bothers me about the suggestion.
A: It bothers you? Why does it bother you?
B: Come on. Hear me out. It will cost too much money.

### Making Sentences Sample Answers
1. Here's what (he might say / they're saying about the incident / can be done).
2. Does anyone want to (take a short break / sit up front / go with Joe)?
3. Hear (them/her) out.
4. Let me (see what's next / circle back to my last point / know).

### Roleplay Sample Answer
Scenario 1
Person 1: Here's what I think. We should delay the project.
Person 2: Does anyone want to weigh in?
Person 3: We can't delay the project.
Person 1: Why not? It's just for a week.
Person 2: Hear him out.
Person 3: Let me play the devil's advocate. What if some of the materials are already shipped?

### Homework Sample Answer
Person 1: Hear me out. Here's what I think. Our supplier is not cooperating, so we should find another supplier. You guys get it, right? Does anyone want to weigh in?
Person 2: Let me play the devil's advocate. What if the current supplier finds out? Then what do we do?

**Meeting Tip**

# How to Effectively Play the Devil's Advocate
효율적으로 반대쪽 입장이 되어 보는 방법

① **Oppose the idea, not the speaker.** 발표자가 아닌 발상을 반대한다.

You're not opposing the person. Focus on the idea itself and find fault in its logic or soundness of argument. Avoid making comments about the speaker.

사람에게 반대하는 것이 아니다. 발상 자체에 집중해서 발상의 논리나 논증의 건전성의 결점을 찾는다. 발표자에 대한 의견은 피한다.

② **Be logical.** 논리적으로 생각한다.

Stay away from emotional expressions such as "I like…" or "I don't like…" Present different or alternative examples, evidence, or insights from what you heard.

'~가 좋다', '~가 좋지 않다' 등의 정서 표현을 피한다. 들은 것과 다르거나 대안이 되는 예시나 증거, 통찰을 제시한다.

③ **Speak for your group, not yourself.** 나 자신 말고 나의 집단을 위해 이야기한다.

Act as the rep for the team when you're being the devil's advocate. Don't try to push your personal agenda.

선의의 비판자 역할을 할 때는 팀의 대표가 되어야 한다. 나의 개인적인 목표를 위한 행동은 하지 않는다.

④ **Don't go too far.** 도를 넘지 않는다.

Avoid getting carried away. Once you've made your point, move on.

너무 지나치게 하지 않는다. 주장을 밝힌 후에는 다음으로 넘어간다.

⑤ **Take turns.** 역할을 바꿔본다.

Don't always have the same person playing the devil's advocate. Let others have a chance as well.

매번 같은 사람이 비판자 역할을 하지 않도록 한다. 다른 사람에게도 기회를 준다.

**Action Plans**

# 8

## We need to set up a timeline for completing the next phase of the project.

 **Learning Objectives**

- Learners can talk about timelines for completing tasks.
- Learners can express the importance of making specific plans.
- Learners can suggest setting up objectives.

 **Warm Up**

**Work with a partner or in a group. Discuss the following questions.**
1. Why are discussions about timelines important?
2. How detailed should plans be?
3. Are your plans as detailed as you would like?

 **Dialogue**

**Practice the dialogue with a partner.**

A: July is right around the corner. **Let's set clear objectives for the next quarter.** First, the Anson project. **We need to set up a timeline for completing the next phase of the project.**

B: You mean market research?

A: Yes. Let's get right into it. What's the timeline for completing the market research? Stephen?

B: I'd say we'll need roughly three months.

A: Three months. That's longer than I thought.

B: **That's if we can get additional staff to help with the research.** If we can't, it'll take longer.

A: Well, we can't hire more people.

B: Yeah, I understand that.

A: Any ideas? Dean?

C: I think Paula and Cathy from my team can probably help out.

A: That's good news. **We're making good progress.**

A: 7월이 코앞입니다. 다음 분기에 대한 분명한 목표들을 정합시다. 먼저 Anson 프로젝트입니다. 프로젝트의 다음 단계 완료를 위한 일정을 설정해야 합니다.
B: 시장 조사 말씀인가요?
A: 네. 바로 본론으로 들어갑시다. 시장 조사 완료 일정이 어떻게 됩니까? Stephen?
B: 대략 3개월이 필요할 겁니다.
A: 3개월이요. 생각했던 것보다 기네요.
B: 그것도 조사를 도울 수 있는 추가 직원들을 확보해야만 가능합니다. 그렇게 못하면, 더 오래 걸릴 거고요.
A: 음, 사람들을 더 채용할 수는 없어요.
B: 네, 이해합니다.
A: 좋은 생각 없어요? Dean?
C: 저희 팀에 있는 Paula와 Cathy가 도울 수 있을 것 같습니다.
A: 좋은 소식이에요. 좋은 진전을 보이고 있습니다.

### ✓ Comprehension Check

**Answer the questions.**

1. What does the chair want to establish?
2. How long does Stephen think the market research will take?

# Vocabulary

**Match the words or expressions with the correct definitions.**

1. clear _____
2. quarter _____
3. objective _____
4. mean _____
5. market research _____
6. right _____
7. roughly _____
8. help out _____
9. progress _____

a. 대략
b. ~을 말하다
c. 돕다, 도와주다
d. 분명한
e. 시장 조사
f. 분기
g. 목표
h. 바로
i. 진전

## ⊕ Bonus Resources

### lend a hand  도움을 주다

A: We need to get this done by tomorrow.  이거 내일까지 끝내야 합니다.
B: I can **lend a hand**.  제가 도와드릴 수 있어요.

lend a hand는 '손을 빌려 주다'로 직역되는데, 말 그대로 나의 손을 이용해서 다른 사람의 일을 돕는다는 뜻이다. 물론 내가 주는 도움이 육체적인 도움이 아니어도 쓸 수 있는 표현이다.

**Grammar Points**

**Read the following and practice making sentences.**

1. We need to set up ~

> set up이라는 단어는 '설정하다', '준비하다' 등 무언가를 만든다는 뉘앙스를 지니면서 다양한 정의를 가지고 있다. 따라서 We need to set up ~은 '우리는 ~을 만들어야 한다'라는 뜻이다.
>
> *We need to set up a new bank account.* 새 은행 계좌를 개설해야 합니다.

a) We need to set up _____. 새 지침을 세워야 합니다.

b) We need to set up _____ with them. 그들과 회의를 잡아야 합니다.

c) We need to set up _____. 비밀번호를 설정해야 합니다.

2. That's if we can ~

> That's if we can ~은 '그건 ~이어야만 가능하다'라는 뜻이다. that은 펼쳐질 수 있는 일을 가리키는 것이고, if we can이 들어갔기에 우리가 어떤 것을 할 수 있어야만 'that'이 가능하다는 것이다.
>
> *That's if we can get hold of them.* 그들과 연락이 돼야만 가능해요.

a) That's if we can _____ to agree. 그건 주인의 동의를 얻어 낼 수 있어야만 가능해요.

b) That's if we can _____ on time. 그건 프로젝트를 제시간에 끝낼 수 있어야만 가능해요.

c) That's if we can _____. 그건 교통혼잡을 피할 수 있어야만 가능해요.

### Write

**Make your own dialogue using the expressions from Grammar Points.**

A: _____

B: _____

A: _____

B: _____

 **Practice**

**Shadowing**

**Listen and repeat.**

1. **Let's** calm down.
   **Let's** hear what she has to say.

2. **We need to set up** a new plan.
   **We need to set up** a task force.

3. **That's if we can** change the date.
   **That's if we can** convince the CEO.

4. **We're** having some problems.
   **We're** getting nowhere.

5. Could you **lend a hand** with the research?

**Making Sentences**

**Practice making sentences. Use the words in the parentheses or use your own. Then, read your sentences to your partner or group. After sharing your sentences, practice saying someone else's sentences.**

1. Let's _____. (go, see, move)

2. We need to set up _____. (team, boundaries, plans)

3. That's if we can _____. (get, reply)

4. We're _____. (do, look, have)

## Roleplay

**Roleplay the following scenarios with a partner. Practice and change roles.**

Scenario 1

> **Two people are talking about setting up a website.**
> **Person 1:** say we need to set up a new website
> **Person 2:** ask Person 1 what the timeline is for setting up the website

Scenario 2

> **People are making plans for a project.**
> **Person 1:** say we need to create a full project schedule
> **Person 2:** ask Person 1 what the timeline for creating it is
> **Person 3:** suggest that we create a task force to do that

## Homework

**Write a short dialogue of two people discussing action plans.**

_____

_____

**Warm Up Sample Answers**
1. They're important because (they set deadlines for specific projects / they're good for measuring progress).
2. Plans should be (really/somewhat) detailed. / Plans should be more flexible.
3. Yes, they are. / No, they are not.

**Comprehension Check Answers**
1. The chair wants to establish a timeline for completing the next phase of the project, which is market research.
2. Stephen thinks it'll take roughly 3 months.

**Vocabulary Answers**
1. d, 2. f, 3. g, 4. b, 5. e, 6. h, 7. a, 8. c, 9. i

**Grammar Points Answers**
1. a) a new policy b) a meeting c) a password
2. a) get the owner b) complete the project c) beat the traffic

**Write Sample Answer**
A: We need to set up a meeting with the owner ASAP.
B: What's the problem?
A: We're having issues with payment. So, can we meet with her?
B: Maybe. That's if we can set up a meeting before she goes on vacation.

**Making Sentences Sample Answers**
1. Let's (go and check / see what happens next / move to the next page).
2. We need to set up (a new team / some boundaries / two separate plans).
3. That's if we can (get approval / reply to their e-mail in time).
4. We're (doing our best / looking at this the wrong way / having fun).

**Roleplay Sample Answer**
Scenario 1
Person 1: We need to set up a new website.
Person 2: What's the timeline for that?
Person 1: We're thinking we should get it up and running by July.
Person 2: Is that doable?
Person 1: Sure. That's if we can find the right person to work on it.
Person 2: Let's find out if Pamela can do it.

**Homework Sample Answer**
Person 1: Let's set clear objectives for the next quarter. We need to set up a timeline for completing the next phase of the project.
Person 2: What's the timeline for the market research? We need to finish that first, right?
Person 1: Yes. The market research should be done by next week.
Person 2: That's if we can get additional staff to help with the research.
Person 1: No worries, Charlie's team is lending a hand.
Person 2: We're making good progress.

**Meeting Tip**

# How to Write a Great Action Plan
훌륭한 액션플랜(실행 계획)을 짜는 방법

### ① Set your goal. 목표를 설정한다.

When setting your goal, use the SMART goals: specific, measurable, achievable, relevant, and time-based.

목표를 설정할 때는 SMART 원칙을 사용한다: S(구체적), M(수치화할 수 있는), A(이룰 수 있는), R(관련 있는), T(시간 제한적).

### ② Make a list of tasks. 업무 리스트를 작성한다.

Divide the goal into individual tasks. This makes the goal less daunting and allows you to move ahead in an organized way.

목표를 개별 업무로 나눈다. 그러면 목표 자체가 덜 벅차게 느껴질뿐더러 짜임새 있게 진행할 수 있다.

### ③ Create a detailed schedule. 세부적인 일정을 짠다.

Aside from the main schedule, each task should have individual deadlines. They can serve as milestones.

주된 일정 외에도, 개별 업무마다 별도의 마감 기한이 있어야 한다. 마감 기한은 이정표 역할을 할 수 있다.

### ④ Assign tasks to team members. 팀원들에게 업무를 배정한다.

Consider the strengths and qualifications of your team members and assign the right task to each person.

팀원들의 장점과 자격을 고려해서 개별적으로 적합한 업무를 맡긴다.

### ⑤ Measure progress. 진척도를 평가한다.

It's important that each task is monitored regularly. Get reports and hold regular meetings to assess progress.

정기적으로 개별 업무를 모니터하는 것은 중요하다. 진행 상황을 평가하기 위한 보고서를 받고 정기 회의를 진행한다.

**Delays**

# 9  We're behind schedule.

 ## Learning Objectives

- Learners can talk about delays in a schedule.
- Learners can give detailed reasons for a delay.
- Learners can discuss how much time they need to catch up.

 ## Warm Up

**Work with a partner or in a group. Discuss the following questions.**

1. Do many of your projects get delayed?
2. What are some reasons they get delayed?
3. How do you see yourself as a project manager?

 **Dialogue**

**Practice the dialogue with a partner.**

A: Let's talk about your project, Harry. How many phases are there?

B: We have four phases.

A: What phase are you in now? Phase 3?

B: No. We're in Phase 2. **We're behind schedule.**

A: You are? How behind are you?

B: Um, two weeks. Well, it's more like three weeks.

A: Three weeks! Wow. That is late. What's causing the delay?

B: **The delay is due to technical issues.** There are other types of issues, but I'd say they're mostly technical ones.

A: When are these issues going to be taken care of?

B: We took care of them last month.

A: I don't get it. If that's the case, why are you still behind schedule?

B: The problems occurred during the last phase. **We had to allocate more time to Phase 1. I need more time to catch up.**

A: 당신 프로젝트에 관해 얘기해 봅시다, Harry. 단계가 몇 개 있죠?

B: 4단계가 있습니다.

A: 지금은 어느 단계에 있죠? 3단계?

B: 아닙니다. 2단계에 있습니다. **일정보다 뒤쳐져 있습니다.**

A: 그래요? 얼마나 뒤처졌나요?

B: 음, 2주요. 음, 3주에 더 가깝네요.

A: 3주요! 와. 그거 늦네요. 뭐 때문에 지연되고 있는 거죠?

B: **기술적 문제 때문에 지연되고 있습니다.** 다른 문제들도 있지만, 대부분 기술적인 것들이라고 봐요.

A: 언제 이 문제들이 해결되나요?

B: 지난달에 문제들을 해결했습니다.

A: 이해가 안 되네요. 그게 사실이면, 왜 아직도 늦어지고 있습니까?

B: 문제들이 지난 단계에서 발생했거든요. **1단계에 시간을 더 할당해야 했습니다. 따라잡는 데 시간이 더 필요합니다.**

### ✓ Comprehension Check

**Answer the questions.**

1. What phase is Harry's project in now?
2. What was the main cause of the delay in the overall schedule?

# Vocabulary

**Match the words or expressions with the correct definitions.**

1. phase _____
2. behind schedule _____
3. due to _____
4. technical issue _____
5. take care of _____
6. case _____
7. last _____
8. allocate _____
9. catch up _____

a. 따라잡다
b. 일정보다 뒤처진
c. 기술적 문제
d. 단계
e. ~을 해결하다, ~을 수습하다
f. ~ 때문에
g. 경우
h. 할당하다
i. 지난

### ⊕ Bonus Resources

**super** 특별히, 엄청

A: I need more time to complete the work.
작업을 끝내기 위해 시간이 더 필요합니다.

B: Okay, but you were **super** confident you'd be done by this week.
좋아요, 그런데 이번 주까지 마무리할 수 있다고 엄청나게 확신하셨었어요.

super는 비격식으로 '특별히', '엄청'을 부사로 나타낼 때 사용한다. 격식 차린 자리에서는 extremely, very 등을 쓰는 편이 낫다.

 **Grammar Points**

**Read the following and practice making sentences.**

**1. The delay is due to ~**

> '지연'을 의미하는 the delay가 '~ 때문에 있다'를 뜻하는 is due to와 함께 쓰이면서 The delay is due to ~는 '~때문에 지연되고 있다'라는 의미가 된다. 이때 to 뒤에는 동사원형이 아닌 명사나 명사구가 나와야 한다.
>
> *The delay is due to a problem with the machine.* 기계의 문제 때문에 지연되고 있습니다.

a) The delay is due to the _____. 최근 폭우 때문에 지연되고 있습니다.
b) The delay is due to a _____. 여러 요인으로 지연되고 있습니다.
c) The delay is due to the _____. 항구 파업 때문에 지연되고 있습니다.

**2. I need more time to ~**

> I need time to ~라고 하면 '~할 시간이 필요하다'를 의미하는데, 여기에 more를 넣으면 '~할 시간이 더 필요하다'는 표현이 만들어진다.
>
> *I need more time to think about it.* 생각할 시간이 더 필요합니다.

a) I need more time to _____. 추가 조사할 시간이 더 필요합니다.
b) I need more time to _____. 준비할 시간이 더 필요합니다.
c) I need more time to _____. 행사를 계획할 시간이 더 필요합니다.

---

### Write

**Make your own dialogue using the expressions from Grammar Points.**

A: _____

B: _____

A: _____

B: _____

 **Practice**

Shadowing

**Listen and repeat.**

1. **We're** ahead of schedule.
   **We're** ready to go.

2. **The delay is due to** a minor error.
   **The delay is due to** several factors.

3. **We had to** stop the work.
   **We had to** cancel the flight.

4. **I need more time to** figure this out.
   **I need more time to** write the e-mail.

5. You've been **super** helpful.

Making Sentences

**Practice making sentences. Use the words in the parentheses or use your own. Then, read your sentences to your partner or group. After sharing your sentences, practice saying someone else's sentences.**

1. We're _____. (certain, right, ready)

2. The delay is due to _____. (lack, accident)

3. We had to _____. (say, go, let)

4. I need more time to _____. (look over, talk, finish)

 **Roleplay**

**Roleplay the following scenarios with a partner. Practice and change roles.**

Scenario 1

> **Two people are talking about a work delay.**
> 
> **Person 1:** ask Person 2 why the work is being delayed
> 
> **Person 2:** say the wiring had to be redone on the second floor

Scenario 2

> **Two people are talking about being behind schedule.**
> 
> **Person 1:** tell Person 2 that the store interior work is behind schedule
> 
> **Person 2:** ask why
> 
> **Person 1:** explain that there were several factors, including a small fire and a redesign of the storefront

 **Homework**

**Write a short dialogue of two people discussing a delay in work.**

_____

_____

### Warm Up Sample Answers
1. Yes, they do. / No, they don't.
2. Some reasons are (the weather / the suppliers / the client / the management).
3. I think (I'm / I'm not) a good project manager. / I'm not sure.

### Comprehension Check Answers
1. It is in Phase 2.
2. Technical issues delayed the overall schedule.

### Vocabulary Answers
1. d, 2. b, 3. f, 4. c, 5. e, 6. g, 7. i, 8. h, 9. a

### Grammar Points Answers
1. a) recent storm  b) variety of factors  c) strike at the port
2. a) do/conduct additional research  b) get ready  c) plan the event

### Write Sample Answer
A: What's causing the delay?
B: The delay is due to some changes in the scope of work.
A: Have we incorporated the changes now?
B: Yes, but I need more time to adjust the schedule.

### Making Sentences Sample Answers
1. We're (certain about that / right on schedule / ready to start the meeting).
2. The delay is due to (their lack of urgency / an unfortunate accident).
3. We had to (say no to the manager / go back to them / let it go).
4. I need more time to (look over the report / talk to everyone / finish the report).

### Roleplay Sample Answer
Scenario 1
Person 1: Why is the work being delayed?
Person 2: The delay is due to the rework. The wiring had to be redone on the second floor.
Person 1: Oh, no. Has that been done?
Person 2: I think so. But I need more time to finish all the inspections.

### Homework Sample Answer
Person 1: We're not going to meet the deadline.
Person 2: What's causing the delay?
Person 1: The delay is due to time constraints. I need more time to finish the sales analysis.
Person 2: I thought your team was done with that.
Person 1: We had to redo the numbers.
Person 2: Is this because of the accounting team?
Person 1: No, no. They are always super helpful. It was a computer error.

**Meeting Tip**

# Managing Delays
지연에 대처하기

### ① Say there might be a delay. 지연이 있을 것이라고 알린다.

It's not a good idea to wait until the delay actually happens. When you think a delay might occur, let the stakeholders know about the possibility in advance. Give the stakeholders time to prepare.

지연 자체가 발생할 때까지 기다리지 않는 것이 좋다. 지연이 발생할 가능성이 있다는 생각이 들면 이해관계자들에게 미리 그 가능성을 알린다. 이해관계자들이 준비할 시간을 주는 것이다.

### ② Say what will be delayed. 무엇이 지연되는지 알린다.

If it's not the entire project that is being delayed, let the stakeholders know that. Be specific about the affected deliverables or milestone. However, you don't need to give full technical details or the reason for the delay.

전체 프로젝트가 지연되는 것이 아니라면 그 사실을 알린다. 영향을 받는 결과물이나 단계가 무엇인지 확실히 말한다. 하지만 지연의 기술적인 세부 사항이나 이유를 알릴 필요는 없다.

### ③ Say how long the delay will be. 얼마나 지연될 것인지 알린다.

Of course, let the stakeholders know the length of the delay. If you're not sure yet, give a rough estimate or tell them you will let them know as soon as you find out.

당연히 지연 기간에 대해 이해관계자들에게 알린다. 아직 확실치 않다면 대략적인 기간을 언급하거나 알게 되면 즉시 알려주겠다고 말한다.

### ④ Say what the options are. 어떤 선택지가 있는지 알린다.

If there are possible ways to shorten or prevent the delay, say so to the stakeholders. If there are no solutions, examine ways to lessen the impact of the delay.

지연 기간을 줄이거나 방지할 방법이 있다면 이를 이해관계자들에게 알린다. 해결책이 없다면 지연이 끼칠 영향을 줄일 수 있는 방법을 찾아본다.

**Progress Report**

# 10 How's the project coming along?

 ## Learning Objectives

- Learners can report on the progress of their work or project.
- Learners can specify where they are in their project.
- Learners can identify issues affecting a project.

 ## Warm Up

**Work with a partner or in a group. Discuss the following questions.**

1. How often do you have to report on the progress of your work?
2. How do you feel when you have to give bad news to superiors?
3. Why are progress reports important?

 # Dialogue

**Practice the dialogue with a partner.**

A: **How's the project coming along?**
B: **We're halfway through the research phase.**
A: Any issues so far?
B: **We're working through some roadblocks.**
A: Roadblocks? Would you like to elaborate on that?
B: Yeah, a researcher quit last week. He'd been with us for ten years, so it was a bit of a shock.
A: Unfortunately, these things happen. What else?
B: An engineer has been out sick for a week.
A: How's the engineer doing? Is it serious?
B: No, she should be back next week. And, um, we had a water leak at the lab.
A: A water leak? Now, that sounds serious.
B: It wasn't so bad. There was some water damage to a few walls. Nothing major.
A: Well, John, I'm glad you're staying on top of it.
B: Of course. **I'll continue keeping tabs on the status of the project.**

A: 프로젝트는 어떻게 되어 가고 있어요?
B: 연구 단계를 반쯤 끝냈습니다.
A: 지금까지 무슨 문제가 있었나요?
B: 몇 개의 걸림돌을 좀 처리하는 중입니다.
A: 걸림돌요? 더 자세히 설명해 주실래요?
B: 네, 연구원 한 명이 지난주 관뒀어요. 우리와 10년을 함께 했기에 좀 충격이었어요.
A: 안타깝게도 흔히 있는 일이죠. 또 다른 건요?
B: 엔지니어 한 명이 일주일간 아파서 결근하고 있고요.
A: 그 엔지니어는 어때요? 심각한 건가요?
B: 아니요, 그녀는 다음 주에 나올 겁니다. 그리고, 음, 연구실에 누수가 있었습니다.
A: 누수요? 자, 그건 심각한 것 같은데요.
B: 그리 큰 문제는 아니었습니다. 몇 개의 벽에 수분 유입이 좀 있었어요. 큰 문제는 아니었어요.
A: 음, John, 이 모든 걸 잘 파악하고 있으니 다행입니다.
B: 물론이죠. 프로젝트 진행 상황을 계속 확인하고 있겠습니다.

## ✓ Comprehension Check

**Answer the questions.**

1. What phase are they in?
2. What are some of the roadblocks they're facing?

# Vocabulary

**Match the words or expressions with the correct definitions.**

1. come along _____
2. halfway through _____
3. roadblock _____
4. quit _____
5. be out sick _____
6. water leak _____
7. lab _____
8. stay on top of _____
9. keep tabs on _____

a. 반쯤 끝낸, 중간에 있는
b. 연구실, 실험실
c. 누수
d. (잘) 되어 가다
e. ~을 잘 파악하고 있다
f. 아파서 결근하다
g. 그만두다
h. ~을 확인하다
i. 장애물, 걸림돌

---

### ⊕ Bonus Resources

### be in a tight spot 어려운 상황에 놓이다

A: How's the final phase coming along? 마지막 단계는 어떻게 되어 가고 있어요?
B: We're in a bit of a tight spot. The client is saying we used the wrong tiles.
약간 어려운 상황에 놓여 있습니다. 클라이언트가 우리가 잘못된 타일을 사용했다고 합니다.

be in a tight spot은 '꽉 조이는 위치에 있다'로 직역되는 관용표현으로, 어렵거나 곤란한 상황에 부닥쳐 있는 것을 뜻한다.

 # Grammar Points

**Read the following and practice making sentences.**

1. We're halfway through ~

> We're halfway through ~는 '~을 반쯤 끝냈다', '~이 반쯤 지났다'를 뜻한다. halfway 뒤에 다른 단어를 사용해 halfway across(~을 반쯤 건넜다)와 halfway up(~을 반쯤 올랐다) 등을 언급할 수 있다.
> *We're halfway through the project.* 프로젝트를 반쯤 끝냈습니다.

a) We're halfway through _____. 올해가 반쯤 지났습니다.
b) We're halfway through _____. 어려운 부분을 반쯤 끝냈습니다.
c) We're halfway through _____. 문제를 반쯤 해결했습니다.

2. I'll continue + ~ing

> I'll continue + ~ing는 '~을 계속하겠다'라는 의미다. I'll keep + ~ing와 유사한 표현이지만, keep은 조금 더 격식 없는 느낌을 준다. 내가 뭔가를 계속하겠다고 하면서 상대방에게 안심시켜 주는 역할을 하는 경우가 많다.
> *I'll continue monitoring the situation.* 상황을 계속 관찰하겠습니다.

a) I'll continue _____. Anna와 계속 일하겠습니다.
b) I'll continue _____ with the secretary. 비서에게 계속 메모를 남기겠습니다.
c) I'll continue _____. 회의에 계속 참석하겠습니다.

## ✏ Write

**Make your own dialogue using the expressions from Grammar Points.**

A: _____

B: _____

A: _____

B: _____

 **Practice**

**Shadowing**

**Listen and repeat.**

1. **How's the** new employee doing?
   **How's the** situation in Tokyo?

2. **We're halfway through** the schedule.
   **We're halfway through** building a prototype.

3. **We're working through** a few problems.
   **We're working through** the larger issues now.

4. **I'll continue** tal**k**ing with her.
   **I'll continue** cal**l**ing him.

5. We **are in a tight spot**.

**Making Sentences**

Practice making sentences. Use the words in the parentheses or use your own. Then, read your sentences to your partner or group. After sharing your sentences, practice saying someone else's sentences.

1. How's the _____? (team, position, mood)

2. We're halfway through _____. (process, cleaning out)

3. We're working through _____. (list, issues)

4. I'll continue _____. (keep, work)

 ## Roleplay

**Roleplay the following scenarios with a partner. Practice and change roles.**

Scenario 1

> **Two people are talking about the progress of a new project.**
>
> **Person 1:** ask Person 2 how the new project is coming along
>
> **Person 2:** say you're halfway through it / you're working through some supplier issues

Scenario 2

> **Two people are talking about the progress of a project.**
>
> **Person 1:** ask how the project is coming along
>
> **Person 2:** say there are some issues / explain some issues with delivery, weather, and overtime

 ## Homework

**Write a short dialogue of two people discussing the progress of a project.**

_____

_____

**Warm Up Sample Answers**
1. I have to report (once a week / twice a month / often).
2. I feel (anxious/confident/okay).
3. They are important because (the stakeholders can plan ahead / all work need to be measured).

**Comprehension Check Answers**
1. They are in the research phase.
2. Some roadblocks are a researcher quitting, an engineer being out sick, and some water damage on a few walls due to a water leak.

**Vocabulary Answers**
1. d, 2. a, 3. i, 4. g, 5. f, 6. c, 7. b, 8. e, 9. h

**Grammar Points Answers**
1. a) the year  b) the hard part  c) (fixing/solving) the problem
2. a) working with Anna  b) leaving messages  c) going to the meetings

**Write Sample Answer**
A: How's the team doing?
B: We're doing good. We're halfway through the new project now.
A: Any problems so far?
B: No, none so far. I'll continue monitoring the progress.

**Making Sentences Sample Answers**
1. How's the (team handling the news / new position working out / mood over there)?
2. We're halfway through (the design process / cleaning out the warehouse).
3. We're working through (the list / the issues at the site).
4. I'll continue (keeping a lookout for any problems / working from home).

**Roleplay Sample Answer**
Scenario 1
Person 1: How's the new project coming along?
Person 2: We're halfway through it.
Person 1: Anything I should know about?
Person 2: We're working through some supplier issues.
Person 1: I hope it's nothing serious.
Person 2: Not at all. I'll continue working with them to solve those issues.

**Homework Sample Answer**
Person 1: How's the project coming along?
Person 2: We're working through some roadblocks.
Person 1: Roadblocks? Are you in a tight spot?
Person 2: No. We're okay. We're still on schedule. We're halfway through the research phase. I'll continue keeping tabs on the status of the project.

**Meeting Tip**

# Giving Status Updates to Executives
경영진에게 진행 상황 업데이트하기

### ① Provide a summary. 요약하여 보고한다.

Give an overall summary of the status of the project. Express your feelings about the status. Also, tell them any worries you might have about any aspect of the project.

프로젝트의 진행 상황을 전체적으로 요약한다. 현황에 대한 내 느낌을 표현한다. 또한 프로젝트에 대해 우려하는 부분이 있다면 알린다.

> *I'm happy to say the project is going well. I'm a little worried about the weather, but I think we'll be fine.*
> 프로젝트가 잘 진행되고 있어 기쁩니다. 날씨가 조금 우려되지만, 괜찮을 것 같습니다.

### ② Give highlights. 중요한 부분을 보고한다.

Highlight any milestones achieved, good work by a team member, or a problem that has been solved.

중요한 단계 도달, 팀원의 좋은 성과, 혹은 해결된 문제 등을 조명한다.

> *The parking system is now complete. Angie Park has done a great job.*
> 주차 시스템이 이제 완성되었습니다. Angie Park가 아주 잘해 냈습니다.

### ③ Wrap it up. 마무리한다.

If you have a request, make it, and at the end, ask them if they have any questions. Remember to end on a positive note.

요청할 것이 있으면 하고, 끝부분에서는 질문이 있는지 물어본다. 긍정적으로 마무리하는 것도 기억한다.

> *Can I give you the photos tomorrow? Okay, do you have any questions?*
> 사진들은 내일 드려도 될까요? 자, 질문 있으세요?

## 11 Zoom/WebEX Meeting Expressions

# Are we all on the same page?

 **Learning Objectives**

- Learners can advise participants to use a specific feature of a virtual meeting app.
- Learners can mention they need to take a call.
- Learners can tell everyone they may need to drop off the meeting early.

 **Warm Up**

**Work with a partner or in a group. Discuss the following questions.**
1. What do you do if you get a call while you're having a virtual meeting?
2. Have you ever had to drop off a virtual meeting early?
3. What are some of the reasons people drop off early?

 # Dialogue

**Practice the dialogue with a partner.**

A: Good morning. It's just the three of us today. **I advise you all to unmute your mics. Are we all on the same page?** Peter?

B: Morning.

A: Mary?

C: Hey, John. Morning.

A: It's Monday, so any of us could get called away during the meeting.

B: Yeah, my boss might call me in anytime now. **If I drop off, please carry on without me.**

A: All right. Let's start the meeting. Mary, I think I hear your phone vibrating.

C: Wow, you're right. **I have to jump on a call.**

A: Will you be long?

C: No, it'll be quick. I'll be right back.

A: Sure. Put your mic on mute.

B: Oh, no. John, my boss just texted me. I'd better go.

A: Of course. I think we should have our meetings on Tuesdays from now on.

A: 좋은 아침입니다. 오늘은 우리 3명뿐입니다. **모두 마이크 음소거를 해제해 주세요. 모두 이해하셨죠?** Peter?

B: 좋은 아침입니다.

A: Mary?

C: 안녕하세요, John. 좋은 아침이에요.

A: 월요일이니까 회의 중 우리 중 누구라도 호출당할 수 있겠어요.

B: 네, 곧 제 상사가 절 부를 수도 있어요. **제가 나가게 되면 저 없이 계속하세요.**

A: 알았어요. 회의 시작합시다. Mary, 당신 전화가 진동하는 게 들리는 것 같은데요.

C: 와, 맞네요. **이 전화 받아야 해요.**

A: 오래 걸리나요?

C: 아니요. 잠깐이면 돼요. 금방 돌아올게요.

A: 좋아요. 마이크 음소거를 설정해 주세요.

B: 아이고, John, 제 상사가 방금 저에게 문자를 보냈어요. 저 가야겠어요.

A: 물론이죠. 이제부터 우리 회의는 화요일에 하는 게 좋을 것 같습니다.

### ✓ Comprehension Check

**Answer the questions.**

1. Why does John think they might be interrupted during the meeting?
2. Who might call Peter in anytime now?

 **Vocabulary**

**Match the words or expressions with the correct definitions.**

1. advise _____
2. unmute _____
3. be on the same page _____
4. Morning. _____
5. call someone away _____
6. anytime now _____
7. drop off _____
8. jump on a call _____
9. put on mute _____

a. 동의하다, 공감하다
b. 좋은 아침입니다. (Good 생략)
c. 권하다
d. 음소거를 설정하다
e. 곧, 금방
f. (회의 등에서) 나가다
g. 음소거를 해제하다
h. 전화를 받다
i. (~를) 호출하다, 불러내다

⊕ **Bonus Resources**

### Will do. 그렇게 할게요.

A: I advise you all to take notes. 모두 메모를 하세요.
B: **Will do.** 그렇게 할게요.

Will do는 주어나 목적어 없는, 마치 콩글리시처럼 느껴지는 표현으로, I will do that을 줄여서 쓴다고 보면 된다. 격식 없는 상황에서 의외로 자주 쓰는 표현으로, 함께 있는 사람들에게 친근감을 준다.

 **Grammar Points**

**Read the following and practice making sentences.**

**1. I advise you all to ~**

> I advise you all to ~는 '~하세요' 하며 뭔가를 권고할 때 사용한다. 같은 장소에 모인 사람들을 말하는 you all은 더 간단하게 everyone으로 써도 무방하다.
> 
> *I advise you all to stay calm.* 모두 침착하세요.

a) I advise you all to _____. 모두 더 조심하세요.

b) I advise you all to _____. 모두 준비하세요.

c) I advise you all to _____ if that happens. 그런 일이 생기면 저에게 알려주세요.

**2. Are we all ~?**

> Are we all ~?은 '우리 다 ~인가요?'를 묻는 패턴으로, 형용사나 전치사, ing 등 다양한 품사가 뒤에 붙는다. are we all 대신 is everyone을 사용할 수도 있는데, 여기서 everyone은 '나'도 포함된다.
> 
> *Are we all set?* 우리 다 준비됐나요?

a) Are we all _____? 우리 다 콘퍼런스에 가는 건가요?

b) Are we all _____? 우리 이제 다 기분 좋은 거죠?

c) Are we all _____? 우리 다 동의하나요?

---

**✏ Write**

**Make your own dialogue using the expressions from Grammar Points.**

A: _____

B: _____

A: _____

B: _____

 **Practice**

**Shadowing**

**Listen and repeat.**

1. **I advise you all to** participate.
   **I advise you all to** volunteer.

2. **Are we all** ready to start?
   **Are we all** in a bad mood?

3. **If I** may, I'd like to add something.
   **If I** could go, I would.

4. **I have to** take it easy for a few days.
   **I have to** ask him tomorrow.

5. Okay, **will do**.

**Making Sentences**

**Practice making sentences. Use the words in the parentheses or use your own. Then, read your sentences to your partner or group. After sharing your sentences, practice saying someone else's sentences.**

1. I advise you all to _____. (consider, read, pause)

2. Are we all _____? (in, worried, blaming)

3. If I _____. (need, understood)

4. I have to _____. (drop, know, take)

 **Roleplay**

**Roleplay the following scenarios with a partner. Practice and change roles.**

Scenario 1

> **People are starting a Zoom meeting.**
> 
> **Person 1:** ask if everyone's here
> 
> **Person 2:** say hold on / you have to look at the list

Scenario 2

> **People are talking about being behind schedule during a Zoom meeting.**
> 
> **Person 1:** advise everyone to look at the agenda
> 
> **Person 2:** say you have to get your copy / say if you don't come back in 10 seconds, start without you

 **Homework**

**Write a short dialogue of people having a Zoom meeting.**

_____

_____

**Warm Up Sample Answers**
1. I (quickly take the call / don't answer / send a text message to the caller).
2. Yes, I have. / No, I haven't.
3. They need to (take a call / go to another meeting / go and see someone / go see a doctor).

**Comprehension Check Answers**
1. Because it's Monday.
2. His boss might call him in.

**Vocabulary Answers**
1. c, 2. g, 3. a, 4. b, 5. i, 6. e, 7. f, 8. h, 9. d

**Grammar Points Answers**
1. a) be more careful  b) get ready  c) let me know
2. a) going to the conference  b) happy now  c) in agreement

**Write Sample Answer**
A: Are we all going to the event?
B: Yes. I advise you all to go.
A: What'll happen if I don't go?
B: Nothing, of course. It's not mandatory.

**Making Sentences Sample Answers**
1. I advise you all to (consider this / read the manual / pause and think).
2. Are we all (in trouble / worried about this / blaming the customer)?
3. If I (need anything, I'll call you / understood you correctly, my answer is no).
4. I have to (drop my boss off / know if she's coming / take another call).

**Roleplay Sample Answer**
Scenario 1
Person 1: Are we all here?
Person 2: Hold on. I have to look at the list. I think we're missing Joseph.
Person 1: Why don't you text him?
Person 2: I have to get my phone from the other room.
Person 3: I'll text him.
Person 1: Thanks. I advise you all to put your phones on vibrate, by the way.

**Homework Sample Answer**
Person 1: Good afternoon. I advise you all to turn on your videos.
Person 2: Will do.
Person 3: Uh, sorry Jerry. I have to jump on a call.
Person 1: Will it take a while?
Person 3: Yes, it might take a while. If I drop off, please carry on without me.
Person 1: Okay. Are we all looking at the agenda? Let's start with the problems with the new app. I'm talking about Zengo 3.

**Meeting Tip**

# Common Virtual Meeting Expressions in English
화상 회의에서 자주 쓰는 영어 표현

### ① Asking for repetition 재차 물을 때

Could you repeat that? 다시 말씀해 주시겠어요?
Can you say that again? 다시 말씀해 주시겠어요?

### ② Asking someone to speak slower 더 천천히 말해달라고 요청할 때

Can you speak a little slower? 더 천천히 말씀하시겠어요?
Could you slow down, please? 더 천천히 말씀하시겠어요?

### ③ Asking someone to speak louder 더 크게 말해달라고 요청할 때

Can you speak up? 더 크게 말씀하시겠어요?
Could you speak a little louder? 조금 더 크게 말씀하시겠어요?

### ④ Screen sharing: me 화면 공유: 본인

Can you see my screen? 제 스크린 보이세요?
Are you able to see my screen? 제 스크린 보이세요?

### ⑤ Screen sharing: others 화면 공유: 다른 사람

You're not sharing. 공유가 안 되고 있는데요.
I can't see your screen. 스크린이 안 보여요.

### ⑥ Taking another call 다른 전화 받을 때

I have to jump on another call. 다른 전화 받아야 해요.
I need to take this call. 전화 받아야 해요.

### ⑦ Unmuting 음소거 해제

Can you turn off mute? 음소거를 해제하시겠어요?
You're on mute. 음소거 상태인데요.

**Zoom/WebEX Troubleshooting**

# 12 I'm experiencing some major connectivity issues.

## Learning Objectives

- Learners can troubleshoot problems that occur during virtual meetings.
- Learners can make suggestions on troubleshooting problems.
- Learners can express what technical issues they are facing.

## Warm Up

**Work with a partner or in a group. Discuss the following questions.**

1. What was a recent technical issue you had with your virtual meeting app?
2. What virtual program app do you use?
3. Which do you prefer: face-to-face meetings or virtual meetings? Why?

 Dialogue

**Practice the dialogue with a partner.**

A: Darren, your screen was gone for a minute.
B: I know. **I'm experiencing some major connectivity issues.**
A: Yeah, you keep dropping off and coming back in.
B: This is my third time today joining the meeting, but I'm still having problems.
C: **Try closing out of Zoom and then reopening it.**
B: Yes, I did that, Emma. Twice.
C: It might be your laptop then.
B: My laptop?
C: Yes. **Have you tried joining from a different device?**
B: No, I haven't, but I'm thinking it's my Wi-Fi. It's given me trouble before.
A: Let's just start and hope Darren's issue gets sorted out.
B: Yeah, guys, don't worry about me. I'll figure it out. I'll go and check the Wi-Fi.
C: Good idea. **Feel free to ask if you need assistance.**
B: All right. I appreciate that.

A: Darren, 당신 화면이 1분 정도 없어졌어요.
B: 알아요. **몇 가지 중대한 연결 문제가 발생하고 있어요.**
A: 그러게요, 계속 나갔다가 들어왔다가 하네요.
B: 이게 제가 오늘 세 번째 회의 들어온 건데, 아직 문제가 있네요.
C: **줌을 닫고 다시 열어 보시죠.**
B: 네, 해봤어요, Emma. 두 번이나요.
C: 그럼 노트북일 수 있어요.
B: 제 노트북이요?
C: 네. **다른 기기로 들어와 보셨나요?**
B: 아니요, 안 해봤지만, 문제는 제 와이파이인 거 같아요. 전에도 그걸로 애먹은 적 있어요.
A: 우리 일단 시작하고 Darren의 문제가 해결되길 바랍시다.
B: 그래요, 여러분, 제 걱정하지 마세요. 제가 해결해 볼게요. 가서 와이파이 확인해 볼게요.
C: 좋은 생각입니다. **도움이 필요하면 편하게 물어보세요.**
B: 알겠어요. 고마워요.

### ✓ Comprehension Check

**Answer the questions.**

1. What kind of issues is Darren experiencing?
2. What does Emma first tell Darren to try doing?

# Vocabulary

**Match the words or expressions with the correct definitions.**

1. major _____
2. connectivity issue _____
3. close out of _____
4. reopen _____
5. might be _____
6. device _____
7. give trouble _____
8. get sorted out _____
9. feel free to _____

a. (문제가) 해결되다
b. 편하게 ~하다
c. 다시 열다
d. 장치, 기구
e. 심각한
f. ~일 수도 있다
g. 애먹이다
h. 연결 문제
i. ~을 닫다, ~에서 나오다

## ⊕ Bonus Resources

### go nowhere 진전이 없다, 효과가 없다

A: Try changing the battery on your keyboard.
키보드 배터리를 한번 교체해 보세요.

B: I did that, too. This is **going nowhere**.
그것도 해봤어요. 이거 진전이 없네요.

go nowhere는 직역으로 '아무 곳도 못 간다'인데, 말 그대로 앞으로 나아갈 수 없다는 뜻으로, 뭔가 해결이 안 될 때 사용한다.

## Grammar Points

**Read the following and practice making sentences.**

**1. Try + ~ing**

> Try ~ing는 '~을 해보세요' 하면서 뭔가를 시도해 보라고 권할 때 쓰는 패턴이다. 조금 더 성의 있게 말하려면 Why don't you try ~ing 패턴을 쓰면 좋다.
> 
> *Try adjusting the volume.* 음량을 조절해 보세요.

a) Try _____ some new ideas. 새로운 아이디어들을 생각해 보세요.

b) Try _____. 당신 브라우저를 열어 보세요.

c) Try _____. 데이터베이스를 검색해 보세요.

**2. Feel free to ~**

> '~하는 걸 자유롭게 느끼세요'로 직역되는 Feel free to ~패턴은 '편하게 ~하세요', '주저 말고 ~하세요' 등, 부담 없이 무언가를 하라고 권할 때 유용한 표현이다.
> 
> *Feel free to take one.* 편하게 하나 가져가세요.

a) Feel free to _____. 편하게 질문하세요.

b) Feel free to _____. 편하게 찾아보세요.

c) Feel free to _____ your suggestions. 편하게 제안을 메일로 보내주세요.

### Write

**Make your own dialogue using the expressions from Grammar Points.**

A: _____

B: _____

A: _____

B: _____

 **Practice**

**Shadowing**

**Listen and repeat.**

1. **I'm** hav**ing** some problems at the office.
   **I'm** work**ing** late.

2. **Try** flick**ing** on the switch.
   **Try** gett**ing** her to talk more.

3. **Have you tried** reopening the app?
   **Have you tried** the coffee?

4. **Feel free to** leave early.
   **Feel free to** use my laptop.

5. This meeting is **going nowhere**.

**Making Sentences**

**Practice making sentences. Use the words in the parentheses or use your own. Then, read your sentences to your partner or group. After sharing your sentences, practice saying someone else's sentences.**

1. I'm _____. (work, take, go)

2. Try _____. (push, close, eat)

3. Have you tried _____? (talk, Thai food, dessert)

4. Feel free to _____. (ask, check, come)

## Roleplay

**Roleplay the following scenarios with a partner. Practice and change roles.**

Scenario 1

> **Two people are talking about a laptop during a Zoom meeting.**
> **Person 1:** say you're having trouble with your laptop
> **Person 2:** suggest turning it off and then on again

Scenario 2

> **Two people are talking about troubleshooting during a Zoom meeting.**
> **Person 1:** say you're experiencing issues with your headphones
> **Person 2:** ask Person 1 to try a different set of headphones or look at the audio settings

## Homework

**Write a short dialogue of two people talking about connectivity issues with Zoom.**

_____

_____

### Warm Up Sample Answers
1. My (webcam/mic/program/connection) (didn't work / kept turning off).
2. I use (Zoom/Skype/WebEx).
3. I prefer (face-to-face meetings / virtual meetings) because (it's easier to communicate / more people can participate / people from different locations can participate).

### Comprehension Check Answers
1. Darren is experiencing major connectivity issues.
2. Emma tells Darren to try closing out of Zoom and then reopening it.

### Vocabulary Answers
1. e, 2. h, 3. i, 4. c, 5. f, 6. d, 7. g, 8. a, 9. b

### Grammar Points Answers
1. a) coming up with  b) opening your browser  c) searching the database
2. a) ask questions  b) look it up  c) email me

### Write Sample Answer
A: Try using the eraser tool.
B: It's not working. Feel free to give it a try yourself if you want.
A: Oh. You're right. Have you tried using the computer over there?
B: Not yet. Let me try that.

### Making Sentences Sample Answers
1. I'm (working with them now / taking some time off / going on vacation).
2. Try (pushing the button / closing the window / eating earlier).
3. Have you tried (talking to him / Thai food before / the dessert)?
4. Feel free to (ask me anything / check the numbers / come in anytime).

### Roleplay Sample Answer
Scenario 1
Person 1: I'm having trouble with my laptop.
Person 2: Try turning it off and then on again.
Person 1: I did. It didn't work.
Person 2: Have you tried checking the setup?
Person 1: Not yet. I'll try checking that.
Person 2: Feel free to call me if you have any further questions.

### Homework Sample Answer
Person 1: I'm experiencing some major connectivity issues.
Person 2: Try closing out of Zoom and then reopening it.
Person 1: I've tried that, but this is going nowhere.
Person 2: Have you tried joining from a different device?
Person 1: No. Maybe I'll try that.
Person 2: Okay. Feel free to ask if you need assistance.

`Meeting Tip`

# Speaking with Confidence during Zoom Meetings
줌 회의 중 자신 있게 말하기

### ① Tone of voice 목소리

Avoid speaking in a monotone. If you do, you'll sound uninterested. Vary your pitch and intonation.

단조롭게 말하지 않는다. 무관심한 듯하게 들릴 수 있기 때문이다. 음높이와 억양에 변화를 준다.

### ② Speed 속도

When people are nervous or excited, they tend to speak too fast. Try to speak slowly, especially if you're having a meeting with non-native English speakers.

사람이 불안하거나 들떠 있을 때 말을 너무 빨리하는 경향이 있다. 특히 영어가 모국어가 아닌 사람들과 회의를 하는 경우에는 천천히 말하도록 노력한다.

### ③ Repeating 반복

When a participant says he or she didn't understand what you said, don't get embarrassed or panic. Smile. Then repeat or rephrase what you said.

어떤 참가자가 내가 한 말을 잘 이해 못했다고 하더라도 당황하거나 놀라지 않는다. 미소를 짓는다. 그다음 다시 말하거나 바꾸어 말해 본다.

### ④ Volume 음량

People tend to speak softly when they are not confident about speaking English. No one expects you to speak perfect English. Sit up straight and speak loudly with confidence.

영어에 자신이 없는 사람들은 작게 말하는 경향이 있다. 아무도 내가 완벽한 영어를 구사하리라고 기대하지 않는다. 똑바로 앉아서 자신 있게 말한다.

### ⑤ Nonverbal communication 비언어적 소통

Unlike telephone calls, people can see you. You can use facial expressions and gestures to help communicate your intentions.

전화 통화와는 달리 사람들이 나를 볼 수 있다. 표정과 제스처를 써서 나의 의사전달을 돕는다.

# PAGODA
# BUSINESS
# BIBLE

Advanced

# WRITING

# 1  Requesting Progress Updates

 **Learning Objectives**

- Learners can request progress updates on a project or task.
- Learners can ask for a timeline.
- Learners can explain the reason for requesting an update.

 **Warm Up**

**Work with a partner or in a group. Discuss the following questions.**

1. Have you ever written an e-mail requesting a progress update?
2. If you have, did you ask for a timeline?
3. Why is it important to get regular updates?

## Sample Writing

**Read the sample e-mail.**

From: jkyoon@paragon.com
To: aking@paragon.com
Subject: AAA Project Timeline

Hi Austin,

**I just wanted to touch base with you on the AAA Project.** I understand that we're halfway through it at this point and that we're on schedule.

**Could you give me an estimated timeline for the remaining tasks?** I'm supposed to make a quick report to Director Han next week. It'd be great if I could give him some specifics about the status of the project. A simple timeline would be fine.

Thanks!

Jake

발신: jkyoon@paragon.com
수신: aking@paragon.com
제목: AAA 프로젝트 일정

안녕하세요, Austin.

**AAA 프로젝트와 관련해서 연락드립니다.** 프로젝트가 현재 절반 정도 완료되었고 일정대로 진행되고 있다는 것을 알고 있습니다.

**남은 업무에 대한 대략적인 일정을 알려주시겠어요?** 다음 주에 한 이사님께 간단하게 보고하기로 되어있습니다. 프로젝트 진행 상태에 대해 더 세부적인 내용을 드릴 수 있으면 정말 좋을 것 같아서요. 간단한 일정표면 됩니다.

고마워요!

Jake

### Comprehension Check

**Answer the questions.**

1. What does Jake want from Austin?
2. Why does he need it?

# Vocabulary

**Match the words or expressions with the correct definitions.**

1. at this point _____
2. estimated _____
3. remaining _____
4. be supposed to _____
5. specifics _____
6. status _____

a. 남은
b. ~하기로 되다
c. 현재
d. 상태, 상황
e. 세부적인 내용
f. 예상되는

## ✓ Vocab Test

**Fill in the blanks with the correct words or expressions.**

at this point / estimated / remaining / was supposed to / specifics / status

1. What items are _____?
2. We're unable to accept that _____.
3. She _____ be in New York last week.
4. Tell me the _____ of the project, please.
5. What is the _____ time of delivery?
6. The lawyers want to know the _____ of the contract.

## ⊕ Bonus Resources

### shift into high gear  박차를 가하다, 속도를 높이다

A: The deadline's coming up fast, George. Your team needs to **shift into high gear**.
마감 기한이 빨리 다가오고 있습니다, George. 당신 팀은 속도를 높여야 해요.

B: We're trying. Our team is already putting in overtime.
저희는 노력하고 있습니다. 저희 팀은 이미 초과 근무를 하고 있어요.

자동차를 몰 때 더 빨리 가려고 '고속 기어로 높이다'라는 말에서 나온 shift into high gear는 말 그대로 무언가를 더욱 빨리, 더 세게 한다는 뜻이다. shift 대신 kick 또는 get이란 단어를 쓰기도 한다.

 **Grammar Points**

**Read the following and practice making sentences.**

1. I wanted to touch base on ~

> I wanted to touch base on ~은 '~와 관련해서 연락하다'라는 뜻이다. touch base는 마치 야구 경기에서 베이스를 만지는 것처럼 무언가를 짚고 넘어가는 느낌을 주는데, 누군가와 특정 쟁점에 대해 연락하거나 논의하는 것을 말한다. on 앞에 with you를 넣는 경우도 많다.
>
> *I wanted to touch base with you on the late shipment.* 지연되는 배송과 관련해서 연락드립니다.

a) I wanted to touch base on _____.
어제 있었던 Joe의 프레젠테이션과 관련해서 연락드립니다.

b) I wanted to touch base on _____. 당신이 언급했던 것과 관련해서 연락드립니다.

c) I wanted to touch base with you on _____. 몇 가지 사항과 관련해서 연락드립니다.

2. Could you give me ~?

> 단순하게 보일 수도 있는 '~을 주시겠어요?'를 표현하는 Could you give me ~?는 무엇이든 상대방에서 요청하는 것이 있으면 구두상이나 필기상이나 쓸 수 있는 좋은 표현이다. give와 me 사이에 to를 넣는 실수는 피하자.
>
> *Could you give me some time to think it over?* 생각할 시간을 좀 주시겠어요?

a) Could you give me _____ why I should accept your explanation?
왜 당신의 설명을 받아들여야 하는지 타당한 이유 하나만 말해 보시겠어요?

b) Could you give me _____ for the client? 고객의 연락처를 주시겠어요?

c) Could you give me _____ on how to deal with the problem?
이 문제를 어떻게 처리해야 할지 아이디어를 좀 주시겠어요?

 **Practice**

**Making Sentences**

**Practice writing sentences. Then, read your sentences to your partner or group.**

**1.** I'm supposed to ~

- _____
- _____
- _____

**2.** It'd be great if ~

- _____
- _____
- _____

**Editing Sentences**

**Correct the mistakes, if any, you find in the e-mail.**

> From: yhkim@paragon.com
> To: cpotter@paragon.com
> Subject: Requesting Updates
>
> Hi Cybil,
>
> I ①<u>wanting</u> to ②<u>touch base</u> on the progress of your negotiation ③<u>with</u> James Harris. I understand that you've met with him twice now.
>
> Could you ④<u>give me</u> an outline of your discussions so far? It'd be ⑤<u>great</u> if you could highlight any agreements you've made.
>
> Regards,
>
> Young

## Real Writing

**Write an e-mail based on the following scenarios. Exchange your e-mail with a partner and check your partner's e-mail for errors.**

`Scenario 1`

> Write an e-mail to Yann, a co-worker. Say you're touching base on the new presentation slides and that you understand Yann's almost done with them. Ask him to give you an idea when you can get them, since you're supposed to practice the presentation with your team next week. Add that it'd be great if you could get them by the end of the week.

`Scenario 2`

> Write an e-mail to a supplier. Indicate that you're touching base regarding a delivery. Ask when you can get the delivery schedule. You need to report it to your boss very soon.

From: nicweathers@paragon.com
To: yannproust@paragon.com
Subject: _____

_____
_____
_____

## Homework

**Write a short e-mail requesting a progress update.**

_____
_____
_____

111

**Warm Up Sample Answers**
1. (Yes, I have / No, I've never) written an e-mail requesting a progress update.
2. (Yes, I did / No, I didn't) ask for a timeline.
3. It's important because (it helps me keep track of everything / I can make good decisions / I feel like I'm part of the team).

**Comprehension Check Answers**
1. Jake wants an estimated timeline for the remaining tasks for the AAA project.
2. He needs it because he has to make a quick report to Director Han next week.

**Vocabulary Answers**
1. c, 2. f, 3. a, 4. b, 5. e, 6. d

**Vocab Test Answers**
1. remaining, 2. at this point, 3. was supposed to, 4. status, 5. estimated, 6. specifics

**Grammar Points Answers**
1. a) Joe's presentation from yesterday b) what you said c) a few/several/some things
2. a) one good reason b) the contact number/information c) some ideas

**Making Sentences Sample Answers**
1. I'm supposed to (have dinner with the guests tonight / attend the meeting this afternoon / apologize to him).
2. It'd be great if (you could join us for dinner / I could get the schedule by tomorrow / the meeting could be pushed back).

**Editing Sentences Answers**
① wanting → wanted

**Real Writing Sample Answer**
Scenario 1
Subject: New Presentation Slides

Hi Yann,

I just wanted to touch base with you on the new presentation slides. I understand you're almost done with them.

Could you give me an idea of when I can get them? I'm supposed to practice the presentation with my team next week. It'd be great if I could get the slides by the end of the week.

Regards,

Nicholas

**Homework Sample Answer**
Subject: Estimated Timeline for Stage 3

Hi Jess,

I wanted to touch base with you on the progress of the Wilson project. I understand that the third stage is moving quite slowly. We really need to shift into high gear.

Could you give me an estimated timeline for the completion of this stage? I'm supposed to meet with our partners early next month. It'd be great if I could tell them we're done with that stage. Let me know.

Regards,

Morgan

**Writing Tip**

# Providing Routine Information
일상적인 정보를 제공할 때

E-mails sharing routine information should be brief and to the point. These e-mails should sound neutral.
일상적인 정보를 공유하는 이메일은 짧고 요점이 명확해야 한다. 이런 이메일은 중립적인 느낌을 주는 게 좋다.

### ① Start with the purpose. 목적에 맞게 시작한다.

Begin by stating the reason for writing the e-mail. Say what information you are providing.
이메일을 작성하는 이유를 먼저 밝히고 시작한다. 내가 제공하는 정보가 무엇인지 언급한다.

- *I wanted to give you an update on the progress of the Avery project.*
  Avery 프로젝트의 진행 상황에 대한 업데이트를 드리고자 합니다.

### ② Provide details. 세부적인 내용을 제공한다.

Then move on to providing specific information that will be helpful for the recipient.
그런 다음 수신자에게 도움이 될 만한 특정 정보를 제공한다.

- *We are currently in the final stage of the project. I estimate that this stage will be completed by November 2. This will mean we'll be done two weeks ahead of schedule. Obviously, this is an estimate of the ideal scenario and there could be unforeseen roadblocks ahead.*
  현재 저희는 프로젝트의 최종 단계에 있습니다. 이 단계는 11월 2일까지 끝날 것으로 저는 추정하고 있습니다. 이는 예정보다 2주 앞당겨 끝날 수 있다는 뜻입니다. 물론 이는 이상적인 시나리오에 대한 추정일 뿐이며 앞으로 예상치 못한 장애물이 있을 수 있습니다.

### ③ End in a courteous way. 정중하게 마무리한다.

Close with a courteous tone. You might say you're available to address any questions or comments from the recipient.
정중한 어조로 마무리한다. 수신자의 질문이나 의견에 대해 답변할 수 있다고 말해도 좋다.

- *I'll continue to update you on the progress. Let me know if you have any questions or comments about the project. Thanks.*
  진행 상황에 대해 계속 업데이트를 드리겠습니다. 프로젝트에 대한 질문이나 의견이 있으시면 알려주세요. 감사합니다.

# 2. Disagreeing with Someone

## Learning Objectives

- Learners can disagree with a recipient.
- Learners can use a polite but firm tone when disagreeing.
- Learners can provide reasons for disagreeing.

## Warm Up

**Work with a partner or in a group. Discuss the following questions.**

1. How often do you write e-mails disagreeing with someone?
2. Have you ever disagreed with your boss via e-mail?
3. Is it difficult for you to find the right expressions when you state your disagreement?

# Sample Writing

**Read the sample e-mail.**

From: craigwang@smartthings.com
To: benanderson@smartthings.com
Subject: Paragon Project Temporary Housing Cost

Hi Benny,

**I have some concerns regarding the costs of this project.** My main concern is the cost of temporary housing. I know you said that the $50,000 quote seems reasonable.

**I have a slightly different view.** To me, $50,000 for a ten-week project seems way too high. In my experience, a project this size requires only half that amount. Considering this, it might be a good idea to get additional quotes from other agencies.

Let me know your thoughts. Thanks.

Regards,

Craig

발신: craigwang@smartthings.com
수신: benanderson@smartthings.com
제목: Paragon 프로젝트 임시 거처 비용

안녕하세요, Benny.

**이번 프로젝트 관련 비용에 대해 몇 가지 우려되는 점이 있습니다.** 제가 가장 우려하는 것은 임시 숙소 비용입니다. 5만 달러 견적이 타당하다고 말씀하신 것은 알고 있습니다.

**저는 좀 다른 의견이 있습니다.** 제 생각에는 10주 프로젝트에 5만 달러는 너무 높은 것 같습니다. 저의 경험으로는 그 정도 프로젝트 규모는 그 금액의 절반만 필요합니다. 이 점을 고려하면 다른 중개업소들에서 추가 견적서를 받는 게 좋을 수도 있을 것 같습니다.

당신의 의견을 알려주세요. 감사합니다.

수고하세요.

Craig

## Comprehension Check

**Answer the questions.**

1. What is Craig's main concern?
2. What does Craig suggest they do?

## Vocabulary

**Match the words or expressions with the correct definitions.**

1. concern _____
2. temporary housing _____
3. reasonable _____
4. view _____
5. in my experience _____
6. might be _____

a. 임시 거처
b. 의견, 관점
c. 내 경험 상
d. 아마/어쩌면 ~일 것 같다
e. 우려, 염려
f. 타당한, 합리적인

### ✓ Vocab Test

**Fill in the blanks with the correct words or expressions.**

concern / temporary housing / reasonable / view / in my experience / might be

1. John and Steve will need _____ when they're in Chicago.
2. Does anyone have a different _____?
3. That's my main _____ regarding the new policy.
4. You know, that _____ true.
5. The price seems quite _____.
6. _____, the best thing to do is just wait.

### ⊕ Bonus Resources

### do the trick 효과가 있다

A: The client won't accept our new schedule. Should I talk to his boss Cindy?
고객이 저희의 새 스케줄을 수락해 주지 않네요. 그분 상사 Cindy와 얘기해 볼까요?

B: Yeah, that should **do the trick**. Cindy is more understanding.
네, 그렇게 하면 통할 겁니다. Cindy는 이해심이 많으세요.

여기서 trick은 '속임수'가 아니라 '요령', '비결'을 뜻한다. 그래서 do the trick은 특정 방식이나 방법이 '~이 비결이다', '~이 요령이다'라는 의미로 쓰인다.

 **Grammar Points**

**Read the following and practice making sentences.**

1. I have some concerns regarding ~

> I have some concerns regarding ~은 '~에 대해 몇 가지 우려되는 점이 있다'를 뜻한다. 비슷한 뜻을 가진 I'm worried about ~보다 조금 더 정중하게 말하고자 할 때 사용할 수 있는 좋은 표현이다.
> 
> 📖 *I have some concerns regarding your proposal.* 그쪽 제안서에 대해 우려되는 점이 있습니다.

**a)** I have some concerns regarding _____.
프레젠테이션에 대해 몇 가지 우려되는 점이 있습니다.

**b)** I have some concerns regarding _____.
방금 그가 말한 것에 대해 몇 가지 우려되는 점이 있습니다.

**c)** I have some concerns regarding _____.
내일 있을 미팅에 대해 몇 가지 우려되는 점이 있습니다.

2. I have a different ~

> 간단한 표현으로 간주할 수 있는 I have a different ~는 '나는 다른 ~을 가지고 있다'를 의미하는데, 상대방과는 다른 의견이나 관점, 질문, 답변 등을 말할 때 유용하게 쓸 수 있다.
> 
> 📖 *I have a different expectation.* 저는 다른 기대를 하고 있습니다.

**a)** I have a different _____. 저는 그것에 대해 다른 의견을 가지고 있습니다.
**b)** I have a different _____. 저는 당신에게 드릴 다른 질문이 있습니다.
**c)** I have a different _____. 저는 이번 상황에 대해 다른 이론을 가지고 있습니다.

# Practice

**Making Sentences**

**Practice writing sentences. Then, read your sentences to your partner or group.**

1. In my experience, ~

   - _____
   - _____
   - _____

2. It might be a good idea to ~

   - _____
   - _____
   - _____

**Editing Sentences**

**Correct the mistakes, if any, you find in the e-mail.**

> From: gusbest@buildnow.com
> To: ilsayates@bu.com
> Subject: About the New Project
>
> Hi Ilsa,
>
> I have some concerns regarding the new project ①<u>in Daejeon</u>. My main concern is ②<u>the distance</u>. I know you said the project manager can commute every day.
>
> I have a different idea. In my experience, driving every day will be too ③<u>exhausted</u>. Considering this, it might be a good idea to ④<u>hire</u> a reliable subcontractor in Daejeon to ⑤<u>oversea</u> the project.
>
> Let me know your thoughts.
>
> Regards,
>
> Gus

# Real Writing

**Write an e-mail based on the following scenarios. Exchange your e-mail with a partner and check your partner's e-mail for errors.**

Scenario 1

> Write an e-mail to Betty, a co-worker. Say you have some concerns regarding her comments about the proposed new format for expense reports, mainly about her view that it's taking too long to fill out. Add that you have a different point of view. A longer form allows people to catch expenses they might not have otherwise.

Scenario 2

> Write an e-mail to a supplier. Express your concerns about their new delivery schedule, especially since the items are needed ASAP. Add that it might be a good idea to ship some of the critical items first, instead of waiting for all items to be consolidated.

From: e.cane@globalist.com
To: b.hahn@globalist.com
Subject: _____

___

___

___

# Homework

**Write a short e-mail disagreeing with a team member about a design element.**

___

___

___

**Warm Up Sample Answers**
1. I (often/sometimes/rarely) write them.
2. (Yes, I have / No, I've never) disagreed with my boss via e-mail.
3. (Yes, it's / No, it's not) difficult to find the right expressions.

**Comprehension Check Answers**
1. His main concern is the temporary housing cost of the project.
2. He suggests that they get additional quotes from other agencies.

**Vocabulary Answers**
1. e, 2. a, 3. f, 4. b, 5. c, 6. d

**Vocab Test Answers**
1. temporary housing, 2. view, 3. concern, 4. might be, 5. reasonable, 6. In my experience

**Grammar Points Answers**
1. a) the presentation b) what he just said c) tomorrow's meeting
2. a) view/opinion about it b) question to ask you c) theory about the/this situation

**Making Sentences Sample Answers**
1. In my experience, (San Francisco has great weather / Mondays are not good for meetings / our boss knows what he's doing).
2. It might be a good idea to (tell the client now / start working on it / go to lunch soon).

**Editing Sentences Answers**
③ exhausted → exhausting, ⑤ oversea → oversee

**Real Writing Sample Answer**
Scenario 1
Subject: New Expense Report Format

Hi Betty,

I have some concerns regarding your comments about the proposed new format for expense reports. My main concern is what you said about it now taking too long to fill out.

I have a slightly different point of view about that. In my experience, a longer form allows us to catch expenses we might not have otherwise. Considering this, it might be a good idea to support this new format.

Regards,

Ethan

**Homework Sample Answer**
Subject: Packaging Color

Hi Avery,

I have some concerns regarding your design ideas. My main concern is your color choice for the packaging. I know you wanted to add some kind of dynamic element by delivering our product wrapped in bright red paper.

I have a slightly different idea about the color. In my experience, all red is not always the best choice. It might be a good idea to at least add one more color to it. A bit of green or yellow would probably do the trick.

Let me know your thoughts.

Regards,

Kim

**Writing Tip**

# Expressing Disagreement in E-mails
이메일에 반대 의견 표현하기

In all business communications, including e-mails, it's important to use polite expressions when disagreeing.
이메일을 포함한 모든 비즈니스 커뮤니케이션 수단에서 반대 입장을 말할 때는 정중한 표현을 쓰는 것이 중요하다.

## ① Disagree politely. 정중하게 동의하지 않는다고 한다.

Use phrases that express regret such as "I'm afraid" or "I'm sorry but" to cushion the impact of your disagreement.
나의 반대 입장에 대한 충격을 완화하기 위해 'I'm afraid'나 'I'm sorry but' 등 유감을 표하는 어구를 사용한다.

- **I'm afraid** I have to disagree. 유감이지만 동의할 수 없습니다.
- **I'm sorry but** I have to disagree. 유감이지만 동의할 수 없습니다.

## ② Say you're not sure. 확신이 안 간다고 얘기한다.

Express uncertainty about the recipient's opinion. That way, that person will feel that you are not directly disagreeing with him or her.
수신자의 의견에 대한 불확실성을 표현한다. 그렇게 하면 상대방은 내가 직접적으로 동의하고 있지 않다는 것을 느낄 수 있을 것이다.

- **I'm not sure** I can agree with what you said about the project.
  이 프로젝트에 대해 말씀하신 내용에 제가 동의할 수 있을지 확실히 모르겠습니다.
- **I'm not too confident that** this is the right policy for the suppliers.
  이것이 납품업체들을 위한 올바른 정책인지 확신이 서지 않습니다.

## ③ Use the word "but." 단어 'but'을 사용한다.

First say something positive about the opinion. Then use the conjunction "but" and express your reservation or disagreement.
먼저 해당 의견에 대해 긍정적인 점을 말한다. 그런 다음 접속사 'but'을 사용하여 의구심이나 반대 입장을 표현한다.

- I see what you're saying, **but** I think you might be missing the point.
  무슨 말씀인지 알겠지만, 의도를 잘못 이해하시는 것 같습니다.
- That's a valid point, **but** I have a different opinion. 일리가 있는 지적이지만, 저는 다르게 생각합니다.

# 3 Making Urgent Requests

 **Learning Objectives**

- Learners can make an urgent request via e-mail.
- Learners can say they understand that the recipient may be busy.
- Learners can express appreciation for the anticipated response from the recipient.

 **Warm Up**

**Work with a partner or in a group. Discuss the following questions.**
1. From whom do you usually get urgent requests?
2. Do you often send urgent requests via e-mail?
3. If so, what are your urgent requests usually about?

## Sample Writing

**Read the sample e-mail.**

From: harveysells@paragon.com
To: lewisclark@paragon.com
Subject: Need Your Status Report!

Hi Lewis,

I'm writing to you because I haven't received a response from you regarding my request for the project status report. **I understand that you may have other commitments.** It's just that I have to include your report in my monthly report to the directors. That report is due this Friday.

**If you could prioritize this matter, it would be very much appreciated.** You would really be helping me out. Thanks!

Regards,

Harvey

발신: harveysells@paragon.com

수신: lewisclark@paragon.com

제목: 당신의 현황 보고서가 필요해요!

안녕하세요, Lewis.

제가 이메일을 드리는 이유는 아직 제가 요청한 프로젝트 현황 보고서에 대한 답변을 받지 못했기 때문입니다. **해야 할 다른 일들도 있다는 건 이해합니다.** 다만 그쪽 보고서를 이사님께 드리는 월례 보고서에 포함시켜야 해서 그렇습니다. 그 보고서는 이번 금요일까지입니다.

**이 건을 우선적으로 처리해 주시면, 정말 감사하겠습니다.** 저를 아주 많이 도와주시는 겁니다. 고마워요!

수고하세요.

Harvey

### Comprehension Check

**Answer the questions.**

1. What does Harvey need from Lewis?
2. Why does he need it?

# Vocabulary

**Match the words or expressions with the correct definitions.**

1. status report _____
2. include _____
3. monthly _____
4. prioritize _____
5. this matter _____
6. help ~ out _____

a. 포함시키다
b. 우선적으로 처리하다
c. ~을 도와주다
d. 현황 보고서
e. 이 건, 이 문제
f. 월례

## ✓ Vocab Test

**Fill in the blanks with the correct words or expressions.**

status report / include / monthly / prioritize / this matter / help me out

1. Would you like a weekly report or a _____ report?
2. We need to _____ this task.
3. The presentation slides should _____ some graphs.
4. What are we doing about _____?
5. Please _____ with this.
6. Could you give me a _____ on this project?

## ⊕ Bonus Resources

### on the double 신속히, 빨리

A: When do you need the report on the Jenkins Project?
  Jenkins 프로젝트 보고서는 언제 필요하시나요?

B: Actually, I need to get it **on the double**. My boss is already asking for it.
  사실, 빨리 받아야 됩니다. 제 상사가 이미 요청하셨거든요.

double, 즉 '두 배'라는 뜻이 담긴 on the double이란 표현은 19세기 군인들에게 보통 걸음보다 두 배로 빨리 걸으라고 한 것에서 유래됐다. fast나 quickly 또는 as soon as possible 대신 쓸 수 있다.

**Grammar Points**

**Read the following and practice making sentences.**

1. I understand that ~

> I understand that ~은 '~은 이해합니다'를 말한다. 상대방이 처한 상황을 충분히 인지하고 있다는 뜻을 지니고 있긴 하지만, 나의 입장도 전하고자 할 때 흔히 사용하는 표현이다.
>
> *I understand that you're under a lot of pressure.* 압박감을 느끼시고 있다는 건 이해합니다.

a) I understand that _____ something new. 새로운 걸 시도하시고 싶다는 건 이해합니다.

b) I understand that _____. 엄청 바쁘시다는 건 이해합니다.

c) I understand that _____. 당신 상사가 화났다는 건 이해합니다.

2. If you could ~, it would be very much appreciated.

> If you could ~, it would be very much appreciated는 '~해주시면, 정말 감사하겠습니다'를 의미한다. 여기서 '할 수 있다'를 뜻하는 could가 들어가지만, 실은 정중하게 상대방에게 특정 행동을 유도하고자 할 때 사용한다.
>
> *If you could let me know, it would be very much appreciated.*
> 저에게 알려주시면, 정말 감사하겠습니다.

a) If you could _____, it would be very much appreciated.
그걸 한번 봐 주시면, 정말 감사하겠습니다.

b) If you could _____, it would be very much appreciated.
그것에 대해 John한테 얘기해주시면, 정말 감사하겠습니다.

c) If you could _____, it would be very much appreciated.
저에게 이메일을 보내주시면, 정말 감사하겠습니다.

 **Practice**

**Making Sentences**

**Practice writing sentences. Then, read your sentences to your partner or group.**

**1.** I'm writing to you because ~

- _____
- _____
- _____

**2.** It's just that ~

- _____
- _____
- _____

**Editing Sentences**

**Correct the mistakes, if any, you find in the e-mail.**

From: btkim@tablesnmore.com
To: vcruz@tablesnmore.com
Subject: Feedback on Lamp Sketches

Hi Vera,

I'm writing to you because I really need your feedback on the lamp sketches I ①<u>send you</u> last week. I understand that you are busy ②<u>with</u> the new project. It's just that I need to ③<u>finalize</u> the design ASAP.

If you could just let me ④<u>know</u> what you think, it would be ⑤<u>very much</u> appreciated. Thanks!

Regards,

Beatrice

## Real Writing

**Write an e-mail based on the following scenarios. Exchange your e-mail with a partner and check your partner's e-mail for errors.**

Scenario 1

> Write an e-mail to Luke, a co-worker in a different division. Say you're writing because you haven't gotten his answer regarding the industry conference next week. You understand that he might not be sure of his schedule yet, but you need to let the organizers know whether he's attending. Ask him to let you know by tomorrow morning.

Scenario 2

> Write an e-mail to a legal consultant. Say you're writing because you need to get his advice ASAP on a recent claim made by a client. Ask the consultant to give you some feedback by the end of the week.

From: brucelim@paragon.com
To: lguiterrez@paragon.com
Subject: _____

_____
_____
_____

## Homework

**Write a short e-mail urgently requesting another person's contact number.**

_____
_____
_____

**Warm Up Sample Answers**
1. I usually get urgent requests from (my boss / co-workers / vendors).
2. (Yes, I / No, I don't) send urgent requests via e-mail often.
3. They are usually about (a project / a delivery issue / a request for information).

**Comprehension Check Answers**
1. Harvey needs Lewis's project status report.
2. He needs it because he has to include it in the monthly report to the directors.

**Vocabulary Answers**
1. d, 2. a, 3. f, 4. b, 5. e, 6.c

**Vocab Test Answers**
1. monthly, 2. prioritize, 3. include, 4. this matter, 5. help me out, 6. status report

**Grammar Points Answers**
1. a) you want to try b) you are really busy c) your boss is angry
2. a) take a look at it/that b) talk to John about it/that c) send me an e-mail

**Making Sentences Sample Answers**
1. I'm writing to you because (I need a favor / you haven't given me an answer yet / I have to ask you a question).
2. It's just that (I'm not convinced / I don't have time / we're all very busy here).

**Editing Sentences Answers**
① send you → sent you

**Real Writing Sample Answer**
Scenario 1
Subject: Please Confirm Your Attendance

Hi Luke,

I'm writing to you because I haven't gotten your answer regarding the industry conference next week. I understand that you might not be sure of your schedule yet. It's just that I have to let the organizers know whether you're attending.

If you could just let me know by tomorrow morning, it would be very much appreciated. Thanks!

Regards,

Bruce

**Homework Sample Answer**
Subject: Jess Craven's Contact Info

Hi Debb,

I'm writing to you because I haven't gotten the contact number for Jess Craven from you yet. I understand that you're busy with the inventory. It's just that I need to talk to Jess on the double. It's about a new contract.

If you could just give me his number ASAP, it would be very much appreciated. Thanks!

Regards,

Nora

**Writing Tip**

# Using Polite Words to Express Urgency
긴급함을 표현할 때 정중한 말 사용하기

When you need someone's quick response, it's tempting to be direct. Sometimes that is necessary. In most situations, however, it is better to use polite words to express urgency. Let's look at some useful words.
누군가의 빠른 답변이 필요한 경우, 단도직입적으로 표현하고 싶을 것이다. 때로는 그럴 필요가 있다. 하지만 대부분의 경우, 정중한 말을 써서 긴급함을 표현하는 것이 좋다. 유용하게 사용할 수 있는 단어를 알아보자.

### ① immediate 즉각적인

> Ex: We need your **immediate** response.  즉각적인 답변이 필요합니다.

### ② earliest (possible) convenience 가급적 빨리

> Ex: Please respond at your **earliest possible convenience**.  가급적 빠른 시간 내에 답변하시기 바랍니다.

### ③ high priority 최우선 순위

> Ex: Ensure that this project remains a **high priority**.  이 프로젝트가 최우선 순위로 유지되도록 해 주세요.

### ④ time-sensitive 시간에 민감한

> Ex: This is an extremely **time-sensitive** matter.  이것은 시간에 매우 민감한 사안입니다.

### ⑤ prompt attention 즉각적인 조치

> Ex: Your **prompt attention** would be greatly appreciated.  즉각적인 조치에 감사드리겠습니다.

### ⑥ urgent 긴급한

> Ex: This is an **urgent** matter.  이것은 긴급한 사안입니다.

# 4 Expressing Gratitude to Someone

 ## Learning Objectives

- Learners can express gratitude to a recipient via e-mail.
- Learners can elaborate on the assistance given by the recipient.
- Learners can offer to return the favor when appropriate.

 ## Warm Up

**Work with a partner or in a group. Discuss the following questions.**

1. How often do you express gratitude to someone via e-mail?
2. Do you often get an e-mail thanking you for something?
3. When was the last time you sent an e-mail thanking someone?

 **Sample Writing**

**Read the sample e-mail.**

From: shpark@ultimatewest.com
To: twdavidson@ultimatewest.com
Subject: AA Project was a Success!

Hi Terry,

I just wanted to drop you a note and give you an update on the AA Project. My team just wrapped up the project last Friday. The client is ecstatic about the results. He even took us out to lunch!

**I can't thank you enough for your help on the project.** Your advice related to the scheduling was invaluable.

**If there's ever anything I can do to return the favor, please don't hesitate to let me know.**

Regards,

Seung-ho

발신: shpark@ultimatewest.com
수신: twdavidson@ultimatewest.com
제목: AA 프로젝트는 성공적이었어요!

안녕하세요, Terry.

AA 프로젝트에 대한 업데이트를 알려드리고자 간단한 메모를 남깁니다. 저의 팀은 막 지난 금요일에 프로젝트를 끝냈습니다. 결과에 대해 고객이 열광하고 있습니다. 저희에게 점심까지 사 주셨습니다!

**프로젝트에 도움을 주셔서 어떻게 감사드려야 할지 모르겠습니다.** 스케줄 계획과 관련된 조언은 정말 유용했습니다.

신세를 갚을 수 있는 무엇이라도 있으면 주저하지 말고 저에게 알려주세요.

좋은 하루 되세요.

승호

### Comprehension Check

**Answer the questions.**

1. Why is Seung-ho writing the e-mail?
2. What is he thanking Terry for?

# Vocabulary

**Match the words or expressions with the correct definitions.**

1. drop a note _____
2. ecstatic _____
3. take ~ out to lunch _____
4. scheduling _____
5. invaluable _____
6. return the favor _____

a. 간단한 메모를 남기다
b. 매우 유용한
c. 신세를 갚다, 보답하다
d. 열광한, 신난
e. ~에게 점심을 사다
f. 스케줄 계획

## Vocab Test

**Fill in the blanks with the correct words or expressions.**

drop me a note / ecstatic / take you out to lunch / scheduling / invaluable / return the favor

1. Let me _____ or dinner sometime.
2. Your skills are _____ to the company.
3. _____ when you can.
4. How can I _____?
5. The CEO is _____ about the sales results.
6. The pricing looks good but the _____ needs work.

## Bonus Resources

### I owe you one. 신세 졌어요.

A: Hey, Pam, I'm so grateful for what you did for me. **I owe you one.**
  있잖아요, Pam, 저를 위해 해주신 일에 감사드려요. 신세 졌습니다.

B: Oh, it was nothing. I'm just glad everything worked out.
  아, 별거 아니었습니다. 모든 게 다 잘 풀려서 그냥 좋기만 하네요.

I owe you one을 직역하면 '난 너에게 하나 빚졌어'가 되는데, 이번에 한 번 빚을 지었기에 언젠가는 그 빚을 갚겠다는 의미가 함께 담겨있다.

 **Grammar Points**

**Read the following and practice making sentences.**

**1.** I can't thank you enough for ~

> I can't thank you enough for ~는 '~에 어떻게 감사드려야 할지 모르겠습니다'라는 뜻이다. '~에 대해 충분히 감사를 드릴 수 없다'로 직역되는 이 표현은 비즈니스 현장에서는 물론, 일상에서도 상대방이 아주 큰 도움을 줬을 때 유용하게 쓸 수 있다.
>
> *I can't thank you enough for giving me a chance.*
> 저에게 기회를 주신 것에 대해 어떻게 감사드려야 할지 모르겠습니다.

**a)** I can't thank you enough for _____.
저희에게 알려주신 것에 대해 어떻게 감사드려야 할지 모르겠습니다.

**b)** I can't thank you enough for _____.
당신의 선물에 대해 어떻게 감사드려야 할지 모르겠습니다.

**c)** I can't thank you enough for _____.
모든 것에 대해 어떻게 감사드려야 할지 모르겠습니다.

**2.** If ~, please don't hesitate to let me know.

> If ~, please don't hesitate to let me know는 '~이 있으면 주저하지 말고 저에게 알려주세요'라는 의미로 쓰인다. 특히 이메일 마무리 부분에서 자주 사용되는데, 나에게 연락하는 것에 대해 부담 갖지 말라는 뜻을 강조하는 역할을 한다.
>
> *If you need my help, please don't hesitate to let me know.*
> 저의 도움이 필요하시면 주저하지 말고 저에게 알려주세요.

**a)** If _____, please don't hesitate to let me know.
어떤 질문이라도 있으시면 주저하지 말고 저에게 알려주세요.

**b)** If _____, please don't hesitate to let me know.
제가 도움이 될 수 있다면 주저하지 말고 저에게 알려주세요.

**c)** If _____, please don't hesitate to let me know.
제안서가 필요하시면 주저하지 말고 저에게 알려주세요.

# Practice

**Making Sentences**

**Practice writing sentences. Then, read your sentences to your partner or group.**

1. I just wanted to drop you a note and ~

   - _____
   - _____
   - _____

2. Your advice was ~

   - _____
   - _____
   - _____

**Editing Sentences**

**Correct the mistakes, if any, you find in the e-mail.**

> From: mileskim@paragon.com
> To: ramonwatts@softall.com
> Subject: Thank You for Your Hospitality
>
> Hi Ramon,
>
> I wanted to drop you ①<u>a notice</u> and let you know we're now back in Korea. My team has just finished ②<u>briefing</u> the director about the trip. He is quite ③<u>pleasant with</u> what we've accomplished with your team.
>
> I can't thank you enough for your ④<u>hospitality</u> while we were in San Jose. Your assistance was quite helpful in many ways.
>
> If you need ⑤<u>any assistance</u> with anything, please don't hesitate to let me know.
>
> Regards,
>
> Miles

 **Real Writing**

**Write an e-mail based on the following scenarios. Exchange your e-mail with a partner and check your partner's e-mail for errors.**

Scenario 1

> Write an e-mail to Liam, a colleague on a different team. Thank him for his help organizing last week's demo. Say that Soo Lee and her team were quite impressed with the demo and that Soo wants to place an order soon. Tell him to let you know if you can return the favor somehow.

Scenario 2

> Write an e-mail to a co-worker. Express your appreciation for that person's help in putting together a recent presentation to the executive committee. The presentation was a success, and you want to return the favor somehow.

From: jaygoh@paragon.com
To: liamconnelly@paragon.com
Subject: _____

_____
_____
_____

## Homework

**Write a short e-mail thanking a coworker for helping you organize the files for a project.**

_____
_____
_____

**Warm Up Sample Answers**
1. I (often/rarely/sometimes) express gratitude to people via e-mail.
2. (Yes, I / No, I don't) often get e-mails thanking me for something.
3. The last time I sent such an e-mail was (yesterday / last week / last month). / I don't remember the last time I sent such an e-mail.

**Comprehension Check Answers**
1. Seung-ho is writing the e-mail to give Terry an update on the AA project.
2. He is thanking Terry for giving him some advice related to scheduling.

**Vocabulary Answers**
1. a, 2. d, 3. e, 4. f, 5. b, 6. c

**Vocab Test Answers**
1. take you out to lunch, 2. invaluable, 3. Drop me a note, 4. return the favor, 5. ecstatic, 6. scheduling

**Grammar Points Answers**
1. a) letting us know b) your gift c) everything
2. a) you have any questions b) I can be of help c) you need a proposal

**Making Sentences Sample Answers**
1. I just wanted to drop you a note and (give you a heads-up / thank you for attending the meeting / invite you to a party).
2. Your advice was (timely / really helpful / great).

**Editing Sentences Answers**
① a notice → a note, ③ pleasant with → pleased with

**Real Writing Sample Answer**
Scenario 1
Subject: Demo was a Success!

Hi Liam,

I just wanted to drop you a note and express my appreciation for your help in organizing last week's demo. Soo Lee and her team were quite impressed with it. Soo wants to place an order with us soon.

I can't thank you enough for your help. We couldn't have done it without you.

If I can return the favor somehow, please don't hesitate to let me know.

Regards,

Jay

**Homework Sample Answer**
Subject: Thanks for the Help!

Hi Eli,

I wanted to drop you a note and give you an update on the project files. They're now in boxes, safely stored in the archives room. My boss is pretty impressed.

I can't thank you enough for your help in organizing all those files. Your advice on how to number the files was invaluable. I owe you one.

If I can offer you any assistance in return, please don't hesitate to let me know.

Regards,

Rose

**Writing Tip**

## Good Reasons to Write Thank You E-mails
감사 이메일을 쓰면 좋은 이유

Saying "thank you" to someone not only makes that person feel good, but yourself as well. Here are some good reasons for writing e-mails expressing appreciation to someone.
누군가에게 감사의 뜻을 전하면 그 사람뿐만 아니라 나 자신도 기분이 좋아진다. 감사 이메일을 쓰면 좋은 이유를 알아보자.

### ① They prompt more good work. 계속 일을 잘하도록 유도한다.

Expressing gratitude to someone does more than make that person feel worthy. Having gotten your thanks, it's natural that the person would want to continue doing good work so as not to let you down.
누군가에게 감사를 표하는 것은 그 사람을 가치 있는 사람으로 느끼게 하는 것 이상의 역할을 한다. 감사를 받은 그 사람은 나를 실망시키지 않기 위해 계속해서 좋은 일을 하고 싶어 하는 것은 당연한 일이다.

### ② They become part of people's files. 기록의 일부가 된다.

A note expressing gratitude for excellent work can become part of the person's file. It can serve as proof of the person's skills and aptitude.
훌륭한 업무 마무리에 대한 감사의 뜻이 담긴 메모는 그 사람의 기록에 일부가 된다. 본인의 기량과 재능의 증거가 될 수 있기 때문이다.

### ③ They boost morale. 사기를 북돋는다.

Saying "thank you" shows that you care about people and their contributions. Making people feel appreciated always helps boost morale.
고맙다고 하는 것은 내가 사람들과 그들의 기여에 관심을 가지고 있다는 것을 보여준다. 사람들이 감사함을 느끼게 하는 것은 사기를 북돋는데 늘 도움이 된다.

### ④ They don't take long to write. 쓰는데 오래 걸리지 않는다.

Sometimes it's good to write something longer, but usually saying "thank you" can be short and quick.
때로는 긴 글을 쓰는 것도 좋지만, 보통 고마움 표시는 짧고 간단할 수 있다.

> *I really appreciate your help.* 도와줘서 정말 고마워요.
> *You're a lifesaver!* 덕분에 살았어요!
> *Thank you so much!* 정말 고마워요!

# 5 Sending a Contract and Requesting Confirmation

## Learning Objectives

- Learners can ask a recipient to review a contract.
- Learners can ask the recipient to confirm the contract.
- Learners can explain the next steps to the recipient.

## Warm Up

**Work with a partner or in a group. Discuss the following questions.**

1. In general, do you send or receive contracts for review via e-mail?
2. What are the contracts usually for?
3. Do you find yourself asking for changes or corrections frequently?

# Sample Writing

**Read the sample e-mail.**

From: scollins@paragon.com
To: harrymackey@alleast.com
Subject: Finalized Contract

Dear Harry,

**The finalized contract is attached for your review and confirmation.** We have made the necessary revisions reflecting your previous comments. Director Han has also given his approval.

**Please review the contract thoroughly and confirm that all the details accurately represent our agreement.** Once it is confirmed, I will send you the official copies via courier.

Please let me know if there are any outstanding issues. Thank you.

Sincerely,

Sally Collins

발신: scollins@paragon.com
수신: harrymackey@alleast.com
제목: 최종 계약서

안녕하세요, Harry.

검토 및 확인을 위해 최종 계약서를 첨부합니다. 이전 의견을 반영하여 필요한 부분을 수정했습니다. 한 이사님도 승인해 주셨습니다.

계약서를 철저히 검토하시고 저희가 합의한 사항들이 정확하게 기재되어 있는지 확인해 주시기 바랍니다. 확인되면, 공식 문서를 택배로 보내드리겠습니다.

특이 사항이 있으면 알려주시기 바랍니다. 감사합니다.

수고하십시오.

Sally Collins

## Comprehension Check

**Answer the questions.**

1. What has Sally attached for Harry's review and confirmation?
2. When will she send the official copies to Harry?

# Vocabulary

**Match the words or expressions with the correct definitions.**

1. finalized _____
2. reflect _____
3. thoroughly _____
4. accurately _____
5. via courier _____
6. outstanding _____

a. 반영하다
b. 정확하게
c. 최종 확정된
d. 아직 처리되지 않은
e. 철저히
f. 택배로

## ✓ Vocab Test

**Fill in the blanks with the correct words or expressions.**

finalized / reflects / thoroughly / accurately / via courier / outstanding

1. The slogan _____ the company's philosophy.
2. You can send it _____.
3. Here's the _____ contract for you to sign.
4. Are there any _____ issues we need to address?
5. He _____ predicted the results.
6. Please review the list _____.

## ⊕ Bonus Resources

### dot the i's and cross the t's  꼼꼼하게 확인하다

A: So, are we all set to send the proposal off to the client?
   그럼, 고객에게 제안서를 보낼 준비가 다 된 건가요?

B: Almost. Let me make sure to **dot the i's and cross the t's** before I send it.
   거의 됐어요. 보내기 전에 꼼꼼하게 확인해야 할 점이 있는지 살펴볼게요.

타이핑이 존재하기 전에 문서를 작성할 때 펜으로 사용했는데, 글을 쓸 때 알파벳 i에는 점을 찍고(dot), t에는 선을 긋는(cross) 것에서 유래된 표현이다.

## Grammar Points

**Read the following and practice making sentences.**

**1.** A is attached for your B.

> A is attached for your B는 '당신의 B를 위해 A를 첨부합니다'를 뜻한다. A는 공식적인 계약서나 제안서 등 공식 문서가 들어가고, B에는 review(검토), suggestions(제의), comments(의견), approval(승인), confirmation(확인), records(보관) 등의 단어를 넣을 수 있다.
>
> 📧 *Our proposal is attached for your comments.* 의견을 주실 수 있도록 저희 제안서를 첨부합니다.

**a)** _____ are attached for your _____.
보관하실 수 있도록 파일들을 첨부합니다.

**b)** _____ is attached for your _____.
검토하실 수 있도록 저희의 표준 계약서를 첨부합니다.

**c)** _____ is attached for your _____.
승인하실 수 있도록 최종 문서를 첨부합니다.

**2.** Please review ~ and confirm that ~

> Please review ~ and confirm that ~은 '~을 검토하시고 ~되었는지 확인해 주시기 바랍니다'라는 뜻으로, 통상적으로 review 뒤에는 중요한 문서를, that 뒤에는 상대방과 사전에 합의한 부분에 대한 언급을 한다.
>
> 📧 *Please review the spreadsheet and confirm that we have included all the numbers.*
> 스프레드시트를 검토하시고 저희가 모든 수치를 포함했는지 확인해 주시기 바랍니다.

**a)** Please review _____ and confirm that _____.
제안서를 검토하시고 모든 세부 사항이 정확한지 확인해 주시기 바랍니다.

**b)** Please review _____ and confirm that _____.
도안을 검토하시고 디자인이 만족스러운지 확인해 주시기 바랍니다.

**c)** Please review _____ and confirm that _____ is included.
새로운 계약서를 검토하시고 우리가 논의한 모든 것이 포함되었는지 확인해 주시기 바랍니다.

# Practice

**Making Sentences**

**Practice writing sentences. Then, read your sentences to your partner or group.**

1. We have made the necessary ~

   - 
   - 
   - 

2. I will send you the official ~

   - 
   - 
   - 

**Editing Sentences**

**Correct the mistakes, if any, you find in the e-mail.**

> From: phabib@paragon.com
> To: adrianbronson@devwest.com
> Subject: Revised Contract for Your Review
>
> Hi Adrian,
>
> The ①<u>revised</u> contract is attached for your review and confirmation. We have made the changes ②<u>you've</u> requested. Our legal team has also given ③<u>it's</u> approval.
>
> Please review the contract and confirm that all the changes have been made. ④<u>Once</u> it is confirmed, I will send you the official contract ⑤<u>via courier</u>.
>
> Please let me know if you have any questions or comments. Thank you.
>
> Sincerely,
>
> Paul Habib

## Real Writing

**Write an e-mail based on the following scenarios. Exchange your e-mail with a partner and check your partner's e-mail for errors.**

Scenario 1

> Write an e-mail to Shane, a client. Indicate that you're attaching the revised contract and that you've made the revisions he asked for. Add that your boss has given his approval. Ask Shane to review it thoroughly. Say that you'll send two copies for his signature once the contract is confirmed.

Scenario 2

> Write an e-mail to a client asking them to review and confirm the attached contract.

From: janiceoh@paragon.com
To: shanewhite@conbuild.com
Subject: _____

## Homework

**Write a short e-mail containing the finalized MOU for the recipient's review and confirmation.**

### Warm Up Sample Answers
1. In general, I (send/receive) contracts for review via e-mail.
2. The contracts are usually for (projects / supplying items / consulting).
3. (Yes, I / No, I don't) find myself asking for changes or corrections frequently.

### Comprehension Check Answers
1. Sally has attached the finalized contract.
2. She will send the copies once the contract is confirmed.

### Vocabulary Answers
1. c, 2. a, 3. e, 4. b, 5. f, 6. d

### Vocab Test Answers
1. reflects, 2. via courier, 3. finalized, 4. outstanding, 5. accurately, 6. thoroughly

### Grammar Points Answers
1. a) The files, records b) Our preliminary contract, review c) The finalized document, approval
2. a) the proposal, all details are correct b) the drawings, the design is satisfactory, c) the new contract, everything we discussed

### Making Sentences Sample Answers
1. We have made the necessary (changes as we've discussed / additions you asked for / corrections in the document).
2. I will send you the official (notice by tomorrow / document via DHM / MOU for your signature).

### Editing Sentences Answers
③ it's → its

### Real Writing Sample Answer
Scenario 1
Subject: Revised Contract

Hi Shane,

The revised contract is attached for your review and confirmation. We have made the revisions you asked for. My boss has also given his approval.

Please review it thoroughly and confirm that all changes have been made to your satisfaction. Once it has been confirmed, I will send you two copies for your signature.

Please let me know if you require anything else. Thank you.

Regards,

Janice

### Homework Sample Answer
Subject: Finalized MOU

Hi Mack,

The finalized MOU is attached for your review and confirmation. We have made all the revisions reflecting our discussions last month. It has taken longer than we'd expected, but we wanted to make sure to dot the i's and cross the t's.

Please review it thoroughly and confirm that the details properly reflect our agreement. Once this has been confirmed, I will send you the official copies via DHM.

Please let me know if you need anything else. Thank you.

Sincerely,

Marley Brown

**Writing Tip**

# Dealing with Potential Objections to Your Message
나의 메시지에 대한 이의 제기 가능성 대응하기

No matter how good you think your message is, there will always be objections from some readers. Whether they voice their objections or keep them to themselves, it is your job to anticipate any objections and deal with them beforehand.
아무리 나의 메시지가 좋다고 생각해도 일부 수신자들로부터 반론이 있기 마련이다. 반대 입장을 직접 언급하든 그냥 생각만 하고 있든, 반론을 예측하고 미리 다루는 것이 나의 임무가 될 것이다.

### ① Mention the possible objections. 이의 제기할만한 내용을 언급한다.

Before you even start writing your e-mail, take some time and consider all the possible objections to your message. Then, address them in the e-mail before the recipient can bring them up. This will show you that you have a comprehensive understanding of the issues and are confident about your message.
이메일을 작성하기 전에, 시간을 내서 나올만한 모든 반론을 고려해 본다. 그런 후 수신자가 말을 꺼내기 전에 미리 다루자. 그러면 내가 문제를 포괄적으로 이해하고 있고 나의 메시지에 대한 확신이 있다는 것을 보여줄 것이다.

### ② Put yourself in their shoes. 그들의 입장에서 생각한다.

Forget about your own agenda for a moment and think about the message from the recipient's perspective. Come up with arguments against your ideas and find solutions to address them.
나의 안건은 잠시 내려놓고 수신자의 입장에서 나의 메시지를 생각해 본다. 나의 아이디어에 대한 반론을 제시해 보고 이에 대한 해결책을 찾아본다.

### ③ Present the pros and cons. 찬반양론을 제시한다.

If you believe the message will not be well-received, present many different options with pros and cons for each. Let the recipient see that you have thought everything through.
내 메시지가 잘 받아들여지지 않을 듯하면, 여러 옵션과 함께 찬반양론을 제시한다. 모든 것에 대해 심사숙고했다는 것을 수신자에게 보여주자.

# 6 Sending a Request to Sign an NDA

 ## Learning Objectives

- Learners can send a request to a contractor or vendor to sign an NDA.
- Learners can explain why such a document is necessary.
- Learners can tell the recipient to send an executed copy via courier.

 ## Warm Up

**Work with a partner or in a group. Discuss the following questions.**

1. How often do you ask others to sign an NDA?
2. When was the last time you were asked to sign an NDA?
3. Do you think an NDA is helpful in protecting valuable information or data?

## Sample Writing

**Read the sample e-mail.**

From: mollyhwang@paragon.com
To: a.ringer@allsupplies.com
Subject: Watto Project NDA

Dear Avery,

We are planning to send you our proprietary drawings for the Watto project. **To ensure the security of confidential information, please review and sign the attached Non-disclosure Agreement (NDA). The NDA is designed to protect sensitive data and prevent its unauthorized disclosure.**

Please note that we need to receive an original executed copy by June 2. We highly recommend using DHM or a comparable courier service.

If you have any questions, please contact me at your earliest convenience.

Sincerely,

Molly

---

발신: mollyhwang@paragon.com
수신: a.ringer@allsupplies.com
제목: Watto 프로젝트 NDA

안녕하세요, Avery.

저희는 당사 소유의 Watto 프로젝트 도면을 보내드릴 계획입니다. 기밀 정보의 보안을 보장하기 위해, 첨부된 비밀 유지 계약서(NDA)를 검토하시고 서명해주시기 바랍니다. 이 NDA는 민감한 자료를 보호하고 승인되지 않은 유출을 방지하도록 만들어졌습니다.

6월 2일까지 서명된 원본 한 부를 저희가 받아야 한다는 점을 유의하십시오. DHM 또는 비슷한 배송 서비스를 이용하시기를 권합니다.

질문이 있으시면, 조속히 연락해 주시기를 바랍니다.

수고하세요,

Molly

### Comprehension Check

**Answer the questions.**

1. What is the NDA designed to do?
2. What does Molly need to receive by June 2?

## Vocabulary

**Match the words or expressions with the correct definitions.**

1. proprietary _____
2. confidential information _____
3. non-disclosure agreement _____
4. be designed to _____
5. executed copy _____
6. comparable _____

a. 소유의
b. 기밀 유지 계약서
c. 서명된 사본
d. 비슷한, 비교할 만한
e. 기밀 정보
f. ~하기 위해 만들어지다

### Vocab Test

**Fill in the blanks with the correct words or expressions.**

proprietary / confidential information / non-disclosure agreement /
was designed to / executed copies / comparable

1. This is our _____ technology.
2. The speech _____ get the audience excited.
3. We need two _____ of the contract.
4. I'm sorry, but that's _____.
5. The _____ product from XYZ Corp. is more expensive.
6. Before we can give you the data, we need a _____ from you.

### Bonus Resources

#### non-negotiable 협상 불가한

A: I think the delivery schedule is acceptable, but we'd like to discuss the discount rate.
배송 일정은 괜찮을 것 같습니다만, 할인율을 논의하고 싶습니다.

B: I'm afraid the rate is **non-negotiable**. We can't change the percentage.
유감이지만 할인율은 협상 불가입니다. 그 할인율을 바꿀 수 없습니다.

협상할 때 회사 방침이나 법적인 문제로 도저히 협상이 불가능한 요소가 있기 마련이다. 이때 '협상의 여지가 있는'을 뜻하는 negotiable에 non을 앞에 붙여서 그 요소를 non-negotiable이라고 하면 된다.

 **Grammar Points**

**Read the following and practice making sentences.**

1. To ensure ~, please ~

> To ensure ~는 '~을 보장하기 위해'이고, please는 '~ 바랍니다'를 뜻한다. 이 두 표현을 한 문장에서 씀으로써 '~을 보장하기 위해, ~을 하시기 바랍니다'라는 의미가 전달된다. 상대방에게 무언가를 지시함에 동시에 이유까지 덧붙이는 것이다.
>
> *To ensure* the success of the project, *please* adhere to the schedule.
> 프로젝트의 성공을 보장하기 위해, 일정을 지켜주시기 바랍니다.

a) To ensure the safety of our workers, please make sure _____.
우리 작업자들의 안전을 보장하기 위해, 반드시 모두가 안전모를 쓰도록 하시기 바랍니다.

b) To ensure a smooth process, please _____.
매끄러운 진행을 보장하기 위해, 설명서를 따르시기 바랍니다.

c) To ensure that the room remains warm, please _____.
방이 따뜻하게 유지되도록 온도계를 조정해주시기 바랍니다.

2. ~ is designed to ~

> ~ is designed to ~는 '~은 ~하도록 만들어졌습니다'를 뜻한다. design이란 단어가 나오면 무언가를 말 그대로 디자인한다는 생각이 먼저 들지만 이런 경우에는 '고안하다'에 더 가깝다.
>
> *The suitcase is designed to resist fire.* 그 여행 가방은 화재에 견딜 수 있도록 만들어졌습니다.

a) _____ is designed to _____.
이 정책은 모든 직원에게 혜택을 주도록 만들어졌습니다.

b) _____ is designed to _____.
이 책은 우주에 대한 기본 지식을 제공하도록 만들어졌습니다.

c) _____ is designed to _____.
이 프로세스는 생산력을 높이도록 만들어졌습니다.

#  Practice

**Making Sentences**

**Practice writing sentences. Then, read your sentences to your partner or group.**

1. Please note that ~

- _____
- _____
- _____

2. We highly recommend ~

- _____
- _____
- _____

**Editing Sentences**

**Correct the mistakes, if any, you find in the e-mail.**

From: blakepimm@alldesigns.com
To: h.yamaguchi@sensdesign.com
Subject: NDA Attached for Review

Dear Hiroshi,

We are ready to start ①<u>discussing</u> the possibility of working together on the design of the new cold storage room for PTC Imports. To ensure the security of ②<u>confidential</u> information, please review and sign the ③<u>attached</u> Non-disclosure Agreement (NDA). The NDA is designed to protect our ④<u>exist</u> proprietary designs and prevent their unauthorized use.

Please note that we need to receive an executed copy before we can start our discussion. We highly recommend using a local ⑤<u>courier service</u>.

If you have any questions, please let me know.

Sincerely,

Blake

## Real Writing

**Write an e-mail based on the following scenarios. Exchange your e-mail with a partner and check your partner's e-mail for errors.**

Scenario 1

> Write an e-mail to Pete, a new vendor. Ask him to review and sign the NDA attached to the e-mail. Say that it's designed to keep all sensitive discussions confidential. Add that you need an executed copy by August 22 and that you recommend using DHM or MNT.

Scenario 2

> Write an e-mail to a potential vendor and ask him/her to sign the attached NDA.

From: isabelahn@paragon.com
To: peterbebout@pariscases.com
Subject: _____

_____
_____
_____

## Homework

**Write a short e-mail asking a business associate to sign an NDA.**

_____
_____
_____

**Warm Up Sample Answers**
1. I (quite often / rarely / sometimes) ask others to sign an NDA. / I've never asked anybody to sign an NDA.
2. The last time I was asked to sign an NDA was (last month / a few months ago / last year). / I've never been asked to sign an NDA.
3. (Yes, I / No, I don't) think it's helpful.

**Comprehension Check Answers**
1. The NDA is designed to protect sensitive data and prevent its unauthorized disclosure.
2. Molly needs to receive an original executed copy of the NDA.

**Vocabulary Answers**
1. a, 2. e, 3. b, 4. f, 5. c, 6. d

**Vocab Test Answers**
1. proprietary, 2. was designed to, 3. executed copies, 4. confidential information, 5. comparable,
6. non-disclosure agreement

**Grammar Points Answers**
1. a) everyone wears a hardhat b) follow the instructions c) adjust the thermometer
2. a) The policy, benefit all employees b) This book, provide basic knowledge about the universe c) The process, raise productivity

**Making Sentences Sample Answers**
1. Please note that (the deadline is July 31 / we have not received your application yet / there is an error in the report).
2. We highly recommend (working from home that week / moving quickly / sending out a request for proposals).

**Editing Sentences Answers**
④ exist → existing

**Real Writing Sample Answer**
Scenario 1
Subject: Need to Sign the NDA

Hi Pete,

We are excited to begin negotiating with you. To ensure the security of confidential information, please review and sign the attached Non-disclosure Agreement (NDA). The NDA is designed to keep all sensitive discussions confidential.

Please note that we need to receive an original executed copy by August 22. We highly recommend using DHM or MNT.

If you have any questions, please let me know.

Sincerely,

Isabel

**Homework Sample Answer**
Subject: Need NDA

Dear Eunice,

We are excited to begin working with your team. To ensure the security of confidential information, please review and sign the attached Non-disclosure Agreement (NDA). The NDA is designed to prevent unauthorized use of any proprietary data owned by our company.

Please note that signing the NDA is non-negotiable. We need the executed copy by early next month. We highly recommend using a courier service.

If you have any questions, don't hesitate to contact me.

Sincerely,

Arthur

**Writing Tip**

# Before You Send: Know the Three Main Types of Non-disclosure Agreement (NDA)
보내기 전에: 비밀 유지 계약서의 3가지 주요 유형을 알아두자

When we think of NDAs, we might first think of one-way NDAs. However, in practice, there are three major types of NDA. Accordingly, before you send an e-mail requesting someone to sign an NDA, let's take a look at the different types of NDAs.

비밀 유지 계약서를 떠올릴 때 우리는 먼저 일방적 NDA를 생각할 수 있다. 하지만 실제로는 3가지 유형의 NDA가 있다. 이에 따라 누군가에게 비밀 유지 계약서를 서명해달라는 이메일을 보내기 전에, 여러 비밀 유지 계약서 종류를 한번 살펴보자.

① 
### Unilateral NDAs 일방적 NDA

Also known as a one-way NDA, this is the most common type of non-disclosure agreement. Only one side is required to disclose confidential information to the other. Some examples include employer-employee NDAs, company-vendor NDAs, and seller-buyer NDAs.

'단방향' NDA로도 알려졌으며, 가장 흔한 종류의 비밀 유지 계약서다. 한쪽만 다른 쪽에게 기밀 정보를 공개하도록 되어 있다. 예를 들어 고용주–고용인 NDA, 회사–납품업체 NDA, 판매자–구매자 NDA 등이 여기에 해당한다.

② 
### Bilateral NDAs 쌍방 NDA

In a bilateral NDA, sometimes called a mutual NDA, both sides need to disclose confidential information to each other. Normally the NDA limits the way both sides can use and share confidential information. Mergers, takeovers, and joint ventures fall into this category.

때로는 상호 NDA로 불리기도 하는 쌍방 NDA에서는 양측이 서로에게 기밀 정보를 공개해야 한다. 일반적으로, 해당 NDA는 양측이 비밀 정보를 사용하고 공유할 수 있는 방법을 제한한다. 합병, 인수와 합작투자 등이 이 범주에 속한다.

③ 
### Multilateral NDAs 다자간 NDA

In multilateral NDAs, at least one party is required to disclose information. The other parties are required to protect that information from being disclosed to outsiders. Usually, the related parties are attempting to start a complex business relationship.

다자간 NDA에서는 적어도 한쪽이 기밀 정보를 공개해야 한다. 다른 쪽은 외부에 해당 정보가 유출되지 않도록 해야 한다. 흔히 관련된 모든 당사자들은 복잡한 거래 관계를 시작하려고 한다.

# 7 Addressing Claims and Complaints

 **Learning Objectives**

- Learners can answer claims and complaints from customers.
- Learners can explain the reason for not accepting a claim.
- Learners can explain what is being done or will be done to address the claims or complaints.

 **Warm Up**

**Work with a partner or in a group. Discuss the following questions.**
1. Do you often receive claim or complaint e-mails?
2. In your experience, do you accept or reject most of the claims or complaints?
3. Is it difficult for you to find the appropriate expressions when rejecting claims?

 **Sample Writing**

**Read the sample e-mail.**

From: pamyoo@kortech.com
To: cindyfenton21@ahoo.com
Subject: RE: Product Damage

Dear Ms. Fenton,

**Thank you for writing to us with your concerns.** After examining the photos you've sent us, we have arrived at the following conclusion.

**Our technical team found evidence suggesting that the damage resulted from usage that falls outside the boundaries of normal application.** Thus, I'm afraid that there will be charges for parts and labor if you wish to repair the speaker.

Let us know how you would like to proceed.

Sincerely,

Pamela Yoo

발신: pamyoo@kortech.com
수신: cindyfenton21@ahoo.com
제목: RE: 제품 손상

안녕하세요, Fenton님.

우려 사항과 함께 이메일을 보내주셔서 감사드립니다. 보내주신 사진을 검토한 결과, 다음과 같은 결론에 도달하게 되었습니다.

저희 기술팀이 정상적인 사용 범주를 벗어나 손상이 발생했다는 근거를 발견했습니다. 따라서, 유감스럽지만 스피커 수리를 원하시면 부품과 인건비 비용이 발생할 거라는 점을 알려드립니다.

어떻게 진행을 원하시는지 알려주시기 바랍니다.

수고하십시오.

Pamela Yoo

**Comprehension Check**

**Answer the questions.**

1. What did Pamela Yoo's team examine?
2. What will Ms. Fenton be charged for if she wishes to repair the speaker?

# Vocabulary

**Match the words or expressions with the correct definitions.**

1. concern _____
2. conclusion _____
3. suggest _____
4. boundary _____
5. normal application _____
6. parts and labor _____

a. 시사하다
b. 우려하는 것, 걱정거리
c. 결론
d. 경계
e. 부품과 인건비
f. 정상적인 사용

## ✓ Vocab Test

**Fill in the blanks with the correct words or expressions.**

concerns / conclusion / suggests / boundaries / normal application / parts and labor

1. The warranty covers all _____.
2. We need to set up some _____.
3. I don't agree with your _____.
4. The report _____ that some employees are unhappy.
5. We have some _____ about the project.
6. The battery wasn't damaged from _____.

## ⊕ Bonus Resources

### draw the line    한계를 긋다, 한도를 정하다

A: The supplier is asking if we can give him three more days.
3일을 더 줄 수 있는지 납품업체가 묻네요.

B: We've already given him five extra days. We have to **draw the line** there.
이미 5일을 더 줬습니다. 거기서 한계를 정해야 합니다.

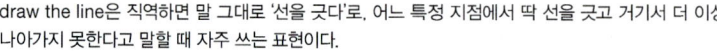

draw the line은 직역하면 말 그대로 '선을 긋다'로, 어느 특정 지점에서 딱 선을 긋고 거기서 더 이상 나아가지 못한다고 말할 때 자주 쓰는 표현이다.

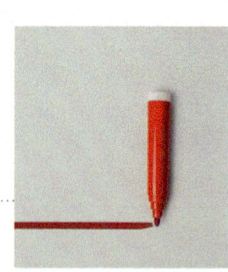

 **Grammar Points**

**Read the following and practice making sentences.**

**1. Thank you for writing to us with your ~**

> Thank you for writing to us with your ~는 '당신의 ~을 이메일로 보내주셔서 감사드립니다'로 번역된다. 영어에는 이메일이라는 표현이 담겨 있지 않지만 write를 '이메일을 보내다'로 간주하면 된다. 캐주얼한 상황에서는 Thank 대신 Thanks를 써도 좋다.
> 
> *Thank you for writing to us with your feedback.* 피드백을 이메일로 보내주셔서 감사드립니다.

a) Thank you for writing to us with your _____.
   소중한 질문을 이메일로 보내주셔서 감사드립니다.

b) Thank you for writing to us with your _____.
   일정과 관련한 우려에 대해 이메일을 보내주셔서 감사드립니다.

c) Thank you for writing to us with your _____.
   생각하신 것에 대해 이메일로 보내주셔서 감사드립니다.

**2. ~ found evidence suggesting that ~**

> ~ found evidence suggesting that ~은 '~이 ~했다는 근거를 발견했습니다'라는 뜻이다. 여기서 suggesting이 함께 나오는 이유는 향후 그 '증거'가 다르게 해석될 수 있을 가능성을 염두에 두고 있기 때문이다.
>
> *We found evidence suggesting that the box was already open.*
> 저희는 박스가 이미 개봉됐었다는 근거를 발견했습니다.

a) Steve found evidence suggesting that _____.
   Steve는 오류가 있다는 근거를 발견했습니다.

b) Our team found evidence suggesting that _____.
   저희 팀이 그림을 보내지 않았다는 근거를 발견했습니다.

c) I found evidence suggesting that _____.
   저는 수치가 부정확했다는 근거를 발견했습니다.

## Practice

**Making Sentences**

**Practice writing sentences. Then, read your sentences to your partner or group.**

1. After ~, we have arrived at the following conclusion.

   - _____
   - _____
   - _____

2. I'm afraid that ~

   - _____
   - _____
   - _____

**Editing Sentences**

**Correct the mistakes, if any, you find in the e-mail.**

From: b.newton@cksupplies.com
To: patholmes@paragon.com
Subject: RE: Inquiry Regarding Order #36434

Dear Patrick,

Thank you for writing ①<u>to us</u> with your concerns. After looking ②<u>through</u> the documents, we have arrived at the following conclusion.

We have found evidence ③<u>suggesting</u> that all the items were shipped in the container. Thus, we regret to inform you that we ④<u>are able</u> to send you additional items as you've requested.

Let us know if we can assist you with ⑤<u>anything else</u>.

Sincerely,

Bob Newton

## Real Writing

**Write an e-mail based on the following scenarios. Exchange your e-mail with a partner and check your partner's e-mail for errors.**

Scenario 1

> Write an e-mail to Martin, a client. You're addressing his concerns regarding the new launch date for a game called Barista Run. You've reviewed the meeting minutes and found evidence suggesting that his company's team leader, Fred Gatz, has agreed to delay the launch date. Because of this, you cannot go back to the original launch date.

Scenario 2

> Write a reply e-mail to a client and deny a request for a replacement of some equipment you've provided. Although the client claims a different model was ordered, you've found evidence that one of his staff had seen a demo of that particular model and accepted it.

From: sking@allgames.com
To: martinherring@gogogames.com
Subject: _____

_____
_____
_____

## Homework

**Write a short e-mail denying a claim to change the type of paper for some textbooks you've provided.**

_____
_____
_____

**Warm Up Sample Answers**
1. (Yes, I / No, I don't) often receive claim or complaint e-mails.
2. In my experience, I (accept/reject) most of the claims or complaints.
3. (Yes, it's / No, it's not) difficult for me to find the appropriate expressions when rejecting claims.

**Comprehension Check Answers**
1. They examined the photos Ms. Fenton sent them.
2. Ms. Fenton will be charged for parts and labor.

**Vocabulary Answers**
1. b, 2. c, 3. a, 4. d, 5. f, 6. e

**Vocab Test Answers**
1. parts and labor, 2. boundaries, 3. conclusion, 4. suggests, 5. concerns, 6. normal application

**Grammar Points Answers**
1. a) valuable questions b) concerns (about / related to) the schedule c) thoughts
2. a) there was an error b) the drawing was not sent c) the numbers were incorrect / not correct

**Making Sentences Sample Answers**
1. After (looking at the samples / considering all the evidence / discussing it with the engineers), we have arrived at the following conclusion.
2. I'm afraid that (your application was not approved / we've decided to not to renew the contract / we cannot accept your claim).

**Editing Sentences Answers**
④ are able → are unable

**Real Writing Sample Answer**
Scenario 1
Subject: RE: Barista Run's Launch Date

Dear Martin,

Thank you for writing to us with your concerns regarding the new launch date for Barista Run. After reviewing the meeting minutes, we have arrived at the following conclusion.

Our project team has found evidence suggesting that your team leader Fred Gatz agreed to delay the game's launch date. Thus, we regret to inform you that we cannot go back to the original launch date.

Please let me know if there is some other way that we can better meet your needs.

Sincerely,

Scott King

**Homework Sample Answer**
Subject: RE: Paper for Textbooks

Hi Albert,

Thank you for writing to us with your concerns about the paper quality of the sample textbook we sent you. After reviewing the contract and past correspondences, we have arrived at the following conclusion.

We have found evidence suggesting that you were aware of the specific paper to be used for the textbooks. The sample paper was sent to you on January 2 via courier. Thus, we regret to inform you that we have to draw the line and deny your request to use a different type of paper.

Let me know if you have any other concerns.

Sincerely,

Chris Christopher

**Writing Tip**

# Responding to Complaints and Claims
항의와 클레임에 대응하기

When you get a complaint or claim via e-mail, keep the following in mind as you plan and actually compose your response.
항의나 클레임 이메일을 받았을 때, 답변을 준비하고 실제로 작성할 때 다음과 같이 고려하자.

### ① Be quick to answer. 빠르게 답변한다.

The writer will probably be waiting anxiously for your reply. If you wait too long to respond, the writer might get upset. Therefore, it's a good idea to try to reply as soon as you can.
발신자는 나의 답변을 애타게 기다리고 있을 것이다. 답변을 너무 오래 지체하면 발신자는 기분이 상할 수 있다. 그러니 가능한 한 빠르게 답변하는 것이 좋다.

### ② Keep your tone friendly. 친절한 어조를 유지한다.

Take extra care to keep your tone professional. In general, you don't want to sound too casual, which may irritate the writer.
전문적인 말투를 유지하도록 특별히 신경을 쓴다. 일반적으로 캐주얼한 어조는 발신자를 불편하게 할 수 있다.

### ③ Show that you've considered everything carefully.
모든 걸 신중히 고려했다는 것을 보여주자.

Let the recipient know you have taken the time to give the complaint or claim a careful consideration. Then tell them why you are forced to deny the request.
수신자에게 항의나 클레임을 아주 신중하게 고려했음을 알리자. 그런 후 왜 그 요구를 거절할 수밖에 없는지 말해준다.

### ④ End in a courteous way. 공손하게 마무리한다.

Close in a helpful, courteous manner. If the writer needs to take some action, make sure to let that person know exactly what to do.
도움이 되면서 정중한 태도로 마무리 짓자. 발신자가 어떤 조치를 취해야 하는 경우, 그게 정확하게 무엇인지 알린다.

# 8 Contract Termination Notice

### Learning Objectives

- Learners can notify a vendor of their decision to terminate or conclude a business relationship.
- Learners can ask the vendor to confirm receipt of the notice.
- Learners can sincerely wish vendors a bright future.

### Warm Up

**Work with a partner or in a group. Discuss the following questions.**
1. Have you ever had to send a contract termination or non-renewal notice?
2. When was the last time you received a contract termination or non-renewal notice?
3. What reasons can you think of for terminating a contract with a vendor?

## Sample Writing

**Read the sample e-mail.**

From: kenpark@paragon.com
To: pattynelson@aaams.com
Subject: Contract Termination Notice

Dear Ms. Nelson,

**I am writing to inform you of our decision to conclude our business partnership with AAA Marketing Solutions.** Our contract specifies that we are to provide three months' notice to terminate the agreement. This e-mail will serve as our official notification.

Please confirm receipt of this notification. **We sincerely appreciate the service you have provided to us to this point.** We wish you the best in all your endeavors.

If you have any questions or comments, please let me know.

Sincerely,

Kenneth Park

발신: kenpark@paragon.com
수신: pattynelson@aaams.com
제목: 계약 종료 통지

안녕하세요, Nelson님.

AAA Marketing Solutions 사와의 사업 협력을 종료하기로 한 결정을 알리기 위해 이메일을 보냅니다. 저희 계약서에는 계약 해지 시 3개월 전 통지를 제공하기로 명시되어 있습니다. 이 이메일이 당사의 공식 통지서 역할을 하겠습니다.

이 통지서의 수령 확인을 부탁드립니다. 지금까지 당사에게 제공해 주신 서비스에 진심으로 감사드립니다. 시도하시는 모든 일에 행운을 기원합니다.

질문이나 의견이 있으시면 알려주세요.

수고하십시오.

Kenneth Park

### Comprehension Check

**Answer the questions.**

1. Why is Kenneth writing to Ms. Nelson?
2. What does he want Ms. Nelson to confirm?

 **Vocabulary**

**Match the words or expressions with the correct definitions.**

1. conclude _____
2. specify _____
3. three months' notice _____
4. to this point _____
5. wish the best _____
6. endeavor _____

a. 3개월 전 통지
b. 명시하다
c. 행운을 기원하다
d. 시도, 노력
e. 종료하다
f. 이 시점까지

### ✓ Vocab Test

**Fill in the blanks with the correct words or expressions.**

concludes / specify / three months' notice / to this point / wish you the best / endeavors

1. To end the contract, you have to give _____.
2. Good luck in your future _____.
3. This _____ my presentation.
4. We _____ of luck.
5. Did they _____ when they want to meet?
6. We have done fine _____.

### ⊕ Bonus Resources

### a matter of formality  형식적인 절차의 이유

A: Here's the official contract. Would you like to sign it now?
여기 공식 계약서가 있습니다. 지금 서명하시겠습니까?

B: Yes. As **a matter of formality**, we should have a contract.
네, 형식적인 절차의 이유로 계약서가 있는 게 좋겠습니다.

a matter of는 '~의 이유'를 뜻하고 formality는 꼭 해야만 하는 형식적인 일을 가리킨다. 비즈니스 등에서 이미 합의된 사항을 공식적인 증거를 남기기 위해 하는 절차를 뜻한다.

## Grammar Points

**Read the following and practice making sentences.**

1. I am writing to inform you of our decision to ~

> I am writing to inform you of our decision to ~는 '~하기로 한 결정을 알리기 위해 이메일을 보냅니다'
> 라는 뜻이다. 다소 격식을 차린 표현인데, 통상적으로 나쁜 소식을 전할 때 주로 쓰인다.
>
> 📧 *I am writing to inform you of our decision to* cancel the promotional event scheduled for next month.
> 다음 달로 예정된 판촉 행사를 취소하기로 한 결정을 알리기 위해 이메일을 보냅니다.

a) I am writing to inform you of our decision to _____.
납품업체를 바꾸기로 한 결정을 알리기 위해 이메일을 보냅니다.

b) I am writing to inform you of our decision to _____.
출시일을 연기하기로 한 결정을 알리기 위해 이메일을 보냅니다.

c) I am writing to inform you of our decision to _____.
Chicago 사무실을 폐쇄하기로 한 결정을 알리기 위해 이메일을 보냅니다.

2. We sincerely appreciate ~

> '~에 진심으로 감사드립니다'를 뜻하는 We sincerely appreciate ~는 격식을 차려서 이메일을 쓸 때 유용
> 하다. 캐주얼한 표현으로 바꾸고자 한다면 sincerely 대신 really를 쓰면 된다.
>
> 📧 *We sincerely appreciate* all your efforts. 당신의 모든 노력에 진심으로 감사드립니다.

a) We sincerely appreciate _____. 당신의 조언에 진심으로 감사드립니다.

b) We sincerely appreciate _____. 행사를 위한 기부금에 진심으로 감사드립니다.

c) We sincerely appreciate _____. 당사의 제품에 대한 관심에 진심으로 감사드립니다.

 **Practice**

**Making Sentences**

**Practice writing sentences. Then, read your sentences to your partner or group.**

1. Our contract specifies that ~

- _____
- _____
- _____

2. Please confirm receipt of ~

- _____
- _____
- _____

**Editing Sentences**

**Correct the mistakes, if any, you find in the e-mail.**

From: ckmin@paragon.com
To: horacepine@gofast.com
Subject: Not Renewing Contract

Dear Horace,

I am writing to inform you of our decision ①<u>not to</u> renew our contract with Go Fast Delivery for next year. Our contract ②<u>specify</u> that we are to send you a non-renewal notice ③<u>by the end of</u> November. This e-mail will serve as that notice.

Please confirm ④<u>receipt</u> of this e-mail. We sincerely appreciate the service you have provided to us during the past year. We hope to work with you again ⑤<u>in</u> the future.

Let us know if you have any questions.

Sincerely,

C.K. Min

## Real Writing

Write an e-mail based on the following scenarios. Exchange your e-mail with a partner and check your partner's e-mail for errors.

**Scenario 1**

> Write an e-mail to Glen, a consultant, informing him of your decision to terminate the contract with Account Pros. You're giving your three-month notice, with the e-mail serving as that notice. Ask him to confirm receipt via e-mail. Thank him and add that you hope to work with him again in the future.

**Scenario 2**

> Write an e-mail to an office cleaning service informing them you will not be renewing the contract next month. You're giving them two weeks' notice as specified in your contract.

From: glenbrooks@accountpros.com
To: rtravolta@abccorp.com
Subject: _____

_____
_____
_____

## Homework

Write a short e-mail terminating a contract.

_____
_____
_____

**Warm Up Sample Answers**
1. (Yes, I've / No, I've never) had to send such a notice.
2. The last time I received such a notice was (a week ago / last month / sometime last year).
3. (The vendor has been doing a bad job. / The company has found a better vendor. / There is no longer any need for the service provided by the vendor.)

**Comprehension Check Answers**
1. He is writing to inform her of his company's decision to conclude their business partnership.
2. He wants her to confirm receipt of the notification.

**Vocabulary Answers**
1. e, 2. b, 3. a, 4. f, 5. c, 6. d

**Vocab Test Answers**
1. three months' notice, 2. endeavors, 3. concludes, 4. wish you the best, 5. specify, 6. to this point

**Grammar Points Answers**
1. a) change suppliers b) delay the launch date c) close the Chicago office
2. a) your advice b) the donations for the event c) your interest in our (company's) products

**Making Sentences Sample Answers**
1. Our contract specifies that (we are to start the work immediately / we are to share the cost for any overtime work / you are to send us a complete schedule).
2. Please confirm receipt of (payment / this e-mail / all the files).

**Editing Sentences Answers**
② specify → specifies

**Real Writing Sample Answer**
Scenario 1
Subject: Contract Termination

Dear Glen,

I am writing to inform you of our decision to terminate the contract with your company. Our contract specifies that we are to provide three months' notice to terminate the agreement. This e-mail will serve as our official notice.

Please confirm receipt of this notification via e-mail. We sincerely appreciate the service you have provided us. We hope to work with you again in the future.

Let us know if you have any questions.

Sincerely,

Ron Travolta

**Homework Sample Answer**
Subject: Contract Termination

Dear Warren,

I am writing to inform you of our decision to conclude our business partnership with your team. Our contract specifies that we are to provide a month's notice to terminate our agreement. This e-mail will serve as that notice.

As a matter of formality, please confirm receipt of this notice. We sincerely appreciate the various services you've provided to us during the past several months. We hope to find an opportunity to work with your team again in the future.

Let me know if you have any questions or comments.

Sincerely,

Hans Cooper

**Writing Tip**

# Useful Expressions to Use When Ending a Contract
계약을 해지할 때 사용할 수 있는 유용한 표현

Even when ending a business relationship, you might want to convey hope for possible collaboration in the future.
비즈니스 계약을 종료하더라도, 미래에 함께 협력할 수 있는 희망을 표현할 수 있다.

## ① Reminding the Recipient about the Contract End Date
계약 종료일에 대해 알리기

> Please be aware that our current contract will officially terminate on December 31, 2023.
> 현 계약서는 공식적으로 2023년 12월 31일에 종료될 것임을 참고하시기 바랍니다.

> This is a friendly reminder that as of July 31, our formal business contract will officially come to an end.
> 7월 31일자로 양사 간의 공식 사업 계약서가 종료될 것임을 알려드리는 바입니다.

> I'd like to remind you that our contractual relationship will come to a close on September 30.
> 9월 30일에 저희의 계약 관계가 종료된다는 점을 알려드리고 싶습니다.

## ② Expressing Appreciation 감사 표현하기

> Thank you for the productive collaboration we have had over the duration of our contract.
> 계약 기간 동안 양사의 생산적인 협력에 대해 감사드립니다.

> I want to express my appreciation for the quality of work your team has provided.
> 그쪽 팀이 제공한 양질의 작업에 감사드리고 싶습니다.

> We are grateful for the contributions your company has made to our projects.
> 당사 프로젝트들에 대한 귀사의 공헌에 감사드립니다.

## ③ Expressing Your Hope to Work Together in the Future
앞으로 함께 일하고 싶다는 희망 표현하기

> I hope we can explore future opportunities to work together again.
> 다시 함께 일할 수 있는 향후 기회를 모색할 수 있기를 기대합니다.

> Our team will continue to follow your company's developments with interest.
> 저희 팀은 귀사의 발전에 관심을 가지고 지켜보겠습니다.

> Please keep us in mind for any future projects where our businesses could work together effectively once again.
> 향후 양사가 다시 한 번 효과적으로 협력할 수 있는 프로젝트가 있으면 저희를 기억해 주시기 바랍니다.

# 9  Declining Invitations

 **Learning Objectives**

- Learners can express gratitude for an opportunity.
- Learners can politely decline invitations.
- Learners can express hope for future opportunities as needed.

 **Warm Up**

**Work with a partner or in a group. Discuss the following questions.**
1. Have you ever had to decline an invitation to an event?
2. Besides using e-mails, in what other ways can you invite people to events?
3. What kinds of invitations do you normally get via e-mail?

# Sample Writing

**Read the sample e-mail.**

From: georgeharris@lookngood.com
To: lucylin@paragon.com
Subject: RE: You're Invited to the Launch!

Hi Lucy,

Thank you so much for inviting me to the product launch party on Friday night. **It's very thoughtful of you to think of me and extend the invitation.**

**Unfortunately, I have a prior engagement.** My family is going out to dinner to celebrate my son's birthday. Otherwise, I would most definitely attend.

Thank you again for the invitation. I'm confident that the event will be a resounding success. Please keep me in mind for your next event.

Best regards,

George

발신: georgeharris@lookngood.com

수신: lucylin@paragon.com

제목: RE: 출시 행사에 초대합니다!

안녕하세요, Lucy.

금요일 저녁에 있을 제품 출시 파티에 저를 초대해 주셔서 정말 감사합니다. **저를 생각해서 초대해 주시다니 대단히 감사합니다.**

**아쉽게도, 저는 선약이 있습니다.** 제 아들의 생일을 축하하기 위해 가족과 외식하려고 하거든요. 그렇지만 않았다면, 확실히 참석했을 겁니다.

초대에 다시 한번 감사드립니다. 행사가 아주 크게 성공할 것이라고 확신합니다. 다음 행사에 저를 잊지 말아 주세요.

수고하십시오.

George

## Comprehension Check

**Answer the questions.**

1. What event has Lucy invited George to?
2. What is George doing on Friday night?

# Vocabulary

**Match the words or expressions with the correct definitions.**

1. product launch _____
2. extend an invitation _____
3. prior engagement _____
4. most definitely _____
5. resounding _____
6. keep ~ in mind _____

a. 선약
b. 제품 출시
c. ~을 잊지 않다, ~을 기억하다
d. 초대를 하다
e. 엄청난, 완전한
f. 확실히

## ✓ Vocab Test

**Fill in the blanks with the correct words or expressions.**

> product launch / extend the invitation / prior engagement / most definitely /
> resounding / keep me in mind

1. Please _____ for your next project.
2. We would like to _____ to join us.
3. Sorry, I have a _____ tomorrow night.
4. The party was a _____ success.
5. When is the _____?
6. I would _____ attend the conference.

## ⊕ Bonus Resources

### out of town 출장 중인

A: Will Josh be coming to the meeting tomorrow?
내일 회의에 Josh가 참석하나요?

B: He really wanted to come, but unfortunately, he's **out of town**. He's in Canada right now.
꼭 참석하고 싶었지만 아쉽게도 그분은 출장 중입니다. 현재 캐나다에 계세요.

'도시 밖에 있는'으로 직역되는 out of town은 말 그대로 해당 동네에 없다는 뜻이다. 업무와 관련해서 언급될 때는 대체로 출장을 뜻한다. 이때 on a business trip이라고 해도 무방하다.

# Grammar Points

**Read the following and practice making sentences.**

1. It's very thoughtful of you to ~

> thoughtful은 '배려심 있는', '사려 깊은'을 뜻하지만, It's very thoughtful of you to ~에서는 상대방에게 깊은 감사의 뜻을 전하는 것이다. very 대신 조금 더 캐주얼하게 really를 쓸 수 있다.
> 
> 📖 *It's very thoughtful of you to say so.* 그렇게 말씀해 주시니 대단히 감사합니다.

    **a)** It's very thoughtful of you to _____.
        이삿짐 옮기는 데 도움을 주시다니 대단히 감사합니다.

    **b)** It's very thoughtful of you to _____.
        파티에 와주시다니 대단히 감사합니다.

    **c)** It's very thoughtful of you to _____.
        저에게 알려주시다니 대단히 감사합니다.

2. Unfortunately, I have a ~

> 아주 기초적으로 보이는 Unfortunately, I have a ~는 의외로 여러 비즈니스 상황에서 자주 쓸 수 있는 유용한 표현이다. 구두상 더 캐주얼한 상황에서는 unfortunately 대신 sorry를 쓰면 더 자연스러울 수 있다.
> 
> 📖 *Unfortunately, I have a meeting right now.* 아쉽지만, 지금 회의가 있습니다.

    **a)** Unfortunately, I have a _____. 아쉽지만, 장례식에 참석해야 합니다.
    **b)** Unfortunately, I have a _____. 아쉽지만, 병원 예약이 있습니다.
    **c)** Unfortunately, I have a _____. 아쉽지만, 일정이 겹칩니다.

## Practice

**Making Sentences**

**Practice writing sentences. Then, read your sentences to your partner or group.**

**1.** Otherwise, I would ~

- _____
- _____
- _____

**2.** I'm confident that ~

- _____
- _____
- _____

**Editing Sentences**

**Correct the mistakes, if any, you find in the e-mail.**

From: troynova@paragon.com
To: mtsynder@coffeeace.com
Subject: RE: Invitation to Gangnam Store's Grand Opening

Hi Mark,

Thank you so much for inviting me to the grand opening this Saturday. It's very thoughtful of you to ①do so.

Unfortunately, I have a ②past commitment. I will be in Jeju with my team for a seminar the ③all weekend. Otherwise, I would definitely attend.

Thanks again for the invitation. I'm confident it will be a ④great success. Please let me know how everything ⑤turns out.

Regards

Troy

## Real Writing

**Write an e-mail based on the following scenarios. Exchange your e-mail with a partner and check your partner's e-mail for errors.**

Scenario 1

> Write a reply e-mail to Cedric, a close client of yours, to say you can't come to the seminar you've been invited to because you have a doctor's appointment in the afternoon. You're getting a full checkup. Ask him to let you know when there is another seminar.

Scenario 2

> Write an e-mail to a business associate, declining an invitation to his/her company's Christmas party. Provide a good reason.

From: neilhan@paragon.com
To: cedricmcarthur@xyzcorp.com
Subject: _____

_____
_____
_____

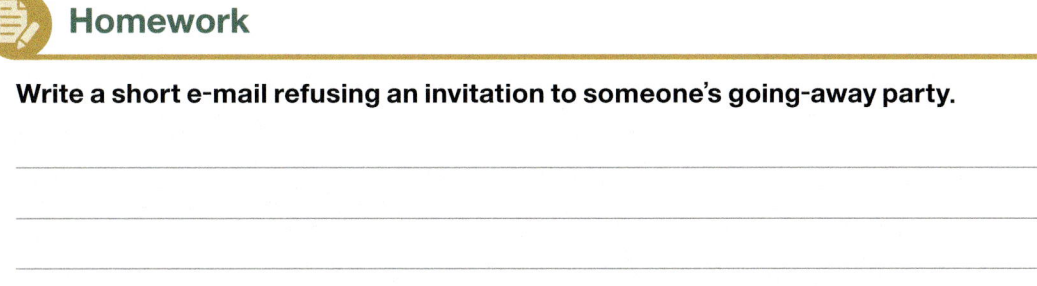 ## Homework

**Write a short e-mail refusing an invitation to someone's going-away party.**

_____
_____
_____

### Warm Up Sample Answers
1. (Yes, I've / No, I've never) had to decline an invitation to an event.
2. You can invite people (by calling them / in person / over the phone)
3. I normally get invited to (parties / meetings / demos / conferences).

### Comprehension Check Answers
1. Lucy has invited George to a product launch party on Friday.
2. He is going out to dinner with his family to celebrate his son's birthday.

### Vocabulary Answers
1. b, 2. d, 3. a, 4. f, 5. e, 6. c

### Vocab Test Answers
1. keep me in mind, 2. extend the invitation, 3. prior engagement, 4. resounding, 5. product launch, 6. most definitely

### Grammar Points Answers
1. a) help me move b) come to the party c) let me know / tell me
2. a) funeral to attend b) doctor's appointment c) scheduling conflict

### Making Sentences Sample Answers
1. Otherwise, I would (go with you / have said yes / be at home right now).
2. I'm confident that (you will do a great job / it'll turn out well / we'll make the deadline).

### Editing Sentences Answers
② past → prior, ③ all → whole/entire

### Real Writing Sample Answer
Scenario 1
Subject: RE: Can You Attend This Week's Seminar?

Hi Cedric,

Thank you so much for inviting me to the seminar. It's very thoughtful of you to extend the invitation to me.

Unfortunately, I have a doctor's appointment in the afternoon. I will be having a full checkup. Otherwise, I would of course be there.

Thanks again for the invitation. I'm confident it will be a highly productive event. Please let me know when there is another seminar.

Regards,

Neil

### Homework Sample Answer
Subject: RE: Sam's Going-away Party

Hi Teresa,

Thank you so much for inviting me to Sam's going-away party. It's very thoughtful of you to extend the invitation to a supplier like me.

Unfortunately, I have a prior commitment. I will be out of town on Thursday afternoon. I'll be in Daejeon the whole day for an industry conference. Otherwise, I would most definitely be there.

Thanks again for the invitation. I'm sure the party will be a blast. Please tell Sam I'll drop by his office on Wednesday before I leave town.

Regards,

Anabelle

**Writing Tip**

# Declining an Invitation Politely
정중하게 초대를 거절하기

### ① Say "thank you." 고맙다고 한다.

Expressing appreciation for inviting you will help lessen the impact of your declining the invitation. It will also tell the recipient you don't take that person for granted. Also, make sure to respond quickly so that the recipient can finalize the list of attendees.

초대에 대한 감사의 마음을 표현하면 초대를 거절했을 때의 충격을 줄이는 데 도움이 된다. 또한 수신자가 초대한 것을 내가 당연하게 여기지 않았다는 것을 알릴 수 있다. 그리고 참석자 명단을 마무리할 수 있도록 수신자에게 빠르게 답변하자.

- **I appreciate** the invitation. 초대해 주셔서 고맙습니다.
  **Thank you** for inviting me. 저를 초대해 주셔서 고맙습니다.
  **I'm honored** to be invited. 초대되어서 영광입니다.

### ② Explain why you have to decline. 거절해야만 하는 이유를 댄다.

Whenever you can, be specific about why you have to turn down the invitation. Having a prior engagement is obviously a good reason.

가능하면 왜 초대를 거절해야 하는지 구체적으로 알린다. 선약이 있다는 것은 당연히 좋은 이유가 될 것이다.

- Unfortunately, I can't attend because I'm currently in Chicago.
  아쉽게도 저는 현재 Chicago에 있어서 참석을 못 합니다.
  But I have another meeting that day. 하지만 그날 다른 회의가 있습니다.
  I'd love to attend, but I will be out of town. 정말 참석하고 싶지만, 출장을 갑니다.

### ③ Keep it short. 짧게 쓴다.

Don't write a long e-mail when you're declining an invitation. Keep it polite but succinct.

초대를 거절할 때는 긴 이메일을 삼가자. 정중하게 하지만 간결하게 유지하자.

# 10  Responding to a Job Application

 **Learning Objectives**

- Learners can send a rejection letter to a job applicant via e-mail.
- Learners can use appropriate language to cushion the impact of the negative news.
- Learners can express hope that the applicant will apply again in the future.

 **Warm Up**

**Work with a partner or in a group. Discuss the following questions.**
1. When was the first time you sent in a job application in English?
2. What should be included in a job application in English?
3. Have you ever accepted or rejected a job application in English?

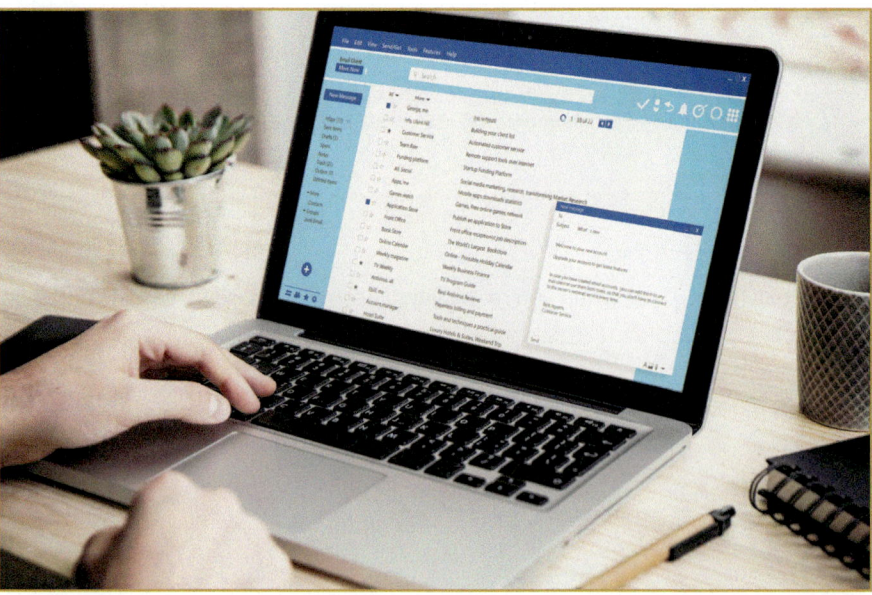

# Sample Writing

**Read the sample e-mail.**

From: aransom@paragon.com
To: haroldpayne22@guougle.com
Subject: Your Job Application

Dear Mr. Payne,

Thank you for taking the time to apply for a career in engineering at Paragon, Inc. **We regret to inform you that we have chosen another candidate for the position. Please know that this decision was not a reflection of your abilities or potential.**

Again, thank you for your interest in Paragon. Should another opportunity arise in the future, we hope you will consider applying again.

We wish you every success in all your endeavors.

Sincerely,

Anne Ransom

발신: aransom@paragon.com
수신: haroldpayne22@guougle.com
제목: 당신의 취업 지원서

안녕하세요, Payne님.

시간을 내어 Paragon 사의 엔지니어링 커리어에 지원해 주셔서 감사드립니다. 해당 직책에 다른 지원자를 선택했음을 알려드리게 되어 유감스럽게 생각합니다. 이번 결정이 귀하의 능력이나 잠재력을 반영한 것이 아니라는 점을 알아주시기 바랍니다.

Paragon에 관심을 가져주셔서 다시 한번 감사드립니다. 향후에 다른 기회가 생기면, 다시 한번 지원을 고려하시기를 바라는 바입니다.

모든 노력의 성공을 기원합니다.

수고하십시오.

Anne Ransom

## Comprehension Check

**Answer the questions.**

1. What does Anne say the decision was not a reflection of?
2. What does she hope Mr. Payne will do should another opportunity arise in the future?

## Vocabulary

**Match the words or expressions with the correct definitions.**

1. take the time _____
2. apply for _____
3. career _____
4. reflection _____
5. potential _____
6. arise _____

a. 시간을 내다
b. 반영
c. 잠재력
d. 커리어, 직장 생활
e. ~에 지원하다
f. 생기다

### ✓ Vocab Test

**Fill in the blanks with the correct words or expressions.**

take the time / apply for / career / reflection / potential / arises

1. She has a lot of _____ as a manager.
2. You should _____ the new position.
3. Have you considered a _____ in accounting?
4. _____ to carefully examine the numbers.
5. This is not a _____ of his true abilities.
6. If the need _____, we will discuss it then.

### ⊕ Bonus Resources

**rest assured (that)** ~라는 것을 확신해도 된다

A: Are you sure that the proposal will be ready by this Thursday?
이번 목요일까지 제안서가 준비될 거라고 확신하시나요?

B: Absolutely. **Rest assured that** you'll get it then.
물론입니다. 그때 받을 수 있으니 안심하세요.

여기서 rest는 '편히 있다'를, assured는 '확실한'을 의미한다. 풀어서 보면 무언가가 확실하니까 편하게 생각해도 된다는 뜻이 전달된다.

# Grammar Points

**Read the following and practice making sentences.**

1. We regret to inform you that ~

> '~라고 알려드리게 되어 유감입니다'를 뜻하는 We regret to inform you that ~은 다소 격식을 차린 표현이다. 수신자에게 나쁜 소식을 전하는 거의 모든 상황에서 유용하게 쓸 수 있다.
> 
> *We regret to inform you that we cannot accept your proposal.*
> 제안서를 수락할 수 없음을 알려드리게 되어 유감입니다.

a) We regret to inform you that we _____.
프로젝트를 연기해야 함을 알려드리게 되어 유감입니다.

b) We regret to inform you that we _____.
계약을 해지하게 되었음을 알려드리게 되어 유감입니다.

c) We regret to inform you that another _____.
다른 입찰자가 선택되었음을 알려드리게 되어 유감입니다.

2. Please know that ~

> Please know that ~은 '~라는 것을 알아주시기 바랍니다'라는 뜻이다. 혹시라도 상대방이 오해하거나 제대로 인지를 못하는 것을 방지하지 위해 무언가를 강조할 때 주로 쓴다.
>
> *Please know that we mean you no harm.* 피해를 드릴 의도가 없다는 것을 알아주시기 바랍니다.

a) Please know that _____. 저희가 최선을 다하겠다는 것을 알아주시기 바랍니다.

b) Please know that _____. 저희가 결과에 만족하지 않다는 것을 알아주시기 바랍니다.

c) Please know that _____. 당신이 맞았다는 것을 알아주시기 바랍니다.

# Practice

**Making Sentences**

**Practice writing sentences. Then, read your sentences to your partner or group.**

1. Thank you for taking the time to ~

   - _____
   - _____
   - _____

2. We wish you success in ~

   - _____
   - _____
   - _____

**Editing Sentences**

**Correct the mistakes, if any, you find in the e-mail.**

From: pamandershr@actpartners.com
To: oliviayoung12@ahoo.com
Subject: Your Application

Dear Ms. Young,

Thank you for applying for the ①<u>position of</u> sales manager at ACT Partners. We regret to inform you that we are not ②<u>able to</u> offer you the position. Please know that this decision was ③<u>based in</u> many considerations.

Again, thank you for your interest in ACT. Should another opportunity arise, we hope you will send us ④<u>an application</u> again.

We wish you success in ⑤<u>all your</u> endeavors.

Sincerely,

Pam Anders

 **Real Writing**

**Write an e-mail based on the following scenarios. Exchange your e-mail with a partner and check your partner's e-mail for errors.**

Scenario 1

> Write an e-mail to Ms. Adebisi, a job applicant, and reject her application. Say that your company has chosen another candidate whose qualifications more closely match your current needs, and that this decision was not a reflection of her experience or abilities. Tell her to consider applying again when another opportunity arises.

Scenario 2

> Write an e-mail to a job candidate rejecting his/her application. Say you have chosen another candidate based on that person's experience.

From: neilhan@accountall.com
To: maraadebisi@kmail.com
Subject: _____

_____
_____
_____

**Homework**

**Write a short e-mail rejecting a job application.**

_____
_____
_____

**Warm Up Sample Answers**
1. The first time was (in 2015 / last year / three years ago).
2. (The title of the position / The name of the company / The candidate's work experience) should be included in the application.
3. (Yes, I have / No, I've never) accepted or rejected a job application in English.

**Comprehension Check Answers**
1. She says that the decision was not a reflection of Mr. Payne's abilities or potential.
2. She hopes that he will consider applying again.

**Vocabulary Answers**
1. a, 2. e, 3. d, 4. b, 5. c, 6. f

**Vocab Test Answers**
1. potential, 2. apply for, 3. career, 4. Take the time, 5. reflection, 6. arises

**Grammar Points Answers**
1. a) need to delay/postpone the project b) are terminating the contract c) bidder was selected/chosen
2. a) we will do our best b) we are not happy with the result c) you were correct

**Making Sentences Sample Answers**
1. Thank you for taking the time to (tell us about the problem / give us the details / call me).
2. We wish you success in (your new business / everything you do / finding the right location).

**Editing Sentences Answers**
③ based in → based on

**Real Writing Sample Answer**
Scenario 1
Subject: Your Job Application

Dear Ms. Adebisi,

Thank you for taking the time to apply for a career in accounting at Account All. We regret to inform you that we have chosen another candidate whose qualifications more closely match our current needs. Please know that this decision was not a reflection of your experience or abilities.

Again, thank you for your interest in Account All. Should another opportunity arise in the future, we hope you will consider applying again.

Sincerely,

Neil Han

**Homework Sample Answer**
Subject: Your Application

Dear Mr. Patel,

Thank you for taking the time to apply for a career at AAA Corp. We regret to inform you that you were not among the candidates slated for an interview. Please know that we have arrived at this decision after a careful review of all the applications. Rest assured that this decision was not a reflection of your abilities or potential.

Again, thank you for your interest. Should another opportunity arise in the future, we invite you to consider applying again.

We wish you success in your job search.

Sincerely,

Wen Lee

**Writing Tip**

## Strategies to Use When Rejecting Job Applications
취업 지원서를 거절할 때 쓸 수 있는 전략

① **Use the applicant's name.** 지원자의 이름을 쓴다.

Don't greet the applicant with "Dear Applicant." Personalize it by using the applicant's last name in the greeting.

'지원자님께'라는 표현을 인사말로 쓰지 말자. 인사말에서 지원자의 성을 써서 개인에게 맞추자.

② **Start by thanking the applicant.** 지원자에게 감사의 뜻을 전하면서 시작한다.

Rather than starting with an expression stating the rejection, thanking the applicant first helps cushion the negative message.

거절을 언급하는 표현으로 시작하는 것보다는 지원자에게 먼저 감사의 뜻을 전하는 것이 부정적인 소식을 완화하는 데 도움이 된다.

③ **Word the rejection in a polite manner.** 거절을 공손하게 표현한다.

Use polite language as much as possible. Sometimes using a passive voice instead of an active voice helps.

가능한 한 공손한 언어를 쓴다. 때로는 능동태 대신 수동태를 쓰는 것도 도움이 된다.

> **Ex** **ACTIVE**: *We did not choose your application.*
> **PASSIVE**: *Your application was not chosen.*
> 능동태: 저희는 당신의 지원서를 선택하지 않았습니다.
> 수동태: 당신의 지원서가 선택되지 않았습니다.

④ **Don't give the applicant false hope.** 지원자에게 헛된 희망을 주지 않는다.

Avoid mentioning that you will keep the current application for future consideration. You can, however, tell the recipient to try applying again in the future.

나중에 다시 고려하기 위해 현 지원서를 보관하겠다는 언급은 피한다. 지원자에게 향후 다시 지원해 보라고는 말할 수는 있다.

⑤ **End by wishing the applicant success in the future.**
지원자의 향후 성공을 기원하면서 마무리한다.

Wishing the application success with future endeavors is an excellent way to close.

향후 시도에 대한 성공을 기원하면서 마무리하는 것은 매우 좋은 방법이다.

# 11 Sharing Policy Updates

 **Learning Objectives**

- Learners can inform recipients of policy changes.
- Learners can provide detailed explanations of policy changes.
- Learners can direct recipients on how to further explore policy details.

 **Warm Up**

**Work with a partner or in a group. Discuss the following questions.**

1. How frequently does your company update its policies?
2. Which policy did your company update recently?
3. How important are policy updates for the company?

## Sample Writing

**Read the sample e-mail.**

From: benpark@aaacorp.com
To: All
Subject: Policy Update: Meeting Room Reservations

Dear Team,

**After much consideration, we're updating our meeting room booking process to ensure fair usage for everyone.** This will take effect on May 10.

Now, you'll need to book rooms through our online system at least 24 hours in advance.

Please take a moment to familiarize yourself with the new system on our intranet and ensure your future meetings are scheduled accordingly. **Should you encounter any difficulties or have suggestions, please don't hesitate to reach out to the administrative team.**

Thank you for your cooperation and understanding.

Benjamin Park

발신: benpark@aaacorp.com
수신: 전 직원
제목: 정책 업데이트: 회의실 예약

모두 안녕하세요.

**많은 고민 끝에, 전 직원이 공평하게 이용할 수 있도록 회의실 예약 절차를 업데이트하게 되었습니다.** 이번 변경은 5월 10일부터 시행될 예정입니다.

앞으로 최소 24시간 전에 온라인 시스템을 통해 회의실을 예약하셔야 합니다.

잠시 시간을 내어 인트라넷에서 새로운 시스템을 숙지하시고, 향후 회의를 일정에 맞춰 예약하시기를 바랍니다. **궁금하신 점이나 제안 사항이 있으시면 언제든지 행정 부서에 문의해 주시기를 바랍니다.**

협조와 이해에 감사드립니다.

Benjamin Park

### Comprehension Check

**Answer the questions.**

1. What does Benjamin say the company is updating?
2. How will everyone book the meeting room?

# Vocabulary

**Match the words or expressions with the correct definitions.**

1. consideration _____
2. take effect _____
3. book _____
4. familiarize _____
5. ensure _____
6. cooperation _____

a. 적용되다, 시행되다
b. 숙지하다, 익숙하게 하다
c. 고민, 고려
d. 협조
e. 예약하다
f. 확실하게 하다

### ✓ Vocab Test

**Fill in the blanks with the correct words or expressions.**

consideration / take effect / book / familiarize / ensure / cooperation

1. I've come to this decision after careful _____.
2. I need to _____ my flight to San Diego.
3. Your _____ will be highly appreciated.
4. The new policy will _____ immediately.
5. Security measures _____ the protection of sensitive data.
6. The new hires should _____ themselves with the company policies.

### ⊕ Bonus Resources

**take stock (of)** (~에 대해) 깊이 생각해 보다

A: We need to **take stock of** the situation before we do anything.
어떤 조치를 취하기 전에 이번 상황에 대해 깊이 생각해 봐야 합니다.

B: I agree. We have to consider everything that is happening right now.
동의합니다. 현재 벌어지고 있는 모든 것을 고려해야 하죠.

원래 take stock은 '재고를 조사하다'라는 뜻이지만 어떤 특정 상황에서 잠깐 멈추고 다음 일을 결정하자는 의미로도 자주 쓰인다. 앞에 놓여있는 모든 것을 고려해서 이것저것 계산을 하는 셈이다.

 **Grammar Points**

**Read the following and practice making sentences.**

1. After much consideration, ~

> After much consideration, ~은 '많은 고민 끝에, ~'를 뜻하며, 어떤 결정이나 행동을 하기 전에 깊이 생각하고 고려한 후에 그 결정이나 행동을 수행했음을 나타낸다. 주로 어려운 결정을 내리거나 중요한 문제에 대한 결정을 내릴 때 사용된다.
>
> 📖 *After much consideration,* I've decided to accept the position.
> 많은 고민 끝에, 그 직책을 수락하기로 했습니다.

a) After much consideration, we _____.
많은 고민 끝에, 피크닉 장소로 공원을 선택했습니다.

b) After much consideration, he _____.
많은 고민 끝에, 그는 초록색 소파를 구매했습니다.

c) After much consideration, I've _____.
많은 고민 끝에, 저는 여행을 취소하기로 했습니다.

2. Should you ~, please ~

> Should you ~, please ~는 '만약 당신이 ~한다면, ~하시기 바랍니다'의 의미를 가지고 있다. 주로 안내문에서 볼 수 있으며, 받는 사람에게 특정 상황에서 받을 수 있는 도움이나 취해야 할 조치를 명확하게 권유하거나 지시할 때 사용된다.
>
> 📖 *Should you* have any questions, *please* contact us.
> 질문이 있다면 언제든지 저희에게 연락해주시기 바랍니다.

a) Should you _____ your order, please _____ before shipment.
주문 취소를 원한다면 배송 전에 저희에게 알려주시기 바랍니다.

b) Should you _____, please _____.
피드백이 있다면 고객 만족도 조사 작성 부탁드립니다.

c) Should you _____, please _____.
추가 정보가 필요하면 사용 설명서를 참고하시기 바랍니다.

# Practice

**Making Sentences**

**Practice writing sentences. Then, read your sentences to your partner or group.**

1. This will take effect ~

   - 
   - 
   - 

2. Please take a moment to ~

   - 
   - 
   - 

**Editing Sentences**

**Correct the mistakes, if any, you find in the e-mail.**

> From: trishwells@happyroll.com
> To: All
> Subject: Important Update on Expense Reporting Policy
>
> Dear everyone,
>
> After much consideration, we're ①revising our expense reporting process to enhance efficiency. This will take effect on June 1.
>
> All expense reports must be ②submit through our new digital platform, accessible via our intranet.
>
> Please take a moment to review the updated guidelines and training materials provided online. Should you encounter any ③challenges or ④have suggestions for improvement, please reach out to the Finance Department.
>
> We ⑤appreciate your cooperation.
>
> Best regards,
>
> Trish

## Real Writing

**Write an e-mail based on the following scenarios. Exchange your e-mail with a partner and check your partner's e-mail for errors.**

Scenario 1

> Write an e-mail to your co-workers updating them on the new office parking policy. Everyone will have to reserve parking spots using a mobile app, which requires downloading and vehicle registration. Advise them to contact the facilities management team with any issues.

Scenario 2

> Write an e-mail to your co-workers and tell them about the company's revised policy on office supplies.

From: isabelcruz@paragon.com
To: All
Subject: _____

_____
_____
_____

## Homework

**Write a short e-mail announcing an updated company policy.**

_____
_____
_____

191

### Warm Up Sample Answers
1. My company updates its policies (regularly / every three months / once a year).
2. My company updated its (dress code / vacation / security) policy.
3. Policy updates are (very/quite/somewhat) important.

### Comprehension Check Answers
1. He says the company is updating its meeting room booking process.
2. They will book the meeting room through the company's online system at least 24 hours in advance.

### Vocabulary Answers
1. c, 2. a, 3. e, 4. b, 5. f, 6 d

### Vocab Test Answers
1. consideration, 2. book, 3. cooperation, 4. take effect, 5. ensure, 6. familiarize

### Grammar Points Answers
1. a) chose the park for the picnic b) bought the green couch c) decided to cancel the trip
2. a) wish to cancel, notify us b) have any feedback, fill out our customer survey c) need further information, refer to the user manual

### Making Sentences Sample Answers
1. This will take effect (in October / on February 15 / immediately).
2. Please take a moment to (complete the survey / review the updated policy / read the company newsletter).

### Editing Sentences Answers
② submit → submitted

### Real Writing Sample Answer
Scenario 1
Subject: Office Parking Policy to Be Updated

Hi all,

After much consideration, we're updating our office parking policy to ensure fair access for all employees. This will take effect from August 16.

Under the new policy, parking spots must be reserved via our mobile app at least 48 hours in advance.

Please take a moment to download the app and register your vehicle if you haven't already. Should you face any issues with the app or have feedback, please reach out to the facilities management team.

Best regards,

Isabel

### Homework Sample Answer
Subject: Update on Company Car Use Policy

Dear all,

After much consideration, we have updated our policy regarding the use of company cars. This will take effect on April 20.

Moving forward, all company car bookings must be made through our new online booking system.

Please take a moment to familiarize yourself with this system and the updated usage guidelines available on our intranet. As you do, take stock of your upcoming travel needs and consider how this change may affect your current car usage patterns.

Should you encounter any difficulties or have any suggestions, please don't hesitate to reach out to the HR Department.

Kind regards,

Romeo

**Writing Tip**

# Useful Expressions to Use When Announcing Company Policy Updates
회사 정책 업데이트를 공지할 때 사용할 수 있는 유용한 표현

When updating company policies, it's crucial to announce changes before they're implemented. This will allow employees to adjust accordingly. For clear communication, here are some expressions you can use in your e-mail.
회사 정책을 업데이트할 때는 시행되기 전에 변경 사항을 공지하는 것이 중요하다. 그러면 직원들이 그에 맞게 조정할 수 있다. 명확한 의사 소통을 위해 이메일에 사용할 수 있는 표현을 다음과 같이 소개한다.

## ① About the Changes 변경 사항에 대해서

- **This e-mail serves as notice for an important update to** our current policy regarding data privacy. These updates are part of our ongoing efforts to enhance the company security.
  이 이메일은 데이터 개인정보 보호에 관한 우리 회사 정책의 중요한 변경 사항을 알리는 공지입니다. 이 업데이트는 회사 보안 강화를 위한 지속적인 노력의 일환입니다.

  **Important revisions have been made to** the company's travel and expense policy.
  중요한 변경 사항은 회사의 출장 및 경비 정책에 대한 것입니다.

  **We are writing to inform all employees about** an upcoming policy adjustment aimed at aligning with new industry standards.
  새로운 산업 표준에 부합하기 위한 정책 조정에 대해 모든 직원에게 알리고자 합니다.

## ② Effective Date 시행일

- **This policy update will take effect** on January 31, at which point all related procedures must be followed.
  이 정책 업데이트는 1월 31일부터 시행되며, 이 시점부터 모든 관련 절차를 따라야 합니다.

  Please note, **these changes will be implemented** starting June 8.
  이러한 변경 사항은 6월 8일부터 시행됩니다.

  **The revised policies will go into effect** starting July 2. 개정된 정책은 7월 2일부터 시행될 예정입니다.

## ③ Action Required 필요한 조치

- **All employees are required to** review the updated policy in detail by November 29.
  모든 직원은 11월 29일까지 업데이트된 정책을 자세히 검토 바랍니다.

  **Please ensure** you understand the new guidelines and adjust your workflows accordingly.
  새로운 지침을 숙지하고 그에 따른 작업 방식에 적응하기 바랍니다.

  **We ask that** all team members review the new policy document available on the company website.
  모든 팀원은 회사 웹사이트에서 제공되는 새 정책 문서를 검토하기 바랍니다.

# 12 Offering Condolences

 **Learning Objectives**

- **Learners can offer condolences via e-mail to recipients who have recently suffered a loss.**
- **Learners can use appropriate, respectful language in the e-mail.**
- **Learners can offer to be of assistance with anything the recipient might need.**

 **Warm Up**

**Work with a partner or in a group. Discuss the following questions.**

1. When did you last send an e-mail offering condolences in English?
2. Have you ever received an e-mail offering condolences in English?
3. Do you find it difficult to navigate the differences in culture when offering condolences?

# Sample Writing

**Read the sample e-mail.**

From: sethlee@paragon.com
To: williampierce@softall.com
Subject: Mila Ferris will be Remembered

Dear Will,

We were all saddened to hear of Mila's passing. I am truly sorry for your loss. Mila will be greatly missed. **She was not only an amazing writer of books but also a kind and friendly person.**

**Please accept our deepest condolences.** I can't even begin to imagine how you must be feeling. Our thoughts are with you.

If there is anything I can do for you, don't hesitate to let me know.

In deepest sympathy,

Seth

발신: sethlee@paragon.com
수신: williampierce@softall.com
제목: Mila Ferris는 기억될 겁니다

안녕하세요, Will.

저희는 모두 Mila의 부고 소식을 듣고 슬픔에 잠겼습니다. 고인의 명복을 빕니다. Mila가 정말 그리울 겁니다. **그녀는 대단한 단행본 작가였을 뿐만 아니라 친절하고 다정한 사람이었습니다.**

**깊은 애도를 표합니다.** 어떤 심정인지 상상조차 못 할 것 같습니다. 저희 마음도 당신과 함께 있습니다.

제가 해드릴 수 있는 일이 있으면 주저하지 마시고 알려주세요.

깊은 애도를 표하면서,

Seth

## Comprehension Check

**Answer the questions.**

1. Who has passed?
2. According to Seth, what kind of person was Mila?

## Vocabulary

**Match the words or expressions with the correct definitions.**

1. passing _____
2. your loss _____
3. amazing _____
4. deepest condolences _____
5. begin to _____
6. imagine _____

a. 당신에게 가까운 사람의 죽음
b. ~하기 시작하다
c. 죽음
d. 상상하다
e. 대단한
f. 깊은 애도

### ✓ Vocab Test

**Fill in the blanks with the correct words or expressions.**

passing / your loss / amazing / deepest condolences / begin to / imagine

1. I can't even _____ describe it.
2. Did you hear about their CEO's sudden _____?
3. _____ how wonderful it would be.
4. I'm sorry for _____.
5. I'd like to offer my _____.
6. Joey is an _____ speaker.

### ⊕ Bonus Resources

**a people person** 사교성이 좋은 사람

A: Cynthia gets along with everyone really well.
   Cynthia는 모든 사람과 정말 잘 어울리네요.
B: She sure does. She's **a people person**. Everyone likes her.
   정말 그렇죠. 사교성 좋은 사람이죠. 다들 좋아해요.

a people person을 직역하면 '사람들의 사람'이 될 만큼, 누구하고든 소통을 잘하고 사람들과 함께 있는 자체를 좋아하는 사람을 뜻한다.

## Grammar Points

**Read the following and practice making sentences.**

1. ~ be not only A but also B.

> ~ be not only A but also B는 '~는 A뿐만 아니라 B다'를 의미한다. A는 기본적인 요소를 언급하는 것이고, B는 그 외에 또는 그 위에 다른 요소가 있음을 말한다. 흔히 형용사나 명사를 쓰며, also 대신 too나 as well을 문장 끝에 붙이기도 한다.
> 
> *Bill is not only smart but nice too.* Bill은 똑똑할 뿐만 아니라 친절하기도 합니다.

a) Wendy was not only _____ but also _____ about the situation.
Wendy는 해당 상황에 대해 기분이 안 좋았을 뿐만 아니라 슬프기도 했다.

b) The project is not only _____ but also _____.
프로젝트는 너무 짧을 뿐만 아니라 너무 비싸기까지 합니다.

c) He was not only _____ but _____ as well.
그는 위대한 사업가였을 뿐만 아니라 훌륭한 아버지기도 했습니다.

2. Please accept ~

> Please accept ~는 '~을 받아 주세요'라는 뜻이다. 기초적이고 간단하지만 사과나 애도, 고마움, 축하 등을 표할 때 비즈니스 이메일에서 아주 유용하게 쓸 수 있다.
> 
> *Please accept my apology.* 제 사과를 받아 주세요.

a) Please accept _____. 저희의 진심 어린 감사를 받아주세요.

b) Please accept _____ on your success. 당신의 성공에 대한 저의 축하를 받아주세요.

c) Please accept _____. 이 작은 선물을 받아주세요.

 **Practice**

**Making Sentences**

**Practice writing sentences. Then, read your sentences to your partner or group.**

1. I can't even begin to imagine ~

   - _____
   - _____
   - _____

2. Our thoughts are with ~

   - _____
   - _____
   - _____

**Editing Sentences**

**Correct the mistakes, if any, you find in the e-mail.**

From: m.fast@xyzcorp.com
To: zenonbrooks@brookspartners.com
Subject: Please accept my condolences

Dear Zenon,

We were all ①<u>saddened</u> to hear of John's death. He will be greatly ②<u>missed</u>. He was not only a great entrepreneur but also a kind person.

Please accept our ③<u>deepest</u> condolences. I can't even begin to ④<u>imagine</u> how everyone is feeling over there. Our thoughts are with you ⑤<u>everyone</u>.

If there is anything we can do, please let us know.

In deepest sympathy,

Maureen

 **Real Writing**

Write an e-mail based on the following scenarios. Exchange your e-mail with a partner and check your partner's e-mail for errors.

Scenario 1

> Write an e-mail to Vicki, a supplier, and say that you were all saddened to hear of the death of Luna, a manager there. Say she was not only a reliable supplier but a wonderful person to be around. Offer your condolences and help with anything Vicki needs.

Scenario 2

> Write an e-mail to a business associate to offer condolences for the loss of his/her spouse.

From: sebtutor@paragon.com
To: vickiaronson@allsupplies.com
Subject: _____

_____
_____
_____

 **Homework**

Write a short e-mail offering someone your condolences.

_____
_____
_____

### Warm Up Sample Answers
1. I last sent such an e-mail (a few months ago / last year / just last week).
2. (Yes, I have / No, I've never) received an e-mail offering condolences in English.
3. (Yes, I / No, I don't) find it difficult. / I think it's difficult in any language, including Korean.

### Comprehension Check Answers
1. Mila Ferris has passed.
2. She was a kind and friendly person.

### Vocabulary Answers
1. c, 2. a, 3. e, 4. f, 5. b, 6. d

### Vocab Test Answers
1. begin to, 2. passing, 3. Imagine, 4. your loss, 5. deepest condolences, 6. amazing

### Grammar Points Answers
1. a) angry, sad b) too short, too expensive c) a great businessman, a wonderful father
2. a) our sincere thanks b) my congratulations c) this small gift

### Making Sentences Sample Answers
1. I can't even begin to imagine (what that is like / how scary that was / how expensive that must be).
2. Our thoughts are with (everyone there / you and your family / all the families).

### Editing Sentences Answers
⑤ everyone → all

### Real Writing Sample Answer
Scenario 1
Subject: Luna's Passing

Dear Vicki,

We were all saddened to hear of Luna's passing last night. We are sorry for your loss. She will be greatly missed. She was not only a reliable supplier but also a wonderful person to be around.

Please accept our deepest condolences. I can't even begin to imagine how you are all feeling. Our thoughts are with you.

If there is anything you need, please let me know.

In deepest sympathy,

Sebastian

### Homework Sample Answer
Subject: Carl's Passing

Dear Mr. Patel,

We were all shocked to hear of Carl's sudden passing. We are so sorry for your loss. He will be greatly missed. He was not only a skilled engineer but also a delightful people person. Everyone here liked him so much.

Please accept our condolences. I can't even begin to imagine how your family must be feeling. Our thoughts are with all of you.

If there is anything any of us can do, please don't hesitate to let us know.

Sincerely,

Ricardo

**Writing Tip**

# Tips When Offering Condolences
조의를 표할 때 쓸 수 있는 팁

### ① Send it early. 일찍 보낸다.

You don't want to wait too long to send the message. The quicker you send it, the more heartfelt it will seem.

메시지 보내는 것을 너무 미루지 말자. 빠르게 보낼수록 더욱 진심 있어 보이기 마련이다.

### ② Focus on the recipient, not yourself. 내가 아니라 수신자에게 주안점을 둔다.

Obviously, if you knew the deceased well, you will also be saddened. However, do not dwell on your own feelings. The message should focus on the recipient's feelings.

고인을 잘 알고 지냈다면 당연히 나도 슬픔을 느낄 것이다. 하지만 나의 감정에 빠져 있지 말자. 메시지는 수신자의 감정에 주안점을 두는 게 맞다.

### ③ Avoid philosophizing about life and religion.
삶과 종교에 대한 철학적 얘기는 피한다.

Don't be tempted to mention a famous philosophical quote or give advice. Simply express your condolences. Also, unless you and the recipient share the same religion, don't mention it.

유명한 철학 명언을 언급하거나 조언은 피하자. 그저 조의만 표하자. 그리고 수신자와 같은 종교를 가지고 있지 않다면 그것에 대해 언급하지 말자.

### ④ Add something personal. 개인적인 요소도 포함한다.

If possible, mention something personal about the deceased. It could be something about the person's personality or special characteristics. You could also talk about a particular experience you shared.

가능하면 고인에 대한 개인적인 이야기를 언급해 보자. 성격이나 특징이 될 수 있다. 함께 한 경험에 대해 말해도 좋다.

- *She was always nice to everyone she met.* 그녀는 만나는 모든 이에게 친절하게 대했습니다.
  *I still fondly remember the business trip I took with him.* 그와 함께 갔던 출장이 아직도 생생하게 기억납니다.

# PAGODA
# BUSINESS
# BIBLE

Advanced

# PRESENTATION

# 1 Hooking Your Audience

 **Learning Objectives**

- Learners can grab the audience's attention at the beginning of a presentation.
- Learners can ask the audience to remember something.
- Learners can mention the name of a product or service at the end of a presentation.

 **Warm Up**

**Work with a partner or in a group. Discuss the following questions.**
1. What is a good way to grab the audience's attention right at the beginning?
2. Do you often give the beginning part of a team's presentation?
3. How big is your audience usually?

## Sample Presentation Script

**Read the presentation aloud.**

**Remember the last time you felt overwhelmed with tasks?** If you're like most people, it was probably just this morning.

We live in an incredibly connected world, with never-ending e-mails, texts, and other messages. With everything going on around us, it's really hard to do our work.

So, how do we alleviate this problem? Sure, you can try to sleep better, eat healthier, and exercise more. But for instant results, you really should get better management software.

**At the forefront of this automation revolution is AweTech.**

마지막으로 업무에 시달렸을 때가 언제인지 기억하시나요? 대부분의 사람들과 같다면, 아마 바로 오늘 아침이었을 겁니다.

우리는 끊이지 않는 이메일, 문자 및 각종 다른 메시지와 매우 연결된 세상에 살고 있습니다. 우리 주변에 일어나는 모든 일로 인해 업무를 수행하기 매우 어려워졌습니다.

그럼, 어떻게 하면 이 문제를 해결할 수 있을까요? 물론, 더 잘 자고, 더 건강하게 먹고, 운동을 더 많이 해볼 수 있습니다. 하지만 보다 더 빠른 결과를 원한다면, 더 좋은 관리 소프트웨어를 구해야 합니다.

이러한 자동화 혁명 선두에는 AweTech가 있습니다.

### ✓ Comprehension Check

**Answer the questions.**

1. According to the speaker, what kind of world do we live in?
2. What is at the forefront of the automation revolution?

# Vocabulary

**Match the words or expressions with the correct definitions.**

1. overwhelmed _____
2. never-ending _____
3. alleviate _____
4. healthier _____
5. forefront _____
6. revolution _____

a. 더 건강한
b. 혁명
c. 압도된
d. 선두
e. 끝이 없는
f. 완화하다

### ✓ Vocab Test

**Fill in the blanks with the correct words or expressions.**

> overwhelmed / never-ending / alleviate / healthier / forefront / revolution

1. I feel much _____ since I began walking to work every day.
2. Anna is _____ with work these days.
3. We are at the _____ of a new social media trend.
4. This is truly a _____ in information technology.
5. It's a _____ cycle.
6. The CEO is trying to _____ our fears about a possible takeover.

### ⊕ Bonus Resources

**at one's wits' end**  어찌할 바를 모르는

A: The new client is never satisfied with our work. I'm **at my wits' end** trying to make him happy.
새로운 고객이 저희 작업에 절대 만족하지 않네요. 그분을 만족시키려고 애쓰는데 전 어찌할 바를 모르겠어요.

B: Yes, I heard he is pretty demanding. 네, 그분 꽤 까다롭다고 들었습니다.

'지혜'나 '분별'을 뜻하는 wits가 '끝'을 가리키는 end 와 있다면 당연히 어떤 한계에 도달했기에, 어떻게 대처할지 모를 수밖에 없다. 너무 걱정되거나 짜증이 나서 진이 다 빠진 상태를 의미하는 표현이다.

 **Grammar Points**

**Read the following and practice making sentences.**

1. Remember the last time you ~?

> Remember the last time you ~?는 '마지막으로 당신이 ~한 것 기억하시나요?'를 뜻한다. 원칙적으로 앞에 붙어야 할 Do you를 생략한 관용표현으로, 수사 의문문 형식으로 질문할 때 자주 쓰는 표현이다.
>
> 📖 *Remember the last time you* were disappointed with your own work?
> 마지막으로 하신 작업에 실망했던 때가 언제인지 기억하시나요?

a) Remember the last time you _____?
   마지막으로 친구를 도와준 때가 언제인지 기억하시나요?

b) Remember the last time you _____?
   마지막으로 컴퓨터 프로그램 때문에 불만스러웠던 때가 언제인지 기억하시나요?

c) Remember the last time you _____?
   마지막으로 임원들에게 프레젠테이션했던 때가 언제인지 기억하시나요?

2. At the forefront of A is B.

> At the forefront of A is B는 'A의 선두에는 B가 있습니다'라는 의미다. A는 어떤 특정 분야를, B는 회사나 단체, 사람을 뜻한다. 일반적인 B is at the forefront of A와는 달리, B를 문장 뒤에 배치하는 것은 B의 역할을 강조하기 위해서다.
>
> 📖 *At the forefront of* IT technology is ABC Corp. 정보통신기술의 선두에는 ABC 사가 있습니다.

a) At the forefront of _____ is Fabo.  고급 재킷의 선두에는 Fabo가 있습니다.

b) At the forefront of _____ is XYZ, Inc.  저렴한 가격의 컴퓨터 선두에는 XYZ 사가 있습니다.

c) At the forefront of _____ is Paragon.  새로운 트렌드의 선두에는 Paragon이 있습니다.

# Practice

**Making Sentences**

**Practice writing sentences. Then, read your sentences to your partner or group.**

1. So, how do we ~?

- 
- 
- 

2. You can try to ~

- 
- 
- 

**Write**

**Write a short presentation script that tells an audience to think about the last time they wanted to do something and how difficult it was to do.**

## Real Presentation

**Read the scenario and write down four key items on the flashcard below. Then, start a presentation with a hook in the form of a question. When another member of your group presents, use the checklist below.**

Scenario

> You are a sales manager for a training and development company, making a presentation to some team leaders from an IT company. You start by asking if they remember the last time that they were less than satisfied with their team's performance. You add that while everyone strives for perfection as leaders, it's really hard to get the results they want with so many things demanding the team's attention. Another question you ask is: How do we get our team to perform better? After stating some possible general solutions, you suggest that the audience should offer a great team performance enhancement training program, Empower All.

### Flashcard

| | |
|---|---|
| 1. | 2. |
| 3. | 4. |

| ✓ Presentation Checklist | Y | N |
|---|---|---|
| The presenter made eye contact with the audience. | | |
| The presenter used gestures and body language. | | |
| The presenter spoke clearly and confidently. | | |
| The presenter correctly used words/expressions from the lesson. | | |

# Homework

**You are speaking to some new customers about your product. Write the beginning part of a presentation where you start with a question to hook your audience. Then, shoot a video of yourself giving the presentation. Your presentation should be at least 2 minutes long. Watch your video and think about how you can improve your presentation.**

---

**Warm Up Sample Answers**
1. A good way is to (ask a compelling question / have them do something).
2. (Yes, I / No, I don't) often give the beginning part of a team's presentation.
3. Usually, I have (only a few / about a dozen / more than thirty) people in the audience.

**Comprehension Check Answers**
1. We live in an incredibly connected world.
2. AweTech is at the forefront of the automation revolution.

**Vocabulary Answers**
1. c, 2. e, 3. f, 4. a, 5. d, 6. b

**Vocab Test Answers**
1. healthier, 2. overwhelmed, 3. forefront, 4. revolution, 5. never-ending, 6. alleviate

**Grammar Points Answers**
1. a) helped (out) a friend b) were frustrated with a computer program c) gave/made a presentation to the executives
2. a) luxury jackets b) affordable computers c) the new trend

**Making Sentences Answers**
1. So, how do we (make this work / create a better working environment / solve this problem)?
2. You can try to (connect with them / ask more questions / be more subtle).

**Write Sample Answer**
Remember the last time you wanted to send a special gift to your top clients? If you're like most people, you probably had a hard time choosing the right gift.
With so many options available, it's really hard to decide on one thing.

**Real Presentation Sample Answer**
Remember the last time you were less than satisfied with your team's performance? If you're like most people, it was probably just today.
We strive for perfection as leaders. With so many things demanding the team's attention, it's really hard to get the results we want.
So, how do we get our team to perform better? Sure, we can try to talk to them, encourage them, and coach them. But to see immediate improvement, we should really offer them a great training program.
At the forefront of team performance enhancement training is Empower All.

**Homework Sample Answer**
Remember the last time you were at your wits' end trying to put together an important report? If you're like most people, it was probably sometime this month.
We're asked to have nice graphics and great data. With so much stuff we can put in, it's really hard to know how to choose the right things.
So, how do we put together a great report? Sure, you can try to use AI programs, use spell checkers, and check your grammar a million times. But for proven results, you should really consider using a state-of-the-art report writing program.
At the forefront of business writing software is BizWrite Ace.

**Presentation Tip**

# How Experts Keep the Audience Engaged
청중의 관심을 사로잡는 전문가의 비결

Keeping your audience focused on your presentation can be a challenge. Here are some expert tips on how to do that. Combining the methods below will ensure a great presentation.
프레젠테이션 내내 청중을 계속 몰입하게 만드는 것은 결코 쉬운 일이 아니다. 다음은 그 방법에 대한 몇 가지 전문가 팁이다. 아래의 방법으로 훌륭한 프레젠테이션을 만들 수 있을 것이다.

## ① Get them to move. 청중을 움직이게 만든다.

A great way to keep the audience engaged is to have them do something physical. If they just sit and listen passively, their focus will wane. You might have them write on handouts, ask them to raise their hands, or do a pair activity. In fact, right at the beginning, you can even have them introduce themselves to the people next to them.
청중을 끌어들이는 아주 좋은 방법은 신체적으로 무언가를 하도록 하는 것이다. 그저 앉아서 소극적으로 듣기만 하면 집중력이 떨어질 것이다. 종이에 뭔가를 쓰게 하거나 손을 들어달라고 하거나 짝을 지어 활동을 시킬 수도 있다. 그리고 아예 시작할 때 옆 사람에게 자기소개를 하게 할 수도 있다.

## ② Add variety to keep their minds engaged. 청중이 계속 참여하도록 다양성을 더한다.

Asking a diverse set of questions is one way to keep the audience involved. You might also add variety by showing videos, graphics, and photos. Making a bold statement can also keep the audience's attention.
청중을 계속 참여시키는 한 가지 방법은 다양한 질문을 던지는 것이다. 영상, 그래픽, 사진을 보여주면서 다양성을 더할 수도 있다. 과감한 발언을 하는 것도 청중의 관심을 계속 끌 수 있다.

## ③ Talk to them. 청중과 대화한다.

Use the word "you" to connect with the audience. Also, you can use expressions to get the audience to imagine or remember something.
'You'라는 단어를 사용하여 청중과 소통한다. 그리고 청중이 무언가를 상상하거나 기억하게 만드는 표현을 써도 좋다.

- Ex *As **you** can see, it's really easy.*
  보시다시피, 아주 쉽습니다.
  ***You** might say things were going great.*
  일이 잘 풀리고 있다고 할 수 있죠.

- Ex ***What if** you had a whole day to yourself?*
  하루 종일 혼자만의 시간이 있다면 어떨까요?
  ***Remember** when you were in high school?*
  고등학교 시절을 기억하시나요?

# 2 Telling a Story

 **Learning Objectives**

- Learners can deliver a core message by telling stories during a presentation.
- Learners can use a good structure when telling a story.
- Learners can express emotions when telling a story.

 **Warm Up**

**Work with a partner or in a group. Discuss the following questions.**
1. Are stories and personal anecdotes in presentations effective?
2. Why do you think stories make us listen attentively?
3. Do you find it easy to talk about yourself in front of an audience?

## Sample Presentation Script

**Read the presentation aloud.**

> **A few years ago, I found myself in a very bad place in my life.**
>
> I had a good job, a supportive family, and great friends. I should've been happy. But I was floundering. I didn't feel centered. I felt I was all over the place, like a rudderless ship. I felt disorganized and without purpose. I needed an answer.
>
> **At some point, I came to the startling realization that the answer had been in front of me the whole tim**e.

몇 년 전, 저는 몹시 어려운 상황에 처해 있었습니다.

좋은 직장, 든든한 가족, 그리고 훌륭한 친구들이 있었죠. 행복했어야 했습니다.
하지만 저는 허우적거리고 있었습니다. 중심도 잡혀 있지 않은 느낌이었습니다. 마치 방향을 잃은 배처럼 이리저리 헤맨 느낌이었습니다. 체계적이지 못하고 목적이 없다고 느껴졌고요. 답이 필요했습니다.

어느 순간, 답은 늘 제 앞에 있었다는 아주 놀라운 깨달음을 얻게 되었습니다.

### ⊘ Comprehension Check

**Answer the questions.**

1. Where did the speaker find himself/herself a few years ago?
2. What was the startling realization?

# Vocabulary

**Match the words or expressions with the correct definitions.**

1. supportive _____
2. flounder _____
3. centered _____
4. all over the place _____
5. rudderless _____
6. startling _____

a. 허우적거리다
b. 아주 놀라운
c. 지지하는
d. 방향이 없는, (배의) 키가 없는
e. 사방에, 엉망인
f. 중심이 잡혀 있는

## ✓ Vocab Test

**Fill in the blanks with the correct words or expressions.**

supportive / flounder / centered / all over the place / rudderless / startling

1. We made a _____ discovery that the contract wasn't signed.
2. The team is like a _____ boat right now.
3. We all need a _____ boss who encourages us.
4. Jane is a very calm and _____ person.
5. The project will _____ if we don't manage it properly.
6. Their director is always _____ with his decisions.

## ⊕ Bonus Resources

### when all is said and done   뭐니 뭐니 해도, 결국에는

A: The customer accepted our apology. She even sent us a thank you e-mail.
  고객이 저희 사과를 받아들였어요. 고맙다는 이메일까지 보냈더라고요.

B: Good to hear. **When all is said and done**, making our customers happy is what's important.
  좋은 소식이네요. 결국 중요한 것은 고객을 만족시키는 거죠.

When all is said and done을 직역하면 '모든 걸 말하고 마친 후에는'이 되는데, '모든 것을 고려하면'이라는 의미가 있다. 이솝 우화 '토끼와 거북이'의 오래된 영어 번역에서 해당 표현이 나왔다고 한다.

**Grammar Points**

**Read the following and practice making sentences.**

1. **I found myself in ~**

> I found myself in ~은 '나는 ~에 있었다'를 뜻한다. 더 간단하게 쓸 수 있는 표현인 I was in과는 달리, '내 의도와 상관없이 ~에 있는 나를 발견하게 되었다'라는 뉘앙스가 강하다. 처한 상황을 말할 수도 있지만 실제 장소를 언급할 때도 쓴다.
> *I found myself in a strange situation.* 저는 이상한 상황에 처해 있었습니다.

a) I found myself in _____. 저는 낯선 사람들과 방에 있게 되었습니다.
b) I found myself in _____. 저는 어제 딜레마에 빠져 있게 되었습니다.
c) I found myself in _____. 저는 새로운 환경에 있게 되었습니다.

2. **I came to the realization that ~**

> I came to the realization that ~은 '~라는 깨달음을 얻었다'를 의미한다. 기본적으로 I realized that ~와 뜻이 유사하지만 '조금 더 깊게 깨닫다'라는 느낌이 강하다. realization 앞에 sudden(갑작스러운)이나 startling(아주 놀라운)과 같은 형용사를 넣기도 한다.
> *I came to the realization that I was wrong.* 제가 틀렸다는 깨달음을 얻었습니다.

a) I came to the realization that _____. 고객이 맞았다는 깨달음을 얻었습니다.
b) I came to the realization that _____. 그분이 비꼬고 있었다는 깨달음을 얻었습니다.
c) I came to the realization that _____. 상황이 아주 나빴었다는 깨달음을 얻었습니다.

# Practice

**Making Sentences**

**Practice writing sentences. Then, read your sentences to your partner or group.**

**1.** I should've ~

- 
- 
- 

**2.** I didn't feel ~

- 
- 
- 

**Write**

**Write a short presentation script that tells the audience about a time you found yourself in a difficult situation.**

**Real Presentation**

**Read the scenario and write down four key items on the flashcard below. Then, do the beginning of a presentation with a personal story that is related to the topic. When another member of your group presents, use the checklist below.**

Scenario

You are a research and development executive for a toy company, making a presentation to the shareholders about the success of a new comic book puzzle line. You start by saying you found yourself in difficult times several years ago, when you were in charge of the jigsaw puzzles unit, which was creating many new puzzles of famous paintings and beautiful scenery. With sales slowing down for the past several years, your team had to figure out some new ways to increase sales. In the end, you came to the realization that you were neglecting the comic book enthusiasts.

### Flashcard

| 1. | 2. |
|---|---|
| 3. | 4. |

| ✓ Presentation Checklist | Y | N |
|---|---|---|
| The presenter made eye contact with the audience. | | |
| The presenter used gestures and body language. | | |
| The presenter spoke clearly and confidently. | | |
| The presenter correctly used words/expressions from the lesson. | | |

# Homework

**You are speaking to some customers about a social media app. Write the beginning part of a presentation where you start talking about something personal about yourself as a lead-in to talking about the app. Then, shoot a video of yourself giving the presentation. Your presentation should be at least 2 minutes long. Watch your video and think about how you can improve your presentation.**

---

**Warm Up Sample Answers**
1. (Yes, they are / No, they are not) effective in presentations.
2. They make us listen attentively because (it's human nature / we want to know what happens).
3. (Yes, I / No, I don't) find it easy talking about myself in front of an audience.

**Comprehension Check Answers**
1. The speaker found himself/herself in a very bad place in his/her life.
2. The answer had been in front of the speaker the whole time.

**Vocabulary Answers**
1. c, 2. a, 3. f, 4. e, 5. d, 6. b

**Vocab Test Answers**
1. startling, 2. rudderless, 3. supportive, 4. centered, 5. flounder, 6. all over the place

**Grammar Points Answers**
1. a) a room with strangers  b) a dilemma yesterday  c) a new environment
2. a) the customer was right/correct  b) he was being sarcastic  c) the situation was really bad

**Making Sentences Answers**
1. I should've (been sad about that / been honest with him / known better).
2. I didn't feel (that great / sad or discouraged / smart at all).

**Write Sample Answer**
Last year, I found myself in a difficult situation with a client.
I had a good relationship with that client. He'd been my client for a few years.
But then, something happened. He began criticizing my service.

**Real Presentation Sample Answer**
Several years ago, I found myself in some difficult times.
I was in charge of the jigsaw puzzles unit. The unit was creating many new puzzles, mostly focused on famous paintings and beautiful scenery. We should've been doing well.
But the sales had been slowing down for years. We had to figure out some new ways to increase sales. My team and I tried to come up with ideas. We needed an answer.
Then, I came to the realization that we were neglecting the comic book enthusiasts.

**Homework Sample Answer**
A few months ago, I found myself in a strange mood.
I was doing well at work and making good money with our social media app. I should've been content.
But I felt a little depressed. I didn't feel content at all. I felt I was always working. I felt incomplete. I needed something more.
At some point, I came to the realization that I was neglecting my personal life. When all is said and done, everyone needs to have a balance.

**Presentation Tip**

# Storytelling Techniques You Can Use for Presentations
프레젠테이션에서 사용할 수 있는 스토리텔링 기법

By nature, people are drawn to story structures. More and more, storytelling techniques are being used in business presentations. Here are three of the major storytelling types you can use.
사람들은 본능적으로 스토리 구조에 끌린다. 점점 더 스토리텔링 기법이 비즈니스 프레젠테이션에서 사용되는 추세다. 세 가지 주요 스토리텔링 유형은 다음과 같다.

## ① The hero's journey 영웅의 여정

This is a very popular storytelling technique used even in Hollywood movies, including *Star Wars: A New Hope*. It involves a hero who embarks on a journey, faces problems, and returns successfully. In a business context, picture your audience embarking on a similar journey.
〈스타워즈 4: 새로운 희망〉과 같은 할리우드 영화에서도 사용되는 아주 인기 있는 스토리텔링 기법이다. 영웅이 여정을 시작하고, 문제에 직면한 후 성공해서 돌아온다. 비즈니스 맥락에서는 청중이 비슷한 여정으로 떠나는 것으로 상상하자.

> *Think about launching a new product. It's like our journey. First, we start with an idea. Then, we...*
> 신제품을 출시한다고 생각해 보세요. 여정으로 떠나는 것 같습니다. 먼저, 아이디어로 시작합니다. 그런 다음...

## ② The middle of the story 스토리 중간

You've probably seen movies that start with a main character already in the middle of an action scene. This is done to grab the audience's attention immediately. They become curious and interested. From there, they get to see how the character got to that point. You can use a similar technique to hook the audience.
아마도 이미 액션 장면 속에서 주인공이 등장하는 영화를 본 적이 있을 것이다. 이는 관중의 관심을 즉시 사로잡기 위함이다. 관중은 호기심이 생기고 흥미를 갖게 된다. 거기서 관중은 그 캐릭터가 어떻게 그 지점까지 왔는지 보게 된다. 청중을 사로잡기 위해 이 비슷한 기법을 사용해 볼 수 있다.

> *Let's start with where we stand now: a 20% increase in quarterly sales. How did we get here? Let's rewind to six months ago.*
> 저희가 현재 어디에 있는지부터 시작합시다. 분기별 매출이 20% 증가했죠. 어떻게 여기까지 왔을까요? 6개월 전으로 되돌아가 보죠.

## ③ A possible future 가능한 미래

This is an effective type of storytelling when you want the audience to take action. You make them envision a potential future by comparing it with their current state. You show a problem and a solution. Then, you also show the audience how to get to the solution.
청중이 어떤 행동을 취하길 바랄 때 효과적으로 사용할 수 있는 스토리텔링 기법이다. 그들의 현재 상태와 비교하여 잠재적인 미래를 상상하게 한다. 문제와 함께 해결책을 보여준다. 그런 다음, 청중에게 해결할 수 있는 방법도 보여준다.

> *Imagine us leading in eco-friendly products next year. I'll share our steps to get there.*
> 내년에 친환경 제품을 선도하는 모습을 상상해 보세요. 그 목표에 도달하기 위한 단계를 공유하겠습니다.

# 3 Building Anticipation

## Learning Objectives

- Learners can ask questions to build anticipation during a presentation.
- Learners can talk about some typical problems the audience commonly faces.
- Learners can offer a solution to a problem after building anticipation.

## Warm Up

**Work with a partner or in a group. Discuss the following questions.**
1. Do you think building anticipation is important during a presentation?
2. What is a good way to build anticipation?
3. Is it necessary to add suspense to build anticipation?

## Sample Presentation Script

**Read the presentation aloud.**

**Have you ever wanted to stop worrying about administrative and billing tasks and just focus on the work that you love?**

I'm willing to bet you're spending most of your working day just on those tasks.
The thing is, those are really, really important tasks. They have to get done. It's just that by the time you're done with them, you're already exhausted.

Enter AweTech 3.0.
**Now you might be wondering what sets our software apart from other products in the market.**

관리와 청구 업무에 대한 걱정을 내려놓고 좋아하는 일에 집중하고 싶었던 적이 있으신가요?

아마도 대부분의 근무 시간을 이러한 업무에만 할애하고 계실 겁니다.
문제는 이러한 업무가 정말 중요한 업무라는 점입니다. 반드시 해야 할 일들이죠. 하지만 그 업무를 마칠 때쯤이면 당신은 이미 지쳐있습니다.

AweTech 3.0을 소개합니다.
여러분께서는 아마 저희 소프트웨어가 시중에 있는 다른 제품과 차별화되는 점이 무엇인지 궁금하실 겁니다.

### ✓ Comprehension Check

**Answer the questions.**

1. What is the name of the product the speaker is introducing?
2. What does the speaker say the audience might be wondering?

 **Vocabulary**

**Match the words or expressions with the correct definitions.**

1. administrative _____
2. focus on _____
3. bet _____
4. by the time _____
5. exhausted _____
6. wonder _____

a. 관리상의
b. 내기를 걸다, 믿는다
c. 궁금해하다
d. ~에 집중하다
e. 진이 다 빠진, 지친
f. ~할 때쯤

### Vocab Test

**Fill in the blanks with the correct words or expressions.**

administrative / focus on / bet / by the time / exhausted / wonder

1. Let's _____ the problem and not get distracted.
2. The team is really _____ from working all week.
3. Most of my duties are _____.
4. I'll _____ the client will call us soon.
5. I _____ if there might be a different way.
6. Lunch will be delivered _____ the meeting is finished.

### Bonus Resources

**stay ahead of the game** (남보다) 앞서 나가다

A: What can we do right now to **stay ahead of the game** in the market?
시장에서 앞서 나가려면 어떻게 해야 할까요?

B: Here are the basics. Put more money and effort into R&D. Recruit the best of the best.
기본적으로 이렇게 해보죠. 연구개발에 더 많은 돈과 노력을 기울이세요. 최고의 인재를 영입하고요.

ahead of the game은 말 그대로 게임에서 이기고 있는 것을 의미한다. 비즈니스에서는 경쟁업체보다 앞서가는 것을 뜻한다. 원래 여기서 game은 스포츠가 아닌 '도박'을 의미 했다고 한다.

**Grammar Points**

**Read the following and practice making sentences.**

1. Have you ever wanted to ~?

> Have you ever wanted to ~는 '당신은 ~하고 싶은 적 있었나요?'라고 질문할 때 쓰는 표현이다. 더 강조하는 느낌을 주고 싶다면 '한 번이라도'를 의미하는 ever라는 단어를 넣는 것을 잊지 말자.
> 
> 📖 *Have you ever wanted to take a road trip in California?*
>   California에서 장거리 자동차 여행을 하고 싶은 적 있으셨나요?

a) Have you ever wanted to _____? 당신의 일상을 바꾸고 싶은 적 있으셨나요?

b) Have you ever wanted to _____? 돈에 대한 걱정을 그만하고 싶은 적 있으셨나요?

c) Have you ever wanted to _____? 더 좋은 친구가 되고 싶은 적 있으셨나요?

2. You might be wondering ~

> You might be wondering ~은 '당신은 ~인지 궁금해하실 겁니다'를 뜻한다. wonder는 무언가가 궁금할 때 curious와 함께 사용하는 단어다. 이 표현을 쓴 후 바로 그 궁금증을 해결하는 내용을 언급하는 경우가 많다.
> 
> 📖 *You might be wondering who that is.* 저분이 누구인지 궁금해하실 겁니다.

a) You might be wondering _____. 회의가 언제일지 궁금해하실 겁니다.

b) You might be wondering _____. 저희가 다음 주 어디로 가는지 궁금해하실 겁니다.

c) You might be wondering _____. 어떤 색상이 선택됐는지 궁금해하실 겁니다.

 **Practice**

**Making Sentences**

**Practice writing sentences. Then, read your sentences to your partner or group.**

**1.** I'm willing to bet ~

- 
- 
- 

**2.** Enter ~

- 
- 
- 

**Write**

**Write a short presentation script that asks the audience members if they have ever wanted to learn something new.**

**Real Presentation**

**Read the scenario and write down four key items on the flashcard below. Then, do the beginning of a presentation where you ask a question and offer a solution to a problem. When another member of your group presents, use the checklist below.**

Scenario

> You are a sales manager for a prepared meal delivery service. You're talking to an audience of office workers. You ask them if they've ever wanted to have more energy throughout the day. You point out that they have no energy in the late afternoon because their lunch is usually a cheap sandwich. They want to eat better, but they don't have the time or the budget. You then introduce your company's Perfect Meals delivery service.

### Flashcard

| 1. | 2. |
|---|---|
| 3. | 4. |

| ☑ Presentation Checklist | Y | N |
|---|---|---|
| The presenter made eye contact with the audience. | | |
| The presenter used gestures and body language. | | |
| The presenter spoke clearly and confidently. | | |
| The presenter correctly used words/expressions from the lesson. | | |

 **Homework**

You are speaking to some customers about a social media campaign service. Write a part of a presentation where you ask a question and offer a solution in the form of your company's service. Then, shoot a video of yourself giving the presentation. Your presentation should be at least 2 minutes long. Watch your video and think about how you can improve your presentation.

---

**Warm Up Sample Answers**
1. (Yes, I / No, I don't) think it's important.
2. A good way is to (tell a personal story / talk about a common problem).
3. (Yes, it's / No, it's not) necessary to add suspense to build anticipation.

**Comprehension Check Answers**
1. The name of the product is AweTech 3.0.
2. The speaker says the audience might be wondering what sets the company's software apart from other products in the market.

**Vocabulary Answers**
1. a, 2. d, 3. b, 4. f, 5. e, 6. c

**Vocab Test Answers**
1. focus on, 2. exhausted, 3. administrative, 4. bet, 5. wonder, 6. by the time

**Grammar Points Answers**
1. a) change your lifestyle b) stop worrying about money c) be a better friend
2. a) when the meeting is b) where we are going next week c) which color was chosen/selected

**Making Sentences Answers**
1. I'm willing to bet (you're not convinced / last year was not a good year / you're having trouble).
2. Enter (a better way to do things / the new version of the software / Seal Right).

**Write Sample Answer**
Have you ever wanted to learn a different language?
I'm willing to bet you've tried that a few times in your life.
The thing is, it's really hard to find the time and the right method.

**Real Presentation Sample Answer**
Have you ever wanted to have more energy throughout the day?
I'm willing to bet you're thinking about that even now.
The thing is, by the time late afternoon comes along, you have no energy because your lunch is usually just a cheap sandwich. It's just that you don't have the time or the budget.
Enter Perfect Meals delivery service.
Now you might be wondering what's so "perfect" about our meals.

**Homework Sample Answer**
Have you ever wanted to get better results from your social media campaigns?
I'm willing to bet you're frustrated with the existing results.
The thing is, there are a lot of different platforms out there. There are a lot of different ways to promote your products. It's just that nothing you've tried so far has been all that effective.
Enter Ace Social PR Services.
Now you might be wondering how you can stay ahead of the game with our services.

**Presentation Tip**

# How to Build Anticipation during Your Presentation
프레젠테이션 중 기대감을 쌓는 방법

Whether it's a movie, a TV episode, a novel, or a presentation, building anticipation is a great way to keep people interested. Here are some ways to build anticipation during a presentation.
영화, TV 방송, 소설 또는 프레젠테이션이든지 간에, 기대감을 쌓는 것은 사람들의 흥미를 유지하는 데에 아주 좋은 방법이다. 프레젠테이션에서 기대감을 쌓는 몇 가지 방법은 다음과 같다.

① **Use the "Rule of Three."** 3의 법칙을 사용한다.

Create keywords or concepts that repeat themselves. They can even be words that start with the same letter, such as Passion, Power, and Performance. Many tales and jokes use the concept of three, including *Goldilocks and the Three Bears*. The repetition of certain types of actions, especially when there is a build-up, can create anticipation.

반복되는 핵심 단어나 아이디어를 만들어 보세요. Passion, Power, Performance와 같이 같은 글자로 시작하는 단어도 좋다. 〈골디락스와 곰 세 마리〉를 포함해서, 많은 이야기와 농담에서 3의 개념을 사용한다. 특히 빌드업이 있을 때, 특정 유형의 행동을 반복함으로써 기대감을 조성할 수 있다.

② **Use foreshadowing.** 복선을 사용한다.

You can start a story with a surprising statement that piques the audience's interest. For example, you might say, "I didn't drive here today. I walked here." Then add, "I'll tell you why soon, but I have to tell you about what happened in the morning first." This will make the audience curious so that they listen to your story.

청중의 관심을 끌 수 있는 놀라운 서술로 이야기를 시작할 수 있다. 예를 들어, '저는 오늘 여기 운전해서 오지 않았습니다. 걸어왔습니다.'라고 말할 수 있다. 그런 다음 '곧 이유를 말씀드리겠지만, 우선 오늘 아침에 무슨 일이 있었는지 알려드려야겠습니다.'라고 덧붙일 수 있다. 이렇게 하면 청중은 호기심을 갖고 나의 이야기에 귀를 기울이게 될 것이다.

③ **Engage the senses and emotions.** 감각과 감정을 사로잡는다.

Don't make your story sound technical, even if you're selling a technical product. Instead, use a lot of details that engage the senses and emotions. The audience will follow your story because you're making them feel like they are in the story. Describe the sights, sounds, and maybe even smells.

기술 제품을 판매하는 상황이더라도, 내용을 기술적으로 들리게 하지 말자. 대신 감각과 감정을 자극하는 많은 디테일을 사용한다. 마치 이야기 속에 빠져 있는 것처럼 청중은 느끼기 때문에 발표자의 이야기에 귀를 기울일 것이다. 시각, 소리, 그리고 냄새까지도 묘사하자.

# 4  Describing a User Experience

 ### Learning Objectives

- **Learners can discuss a user experience to showcase a product or service.**
- **Learners can pose a problem and a solution provided by their product or service.**
- **Learners can use storytelling techniques when describing a user experience.**

 ### Warm Up

**Work with a partner or in a group. Discuss the following questions.**
1. Do you think talking about an actual user experience is helpful during a sales presentation?
2. What should be included when describing a user experience?
3. How many user experiences should be included in a presentation?

## Sample Presentation Script

**Read the presentation aloud.**

**This product was specifically designed with small business owners in mind.**

Most of our clients report that they now spend 90 minutes or less per day on administrative tasks. **To put things in perspective, the average small business owner spends at least four hours every day on these tasks.**

I'd like to share a story about Emily, a small clothing shop owner who streamlined her business using Biz 2.0.

Emily, like many of you, started her business because she thought she'd feel freer and be more independent. She opened her shop, but then the reality hit her: she was spending more time doing paperwork than selling clothes.

Then she decided to give Biz 2.0 a try, and everything changed.

이 제품은 소상공인을 염두에 두고 특별히 고안되었습니다.

대부분의 고객이 하루에 90분 이하를 관리 업무에 소비하고 있다고 합니다. 제대로 이해하시도록 말씀드리자면, 평균 소상공인은 이러한 작업에 매일 최소 4시간을 소비하고 있습니다.

Biz 2.0을 사용하여 업무를 간소화시킨 작은 옷 가게 주인, Emily의 이야기를 들려드리고 싶네요.

여러분 중 많은 분께서 그러셨듯이, Emily는 더 자유롭고 독립적으로 일할 수 있을 거라는 기대로 사업을 시작했습니다. 하지만 막상 가게를 열고나니, 현실에 마주하게 되었습니다. 옷을 파는 것보다 서류 작업에 더 많은 시간을 보내고 있었죠.

그러던 중 Biz 2.0을 한번 써 보기로 결심했고, 모든 것이 달라졌습니다.

### ✓ Comprehension Check

**Answer the questions.**

1. The product was designed with whom in mind?
2. What was Emily spending more time doing than selling clothes?

# Vocabulary

**Match the words or expressions with the correct definitions.**

1. mind _____
2. perspective _____
3. streamline _____
4. reality _____
5. paperwork _____
6. try _____

a. 관점, 시각
b. 효율적으로 하다
c. 생각
d. 현실
e. 서류 작업
f. 시도

## Vocab Test

**Fill in the blanks with the correct words or expressions.**

mind / perspective / streamline / reality / paperwork / try

1. We need to _____ the process.
2. Keep in _____ that the project is still ongoing.
3. The _____ is that we are in trouble.
4. Let's look at this from a different _____.
5. I still have a lot of _____ to finish.
6. It's worth a _____, don't you think?

## Bonus Resources

### on top of the world 기뻐서 날아갈 것 같은

A: Congratulations on your promotion! You must be so happy.
  승진 축하드립니다! 정말 기쁘시겠어요.

B: Thanks. I am! I'm **on top of the world** right now.
  네, 고맙습니다! 지금 날아갈 것 같아요.

기분이 아주 좋거나 매우 행복할 때 세상 꼭대기에 있는 것처럼, 영어로 on top of the world라는 표현을 사용한다. 20세기부터 자주 쓰이는 이 표현은 유명한 Carpenters의 노래 제목으로도 알려져 있다.

# Grammar Points

**Read the following and practice making sentences.**

1. A was designed with B in mind.

> A was designed with B in mind는 'A는 B를 염두에 두고 고안되었습니다'를 의미하는데, 간단하게 말하면 B를 위해 만들어졌다는 뜻이다. 이 표현은 고안하는데 상당한 고민과 노력이 있었다는 뉘앙스가 강하다.
>
> 🔲 *The office building was designed with the needs of mid-size companies in mind.*
> 그 사무실 건물은 중소기업의 요구 사항을 염두에 두고 고안되었습니다.

a) _____ were designed with _____ in mind.
그 새로운 의자들은 편안함을 염두에 두고 고안되었습니다.

b) _____ was designed with _____ in mind.
그 모자는 패션과 유용성 두 가지를 염두에 두고 고안되었습니다.

c) _____ was designed with _____ in mind.
그 놀이터는 안전을 염두에 두고 고안되었습니다.

2. To put things in perspective, ~

> To put things in perspective, ~는 '제대로 된 시각에서 보기 위해 (말하자면)~'로 해석할 수 있다. 이는 복잡한 사항들을 더 쉽게 이해할 수 있도록 비교하거나 예를 들어 설명함으로써, 보다 정확하고 공정하게 판단을 가능하게 하는 데 목적이 있다.
>
> 🔲 *To put things in perspective, we had a much higher turnover rate last year.*
> 제대로 이해하시도록 말씀드리자면, 작년에 이직률이 더 높았습니다.

a) To put things in perspective, _____ on our team.
제대로 이해하시도록 말씀드리자면, 저희 팀에는 엔지니어 10명이 있습니다.

b) To put things in perspective, _____ a story.
제대로 된 시각에서 보기 위해 이야기를 하나 들려드리겠습니다.

c) To put things in perspective, _____ 50 million people.
제대로 이해하시도록 말씀드리자면, 한국은 5천만 명이 넘는 인구가 있습니다.

 **Practice**

**Making Sentences**

**Practice writing sentences. Then, read your sentences to your partner or group.**

1. Like many of you, ~

- 
- 
- 

2. ~ decided to give ~ a try.

- 
- 
- 

**Write**

**Write a short presentation script that tells an audience about a product that was designed with a certain profession in mind.**

**Real Presentation**

**Read the scenario and write down four key items on the flashcard below. Then, tell a story about an end-user who is happy with a product you're selling. When another member of your group presents, use the checklist below.**

Scenario

You are a salesperson for a smartphone accessory company. You're talking to an audience of potential customers. You're showcasing a new smartphone case with a card insert slot specifically designed for busy commuters. This year, your company has sold 10 million of these smartphone cases, which is 8 million more than last year's models that had no card insert slot. Then, you tell the audience a story about Ian, a recent college graduate working at an architectural firm who takes the subway to work every day. Ian used a pre-paid transit card, which he had to take out every time he used the subway. Using the smartphone case now, however, he's so much happier.

### Flashcard

| 1. | 2. |
|---|---|
| 3. | 4. |

| ✓ Presentation Checklist | Y | N |
|---|---|---|
| The presenter made eye contact with the audience. | | |
| The presenter used gestures and body language. | | |
| The presenter spoke clearly and confidently. | | |
| The presenter correctly used words/expressions from the lesson. | | |

# Homework

**You are speaking to some customers about a restaurant ordering system. Write a part of a presentation where you tell a story about an actual user. Then, shoot a video of yourself giving the presentation. Your presentation should be at least 2 minutes long. Watch your video and think about how you can improve your presentation.**

---

**Warm Up Sample Answers**
1. (Yes, I / No, I don't) think it's helpful.
2. (The problems the user faced / Specific products or services) should be included.
3. (Only one / A few / As many as possible) should be included.

**Comprehension Check Answers**
1. The product was designed with small business owners in mind.
2. She was spending more time doing paperwork than selling clothes.

**Vocabulary Answers**
1. c, 2. a, 3. b, 4. d, 5. e, 6. f

**Vocab Test Answers**
1. streamline, 2. mind, 3. reality, 4. perspective, 5. paperwork, 6. try

**Grammar Points Answers**
1. a) The new chairs, comfort b) The hat, both fashion and utility c) The playground, safety
2. a) there are ten engineers b) let me tell you c) Korea has over

**Making Sentences Answers**
1. Like many of you, (James was not satisfied with his job / he wanted more in life / Cindy didn't know what the problem was).
2. (He/She/They) decided to give (our products / that idea / business books) a try.

**Write Sample Answer**
This mouse was specifically designed with designers in mind.
This mouse, with regular use, can last a year without needing a battery change. To put things in perspective, typical users have to switch batteries every three months.

**Real Presentation Sample Answer**
Our new smartphone case with a card insert slot was specifically designed with busy commuters in mind.
We've already sold 10 million of these this year. To put things in perspective, we only sold about 2 million smartphone cases all last year, before we added the card insert slot.
Let me tell you about Ian, a recent college graduate working at an architectural firm downtown.
Ian, like many of you, uses the subway to get to work every day. He uses a pre-paid transit card. He had been frustrated because he had to take out the card every time he used the subway.
Then he decided to give our smartphone case a try, and now, he's so much happier.

**Homework Sample Answer**
Our table service POS was specifically designed with restaurant owners in mind.
With the POS, a single employee can handle an average of 90 customers in a six-hour dinner shift. To put things in perspective, without the POS, we estimate that the maximum number they could serve would be about 30.
I'd like to share a story about Janet, the owner of a small Italian restaurant, who had our system installed last month.
Janet, like many of you, started small and grew her business with hard work. Because of this, she kept hiring more and more staff, but then the reality hit her: she was spending way too much money on labor.
Then she decided to give our POS a try, and now she's on top of the world.

**Presentation Tip**

# When Presenting User Experience Research Findings
사용자 경험 조사 결과를 발표할 때

## ① Identify who your audience is. 청중이 누구인지 파악한다.

Different teams and departments will have specific needs and will be interested in particular set of results from your research. Hence, figure out what your audience wants and tailor your presentation to them.

팀과 부서마다 그들만의 요구 사항이 있고 특정한 결과에 관심이 있을 것이다. 따라서 청중이 무엇을 원하는지 파악하고 프레젠테이션을 그들에게 맞게 조정하자.

## ② Explain concisely. 간결하게 설명한다.

You can hand out a full report for the audience to read later. For the presentation itself, focus on the main points and keep everything concise.

전체 보고서는 청중이 나중에 읽을 수 있도록 나눠주면 된다. 프레젠테이션 자체에서는 핵심 요점에 초점을 맞추고 모든 내용을 간결하게 전달한다.

## ③ Describe your methods. 조사 방법을 설명한다.

Tell the audience how you signed up the participants, conducted the study or questionnaire, and did the analysis. Use plain language so that even the non-technical people in the audience will understand.

참여자 모집 방법, 조사 진행 과정, 그리고 분석 방법을 청중에게 알려준다. 청중 중 비전문가도 알아들을 수 있도록 쉬운 말을 사용하자.

## ④ Summarize your data. 데이터를 요약한다.

Data should not be dumped on your audience. Instead, give them only the carefully selected essential data. Focus on providing a summary of useful insights gained from the sizable data you've collected.

데이터를 청중에게 무작정 던지는 것은 삼가자. 대신 신중히 고른 필수 데이터만 공유한다. 수집한 방대한 데이터에서 얻은 유용한 통찰력을 요약하는 데 집중하자.

## ⑤ Recommend action. 다음 조치를 권장한다.

The audience now has the data and the insights. The final aspect of your presentation is to make recommendations for action based on what you've discussed. Acting on the insights gained from the data is as important as collecting the data itself.

이제 청중에게 데이터와 통찰력을 알린 상태이다. 프레젠테이션의 마지막 부분은 논의한 내용을 기반으로 조치를 권장하는 것이다. 데이터로부터 얻은 통찰력에 따라 행동하는 것은 자료 데이터를 수집한 만큼이나 중요하다.

# 5 Comparing and Contrasting

 **Learning Objectives**

- Learners can compare things during a presentation.
- Learners can contrast things during a presentation.
- Learners can discuss the background related to the development of a product or service.

 **Warm Up**

**Work with a partner or in a group. Discuss the following questions.**
1. How easy is it for you to discuss the similarities or differences between two products or services?
2. What phrases do you use when comparing or contrasting things?
3. Do you often make presentations where you compare or contrast things?

## Sample Presentation Script

**Read the presentation aloud.**

> **The first-ever version of our software was nowhere near as comprehensive as our current version. While both versions have a similar design, they differ in terms of the number of features and data processing speed.**
>
> The first version offered about ten useful features such as simple data entry and reporting, whereas the current version has more than 50, including better analysis tools.
> Of course, the computer processor speed itself has increased since the release of the first version.
>
> At the same time, however, we also faced the challenge of rising customer expectations and requirements. To catch up, we had to try and adjust a few parts and even add more features.
>
> 저희 소프트웨어의 첫 번째 버전은 현재 버전에 비하면 과히 포괄적이지 못했습니다. 두 버전 모두 비슷한 디자인을 가졌지만, 기능 수와 데이터 처리 속도 면에서 차이가 있습니다.
>
> 첫 번째 버전은 간단한 데이터 입력과 보고서 작성과 같은 유용한 기능 10가지를 제공한 반면, 현재 버전은 더 나은 분석 도구를 비롯해 50가지 이상의 기능을 제공합니다.
> 물론, 첫 번째 버전 출시 이후 컴퓨터 프로세서 속도 자체가 빨라졌죠.
>
> 하지만 이와 동시에 고객의 높아지는 기대치와 요구 사항이 커졌습니다. 이를 따라잡기 위해, 몇몇 부분을 조정하고 더 많은 기능을 추가해야 했습니다.

### ✓ Comprehension Check

**Answer the questions.**

1. The two software versions differ in terms of what?
2. To catch up, what did the speaker's company have to try and do?

# Vocabulary

**Match the words or expressions with the correct definitions.**

1. first-ever _____
2. nowhere near _____
3. comprehensive _____
4. in terms of _____
5. customer expectations _____
6. adjust _____

a. 도저히 미치지 못한, 거리가 먼
b. 고객의 기대
c. 포괄적인, 종합적인
d. 조정하다
e. ~면에서, ~에 관해서
f. 최초의, 생전 처음의

## ✓ Vocab Test

**Fill in the blanks with the correct words or expressions.**

first-ever / nowhere near / comprehensive / in terms of / customer expectations / adjust

1. We are _____ where we need to be.
2. Meeting _____ is very important.
3. This is my _____ trip to Canada.
4. Why don't we _____ the forecast a little bit?
5. I wanted a _____ report, not a summary.
6. _____ task completion speed, I finish my daily tasks quite quickly.

## ⊕ Bonus Resources

### Let's be honest. (우리) 솔직해져요.

A: **Let's be honest**, you want a bigger discount, and we want a bigger contract. Isn't that where we are at this point?
  솔직히 말해서, 그쪽은 더 큰 할인을 원하고 저희는 더 큰 계약을 원하는 겁니다. 저희가 있는 상황이 그렇지 않나요?

B: Yes, that is where we are at this point. 네, 지금 저희가 있는 상황입니다.

Let us be honest는 말 그대로 '우리 솔직해집시다'를 뜻한다. 나와 상대방 둘 다 아는 사실이니 말을 돌리거나 너무 정중하게 얘기하지 말고 그저 솔직하게 의견을 나누자는 뜻이다.

# Grammar Points

**Read the following and practice making sentences.**

1. A was nowhere near as ~ as B.

> A was nowhere near as ~ as B는 'A는 B에 비하면 과히 ~이지 못했다'라는 의미다. A와 B를 동일한 조건에서 비교할 때 쓰는 표현으로 as와 as 사이에 해당하는 상황에 적절한 형용사를 넣어서 쓰면 된다.
> 
> *This project was nowhere near as big as the last one.*
> 이번 프로젝트는 지난 프로젝트에 비하면 과히 크지 않았습니다.

a) Sam's presentation was nowhere near as _____.
   Sam의 프레젠테이션은 Matthew의 프레젠테이션에 비하면 과히 길지 않았습니다.

b) Their presentation was nowhere near as _____.
   그들의 프레젠테이션은 저희 프레젠테이션에 비하면 과히 체계적이지 못했습니다.

c) The old car was nowhere near as _____.
   예전 자동차는 그 새로운 SUV에 비하면 과히 비싸지 않았습니다.


2. A differ in terms of B.

> A differ in terms of B는 'A는 B면에서 다르다'라는 의미로, 비슷한 두 가지를 대조할 때 유용한 표현이다. A는 항상 두 가지 이상의 사람이나 단체, 또는 물체를 나타내고, B는 그중에서 한 가지 이상의 차이점을 의미한다.
> 
> *The products differ in terms of pricing and options.* 그 제품은 가격과 옵션 면에서 다릅니다.

a) The two law firms differ in terms of _____. 그 두 로펌은 대변하는 고객 면에서 다릅니다.

b) The countries differ in terms of _____. 그 나라들은 지리와 기후 면에서 다릅니다.

c) The companies differ in terms of _____. 그 회사들은 규모와 산업 분야 면에서 다릅니다.

 **Practice**

**Making Sentences**

**Practice writing sentences. Then, read your sentences to your partner or group.**

1. At the same time, however, ~

   - 
   - 
   - 

2. We had to try and ~

   - 
   - 
   - 

**Write**

**Write a short presentation script that compares and/or contrasts two different products.**

**Real Presentation**

**Read the scenario and write down four key items on the flashcard below. Then, compare and/or contrast two company events. When another member of your group presents, use the checklist below.**

Scenario

> You are a human resources executive making a presentation about this year's company retreat to other executives. You're comparing last year's retreat with this year's. They were both held at the same resort, but they were different in terms of the number of attendees, which was double that of last year, and the money spent. The main differences this year were that you had more time to prepare and that some family members attended, so you had to create special activities for both the spouses and the children.

### Flashcard

| 1. | 2. |
|---|---|
| 3. | 4. |

| ✓ Presentation Checklist | Y | N |
|---|---|---|
| The presenter made eye contact with the audience. | | |
| The presenter used gestures and body language. | | |
| The presenter spoke clearly and confidently. | | |
| The presenter correctly used words/expressions from the lesson. | | |

 **Homework**

You are speaking to some executives at your company about this year's sales results. Write a part of a presentation where you compare last year's sales with this year's. Then, shoot a video of yourself giving the presentation. Your presentation should be at least 2 minutes long. Watch your video and think about how you can improve your presentation.

---

**Warm Up Sample Answers**
1. It's (not very / somewhat / quite) easy.
2. I use phrases like (in contrast / in comparison / whereas).
3. (Yes, I / No, I don't) often make presentations where I compare or contrast things.

**Comprehension Check Answers**
1. They differ in terms of the number of features and data processing speed.
2. The company had to try and adjust a few parts and add more features.

**Vocabulary Answers**
1. f, 2. a, 3. c, 4. e, 5. b, 6. d

**Vocab Test Answers**
1. nowhere near, 2. customer expectations, 3. first-ever, 4. adjust, 5. comprehensive, 6. In terms of

**Grammar Points Answers**
1. a) long as Matthew's b) organized as ours c) expensive as the new SUV
2. a) clients they represent b) geography and climate c) size and industry

**Making Sentences Answers**
1. At the same time, however, (customers were generally dissatisfied / sales declined / we weren't sure about the possible response).
2. We had to try and (maintain composure / be fair / make it work).

**Write Sample Answer**
The old computer was nowhere near as good as this new one. While they are about the same price, they differ in terms of performance.

**Real Presentation Sample Answer**
Last year's company retreat was nowhere near as extravagant as this year's. While both were held at the same resort, they differed in terms of the number of people attending and the amount of money spent.
We had 30 attendees last year, whereas we doubled that number this year.
Of course, we also had more time to prepare.
At the same time, we also had some family members joining us. We had to try and create special activities for both the spouses and the children this time around.

**Homework Sample Answer**
Our sales last year were nowhere near as robust as this year's sales. While both years showed good growth, they differed in terms of volumes sold and the actual profits.
We sold about 250,000 units in total last year, whereas we sold more than 400,000 this year.
Of course, we knew that our toasters and speakers would continue to sell well.
At the same time, however, we did introduce a line of high-priced, high-end microwaves. Let's be honest, we had to try and convince the world that they were worth the money.

**Presentation Tip**

# When Comparing Your Products with Your Competitors'
자사 제품과 경쟁사의 제품을 비교할 때

During a presentation to customers, you might highlight the value of your products by comparing them to those of your competitors. Here are the steps from preparing the comparisons to presenting them.
고객 대상으로 하는 프레젠테이션 중에는 경쟁사 제품과 비교하여 자사 제품의 가치를 강조할 수 있다. 비교 자료를 준비하는 단계부터 발표하는 단계까지는 다음과 같다.

① **Know who the competitors are.** 경쟁사가 누구인지 파악한다.

Identify the key competitors in your market and industry. Think about their strengths and weaknesses. Obviously, you should consider their pricing strategies and positioning in the market.
시장과 업계의 주요 경쟁사를 파악한다. 그들의 장단점을 고려해 본다. 물론 시장에서 그들의 가격 전략과 위치도 고려해야 한다.

② **List the features of competitors' products.** 경쟁사 제품의 특성을 나열한다.

In addition to the features, consider the benefits provided to consumers. Ask yourself what main features and benefits your customers will see as the most important. How do those products meet the needs of the customers?
제품의 특성 외에도 소비자에게 제공하는 이점도 고려한다. 고객이 가장 중요하다고 여기는 주요 특성과 이점이 무엇인지 스스로에게 물어보자. 이러한 제품이 고객의 요구를 어떻게 충족시킬 수 있을까?

③ **Create a comparison table.** 비교표를 만든다.

Now, go into more detail and create a spreadsheet listing the features and benefits of your products and those of your competitors. Make sure to rate each feature and benefit. For example, you can assign a number from 1 to 5.
이제 더 구체적으로 들어가서 자사 제품 및 경쟁사 제품의 특성과 이점을 나열하는 스프레드시트를 만든다. 각 특성과 이점에 점수를 매겨본다. 예를 들어 1에서 5까지의 숫자를 입력할 수 있다.

④ **Present the comparisons to your customers.** 고객에게 비교 자료를 제시한다.

Let the customers see the comparison in a chart or bullet points. Be clear and persuasive with the comparisons. Avoid being negative about your competitors. Instead, highlight the strengths of your products.
차트나 핵심 내용을 통해 비교 자료를 보여준다. 명확하고 설득력 있게 내용을 전달하자. 경쟁사에 대해 부정적으로 언급하는 것은 피한다. 대신 자사 제품의 강점을 강조하자.

# 6 Indicating Importance and Priority

 **Learning Objectives**

- Learners can indicate the important points in their presentations.
- Learners can talk about current trends.
- Learners can discuss what sets their companies, products, or services apart from others.

 **Warm Up**

**Work with a partner or in a group. Discuss the following questions.**
1. How important is it to discuss what differentiates your product or service from others?
2. What are some adjectives you can use for your products or services?
3. Besides price, what other factors do you think are important to customers?

## Sample Presentation Script

**Read the presentation aloud.**

> **It's worth noting that our software has the best built-in data security features.**
>
> As you all know, data security has become a major priority for companies across the globe. And it's no wonder too, with the never-ending streams of news articles about rampant hacking and theft of intellectual property.
>
> Sure, it's true that all software comes with some sort of security feature these days. **What sets our software apart is its simplicity and ease of use.**

저희 소프트웨어가 최고의 데이터 보안 기능이 탑재되어 있다는 것은 주목할 만한 가치가 있습니다.

여러분도 아시다시피, 데이터 보안은 전 세계 기업에게 주요 우선순위가 되었습니다. 그리고 끊임없이 발생하는 해킹과 지식재산권의 절도에 관한 뉴스가 끊이지 않는 것도 놀랄 일이 아니죠.

물론, 요즘 모든 소프트웨어에 어느 정도의 보안 기능이 포함되어 있다는 것은 사실입니다. **저희 소프트웨어를 차별화하는 것은 간편성과 사용 편의성입니다.**

### ✓ Comprehension Check

**Answer the questions.**

1. What does the software have that is the best?
2. What sets the software apart?

## Vocabulary

**Match the words or expressions with the correct definitions.**

1. worth noting _____
2. security _____
3. priority _____
4. across the globe _____
5. rampant _____
6. theft _____

a. 주목할 가치가 있는
b. 우선 사항
c. 전 세계의
d. 절도
e. 만연하는
f. 보안

### ✓ Vocab Test

**Fill in the blanks with the correct words or expressions.**

worth noting / security / priority / across the globe / rampant / theft

1. Anything _____ about this design?
2. We can't tolerate _____ of company property.
3. Consumers _____ love the new tablet.
4. The company invests heavily in _____ measures.
5. Inflation is _____ in many countries.
6. That is our number one _____.

### ⊕ Bonus Resources

### a big deal 엄청난 일

A: I heard you just signed a contract for the Vans project. Congratulations!
Vans 프로젝트 계약을 막 체결하셨다고 들었어요. 축하드립니다!

B: Thanks. This is **a big deal** for us. It's probably our largest project ever.
감사합니다. 저희에게 엄청난 일이죠. 아마 당사 사상 최대의 프로젝트일 겁니다.

'큰 거래'로 직역되는 a big deal은 흔히 비즈니스상 회사에서 중요한 일이나 거래를 뜻한다. big deal은 '그게 무슨 대수야'라고 무언가를 무시할 때 쓸 수 있으니 주의가 필요하다.

# Grammar Points

**Read the following and practice making sentences.**

1. It's worth noting that ~

> worth는 '~ 가치가 있는', 'note는 '~에 주목하다'를 뜻하기에 It's worth noting that ~은 '~은 주목할 만한 가치가 있습니다'를 의미하는 표현이다.
> 
> *It's worth noting that we've won many awards this year.*
>   올해 저희가 많은 상을 탔다는 것은 주목할 만한 가치가 있습니다.

a) It's worth noting that _____.
   모든 사람들이 동의하는 것이 아니라는 것은 주목할 만한 가치가 있습니다.

b) It's worth noting that _____.
   설탕 가격이 올랐다는 것은 주목할 만한 가치가 있습니다.

c) It's worth noting that _____.
   저희가 신입 엔지니어 두 명을 고용했다는 것은 주목할 만한 가치가 있습니다.

2. What sets A apart is its B.

> set apart는 '구별하다', '차별화하다'를 뜻한다. What sets A apart is its B는 'A를 차별화하는 것은 B입니다'를 의미하며, B가 A의 돋보이는 특징을 말한다.
> 
> *What sets us apart is our commitment to excellent service.*
>   저희를 차별화하는 것은 최상의 서비스를 위한 헌신입니다.

a) What sets the pen apart is its _____. 그 펜의 차별성은 고급스러운 디자인입니다.

b) What sets the team apart is its _____. 그 팀을 차별화하는 것은 구성원입니다.

c) What sets the bicycle apart is its _____. 그 자전거의 차별성은 가벼운 무게입니다.

## Practice

**Making Sentences**

**Practice writing sentences. Then, read your sentences to your partner or group.**

1. It's no wonder too, with ~

   - 
   - 
   - 

2. It's true that ~

   - 
   - 
   - 

**Write**

**Write a short presentation script that highlights what sets a product apart from others.**

# Real Presentation

**Read the scenario and write down four key items on the flashcard below. Then, indicate the importance of the presentation's occasion and discuss what sets your company apart from others. When another member of your group presents, use the checklist below.**

Scenario

> You are the owner of a small business. You're making a presentation at the beginning of the year to your executives. It's the company's fiftieth anniversary, which you say is quite an achievement for a family business like yours, since many companies go out of business within just a few years. Highlight that your company's success stems from having the finest employees in the industry. Acknowledge that competitors also value talent and try to hire the best, but emphasize that the attractive employee benefits package is what sets your company apart.

### Flashcard

| 1. | 2. |
|---|---|
| 3. | 4. |

| ✓ Presentation Checklist | Y | N |
|---|---|---|
| The presenter made eye contact with the audience. | | |
| The presenter used gestures and body language. | | |
| The presenter spoke clearly and confidently. | | |
| The presenter correctly used words/expressions from the lesson. | | |

 ## Homework

**You are speaking to some buyers about a product that has won an award. Write a part of a presentation where you highlight the importance of the award. Then, shoot a video of yourself giving the presentation. Your presentation should be at least 2 minutes long. Watch your video and think about how you can improve your presentation.**

___

___

___

---

#### Warm Up Sample Answers
1. I think it's (quite / somewhat / not that) important.
2. They are (fast / affordable / user-friendly).
3. I think (quality / customer service / durability) is important to customers.

#### Comprehension Check Answers
1. It has the best built-in data security features.
2. Its simplicity and ease of use set it apart.

#### Vocabulary Answers
1. a, 2. f, 3. b, 4. c, 5. e, 6. d

#### Vocab Test Answers
1. worth noting, 2. theft, 3. across the globe, 4. security, 5. rampant, 6. priority

#### Grammar Points Answers
1. a) not everyone agrees b) sugar prices have risen/increased c) we've hired two new engineers
2. a) luxurious design b) members c) lightweight

#### Making Sentences Answers
1. It's no wonder too, with (all the confusion / everything that's going on / the problems we have).
2. It's true that (we had a good year / the CEO was upset / the project is having problems).

#### Write Sample Answer
It's worth noting that we manufacture the thinnest headphones in the industry.
As you all know, it's important to make them as thin as possible.

#### Real Presentation Sample Answer
It's worth noting that our company is celebrating its fiftieth anniversary this year.
As you all know, that is quite an achievement for a family business like ours. Many companies go out of business within just a few years of starting, but not ours. And it's no wonder too, with our team being the finest in the industry.
Sure, it's true that our competitors also value talent and try to hire the best. What sets us apart is our attractive employee benefits package.

#### Homework Sample Answer
It's worth noting that we won this year's Best Design Award for a new product.
As you all know, this is a big deal for any company. And it's no wonder too, with the level of competition for this award being so high and the publicity from winning it being so valuable.
Sure, it's true that there are other well-designed products out there. What sets the All-mop apart is its incredible durability.

**Presentation Tip**

# Effective Ways to Emphasize Importance
중요성을 강조하는 효과적인 방법

In any presentation, there will be a few major points that are especially important. To convey the importance of these points, here are some tactics you can use.
모든 프레젠테이션에는 특히 중요한 몇 가지 주요 포인트가 있기 마련이다. 이러한 요점의 중요성을 전달하기 위해 사용할 수 있는 몇 가지 전략을 알아보자.

## ① Use repetition. 반복해서 말한다.

In a normal conversation, saying the same thing over and over again may not be advisable. However, in a presentation, go ahead and repeat important points at appropriate intervals. You can also put the important points right into your slides.

일상 대화에서는 같은 말을 반복하는 것이 좋지 않을 수 있다. 하지만 프레젠테이션에서는 적절한 간격을 두고 중요한 요점을 반복해서 말하자. 또한, 해당 주요 요점을 슬라이드에 바로 담아두는 것도 좋다.

## ② Say it's important. 중요하다고 말한다.

This may sound obvious, but you can simply tell the audience if something is important. This will likely catch the attention of anybody whose mind has wandered off. You can say, "Let me make an important point here." You might even just say, "This is important."

당연하게 들릴 수 있지만, 중요한 내용이라면 청중에게 바로 간단히 말할 수 있다. 이렇게 하면 관심이 다른 곳에 가 있던 사람들이 주목할 수 있게 만들 것이다. '여기서 중요한 요점을 말씀드리겠습니다'라고 말할 수 있다. '이것은 중요합니다'라고도 말할 수 있다.

## ③ Speak slower. 더 천천히 말한다.

In a presentation, you should already be speaking slower than usual. When you're getting ready to make an important point, you might want to slow down even more. It helps to create anticipation for what you are about to say.

프레젠테이션할 때는 평소보다 이미 더 느리게 말하고 있어야 한다. 중요한 요점을 말하려고 할 때는 더욱더 천천히 말하는 것이 바람직하다. 말하고자 하는 것에 대한 기대감을 조성하는 데 도움이 된다.

# 7  Describing a Process or Sequence

 **Learning Objectives**

- Learners can describe a process or sequence to an audience.
- Learners can give extended instructions on how to use a product.
- Learners can use proper transitions when describing a process.

 **Warm Up**

**Work with a partner or in a group. Discuss the following questions.**

1. How easy is it for you to describe a process in English?
2. What was the last item you had to describe the process for?
3. Is it easier to follow instructions on a sheet or from someone talking you through it?

**Sample Presentation Script**

**Read the presentation aloud.**

> First, go ahead and log on. **Once you've done that, head on over to the top right-hand corner and click "My Dashboard."** It looks almost like a car's dashboard, doesn't it?
>
> From there, select any of the items on the dashboard and input your information to complete your task. When you're done inputting everything, click the "Submit" button to request approval from your direct supervisor.
>
> **Then, last but not least, once the approval is complete, print the approval document and store it in a folder, and you're all set.**
>
> There's nothing else you need to do or worry about. Everything about the software is really intuitive. We made it easy to save time through this new approval process.

먼저, 로그인하세요. 그렇게 하신 후, 오른쪽 상단으로 가서 '내 대시보드'를 클릭합니다. 마치 자동차 대시보드처럼 보이지 않나요?

거기서, 대시보드에 있는 항목 중 하나를 선택해서 정보를 입력하고 업무를 처리합니다. 모두 입력하셨으면 '제출' 버튼을 클릭하여 직속 상사로부터 승인을 요청하세요.

그런 다음 마지막으로 결재가 완료되면, 결재 문서를 출력하여 폴더에 보관하기만 하면 그것으로 끝입니다.

그 외에 하셔야 할 일이나 걱정할 일이 전혀 없습니다. 이 소프트웨어에 대한 모든 것은 정말 직관적이거든요. 이 새로운 결재 절차를 통해 시간을 쉽게 절약하실 수 있도록 제작되었습니다.

### ✓ Comprehension Check

**Answer the questions.**

1. What should one do after logging on?
2. What is the last thing that one should do?

# Vocabulary

**Match the words or expressions with the correct definitions.**

1. go ahead _____
2. log on _____
3. right-hand _____
4. submit _____
5. approval _____
6. intuitive _____

a. 로그인하다
b. 승인
c. ~하세요
d. 직관적
e. 오른쪽의, 우측의
f. 제출하다

## ✓ Vocab Test

**Fill in the blanks with the correct words or expressions.**

go ahead / log on / right-hand / submit / approval / intuitive

1. We drive on the _____ side in Korea.
2. I need to get my boss's _____ first before I proceed.
3. _____ and call her now.
4. John has an _____ sense of what works.
5. You have to _____ to the website first.
6. Tell the candidates to _____ a copy of their driver's licenses.

## ⊕ Bonus Resources

### smooth sailing  순조로운 진행

A: Once we finish the landscaping, it'll all be **smooth sailing** from there.
조경 작업만 마치면, 거기서부터는 순조롭게 진행이 될 겁니다.

B: Right. The only problem is that we haven't started the landscaping work yet.
맞습니다. 문제는 저희가 아직 조경 작업을 시작하지 않았다는 거죠.

smooth sailing이란 표현은 거친 파도가 없는 '순조로운 항해'라는 의미인데 어려움 없이 아주 매끄럽게 진행이 되고 있다는 것을 말한다.

# Grammar Points

**Read the following and practice making sentences.**

1. **Once you've done that, ~**

   once는 '하자마자'를 뜻하므로, Once you've done that ~은 '당신이 그것을 하자마자'로 직역된다. 하지만 '당신이 그것을 해야만'이란 뉘앙스가 강하다. 번역상 '그렇게 하시면', '그렇게 하신 후'가 적합하다고 볼 수 있다.

   ▶ *Once you've done that, everything will fall into place.* 그렇게 하시면, 모든 것이 제 자리를 잡을 것입니다.

   a) Once you've done that, _____. 그렇게 하시면, 저희 쪽으로부터 이메일을 받으실 것입니다.
   b) Once you've done that, _____. 그렇게 하신 후, 기다리기만 하면 됩니다.
   c) Once you've done that, _____. 그렇게 하시면, 새로운 창이 열릴 겁니다.

2. **Last but not least, ~**

   직역하면 '마지막이지만 결코 중요하지 않은 것은 아닌'이 되는데, 이는 무언가를 나열한 여러 가지 중 마지막으로 언급되는 것을 의미한다. 따라서, '마지막이지만 중요한' 점을 강조하고 싶다면, Last but not least를 사용하면 된다.

   ▶ *Last but not least, here we see a photo of the completed project.*
   마지막으로, 여기 완성된 프로젝트 사진을 볼 수 있습니다.

   a) Last but not least, _____. 마지막으로, 저희의 특별한 손님을 환영해 줍시다.
   b) Last but not least, _____. 마지막으로, 이것은 신규 제품의 모형입니다.
   c) And last but not least, I'd like to _____. 그리고 마지막으로, 팀원에게 축하의 마음을 전합니다.

 **Practice**

**Making Sentences**

**Practice writing sentences. Then, read your sentences to your partner or group.**

1. When you're done ~ing, ~

   - 
   - 
   - 

2. We made it ~

   - 
   - 
   - 

**Write**

**Write a short presentation script that describes some steps for using a product for the first time.**

**Real Presentation**

**Read the scenario and write down four key items on the flashcard below. Then, go through a detailed step-by-step process for using a product. When another member of your group presents, use the checklist below.**

Scenario

> You are a rep from a digital camera manufacturer. Today, you're showing some customers how to use your camera to take product photos they can use for their blogs. You start out by telling them to place a black or white sheet on a table and set the product they'll be photographing on the sheet. You tell them to make sure the lighting is focused on the product, view the product from different angles, and then take as many photos as they need. Also mention that the camera is so intuitive, the photos can be edited later.

**Flashcard**

| 1. | 2. |
|---|---|
| 3. | 4. |

| ☑ Presentation Checklist | Y | N |
|---|---|---|
| The presenter made eye contact with the audience. | | |
| The presenter used gestures and body language. | | |
| The presenter spoke clearly and confidently. | | |
| The presenter correctly used words/expressions from the lesson. | | |

# Homework

**You are talking to a group of social media followers of your company's meal kit products. Write a part of a presentation where you show them how to cook something with the meal kit. Then, shoot a video of yourself giving the presentation. Your presentation should be at least 2 minutes long. Watch your video and think about how you can improve your presentation.**

---

**Warm Up Sample Answers**
1. It's (fairly / quite / not very) easy.
2. The last item was (a vacuum cleaner / an alarm clock / some do-it-yourself furniture).
3. It's easier to follow instructions (on a sheet / from someone talking me through it).

**Comprehension Check Answers**
1. One should head on over to the top right-hand corner and click "My Dashboard."
2. One should print the approval document and store it in a folder once the approval is complete.

**Vocabulary Answers**
1. c, 2. a, 3. e, 4. f, 5. b, 6. d

**Vocab Test Answers**
1. right-hand, 2. approval, 3. Go ahead, 4. intuitive, 5. log on, 6. submit

**Grammar Points Answers**
1. a) you'll get/receive an e-mail from us b) you just have/need to wait c) a new window will pop up
2. a) let's welcome our special guest b) this is a mock-up of the new product c) I'd like to congratulate the team

**Making Sentences Answers**
1. When you're done (talking on the phone, please come see me / eating, go talk to Joey / writing that e-mail, let me take a look at it).
2. We made it (simple to use / easy to open / bigger this time).

**Write Sample Answer**
First, go ahead and open the box carefully. Once you've done that, take out the speaker and turn the power on.
From there, go to your phone and check the Bluetooth menu for the speaker's icon.

**Real Presentation Sample Answer**
First, go ahead and place a black or white sheet on a table. Once you've done that, set the product you'll be photographing on the sheet. Easy enough, right?
From there, make sure you have the lighting focused on the product. When you're done adjusting the lighting, try viewing the product from different angles.
Then, last but not least, take as many photos as you need with our camera.
If the photos seem too dark or the coloring seems off, don't worry. Everything about our camera is very intuitive. We made it easy to edit the photos later.

**Homework Sample Answer**
First, go ahead and spread the dough on the table. Once you've done that, put some tomato sauce on the dough. It's already beginning to look like a pizza, isn't it?
From there, put some cheese on top of the sauce. When you're done putting the cheese on, add some spices for extra flavor.
Then, last but not least, put the toppings you want all over the cheese.
Now it's all smooth sailing. There's nothing else to do but put the pizza in the oven. We made it easy for you to make a great pizza any time you get the urge.

> **Presentation Tip**

# Showing and Talking about a Process or Sequence
### 과정이나 순서를 보여주고 설명할 때

When showing and explaining a long process or sequence to an audience, you might be tempted to try and fit everything into one slide. From an audience's point of view, the process or sequence will look cluttered. Let's take a look at this regular method, as well as a new, different way.

청중에게 긴 과정이나 순서를 보여주고 설명할 때, 한 장의 슬라이드에 모든 것을 담으려는 욕구가 있을 것이다. 청중 입장에서는 해당 과정이나 순서가 어수선하게 보일 수밖에 없다. 이 기존 방법과 다른 새로운 방법을 한번 보자.

① 
## The traditional way 기존 방식

Let's say there are nine steps in a task. You might place the first three steps from left to right. Thus, you'll have three rows, each with three steps. Each step has an arrow pointing to the next one. After the third step, an arrow points down to the next row's first step, which is the fourth step. Similarly, after the sixth step, an arrow directs you to the first step of the third row, which is the seventh step.

하나의 작업에 9개의 단계가 있다고 가정해 보자. 처음 세 단계를 왼쪽에서 오른쪽으로 배치할 수 있다. 그러면 각각 세 개의 단계가 있는 세 줄이 생긴다. 단계마다 다음 단계를 가리키는 화살표가 있다. 세 번째 단계 이후에는 다음 줄의 첫 번째 단계, 즉 네 번째 단계를 가리키는 화살표가 아래로 향한다. 마찬가지로, 여섯 번째 단계 이후에는 다음 줄의 첫 번째 단계인 일곱 번째 단계를 가리키게 된다.

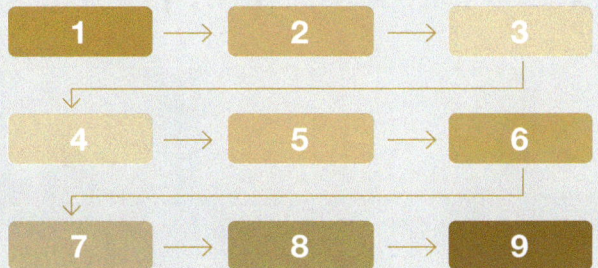

② 
## A new way 새로운 방식

To make everything look tidier, consider dividing the entire process into sub-groups. For instance, you could take the nine steps and organize them into three groups of three steps each. Then, present each group on a separate slide, with each slide showing only three steps. This way, everything becomes much easier to follow.

모든 것을 더 깔끔하게 보이게 하려면, 전체 과정을 하위 그룹으로 나눌 수 있다. 예를 들어, 9개 단계를 세 단계로 이루어진 세 그룹으로 구성할 수 있다. 그런 다음 각 그룹을 각각의 슬라이드에 정리하고 각 슬라이드에는 세 단계만 보여준다. 이렇게 하면 모든 것이 훨씬 쉽게 따라갈 수 있다.

# 8 Talking about Finances

 ## Learning Objectives

- Learners can talk about finances in general.
- Learners can provide relevant background information.
- Learners can mention anticipated financial numbers.

 ## Warm Up

**Work with a partner or in a group. Discuss the following questions.**

1. Do you like discussing finances?
2. How often do you talk about finances during a presentation?
3. Is it difficult for you to discuss poor financial performance?

# Sample Presentation Script

**Read the presentation aloud.**

> **The numbers indicate that our operating expenses have been well-managed and within budget.** This translates into a healthy pre-tax income figure, which we see right there in bold black. Not bad, considering the current problems in the Middle East, Europe, and elsewhere.
>
> With the new products rolling out next quarter, I'd venture to say we should see an even better number soon.
>
> Our forecasts reflect this. **We anticipate a strong growth rate of 25% in the coming year.**

이 수치는 저희 운영비가 예산 범위 내에서 잘 관리되고 있음을 나타내고 있습니다. 이는 좋은 세전 수익 수치로 이어지며, 바로 저기 검은색으로 볼드처리된 수치를 볼 수 있습니다. 중동, 유럽, 그리고 다른 지역의 현 상황을 고려하면, 나쁘지 않습니다.

다음 분기에 신규 제품이 출시되면서, 곧 이보다 더 좋은 수치를 볼 수 있을 거라고 감히 말씀드립니다.

저희의 예측도 이를 보여줍니다. 내년에는 25%의 높은 성장률을 예상합니다.

### ✓ Comprehension Check

**Answer the questions.**

1. What do the numbers indicate?
2. What growth rate does the speaker anticipate for the coming year?

# Vocabulary

**Match the words or expressions with the correct definitions.**

1. indicate _____
2. translate into _____
3. healthy _____
4. roll out _____
5. forecast _____
6. the coming year _____

a. 나타내다
b. 좋은, 건전한
c. 예측
d. 내년
e. ~로 이어지다
f. 출시하다

### ✓ Vocab Test

**Fill in the blanks with the correct words or expressions.**

indicates / translate into / healthy / rolled out / forecast / the coming year

1. We _____ the new hairdryer last year.
2. The data _____ that consumers prefer the newer models.
3. The _____ predicts a 10% increase in sales next quarter.
4. Happier customers _____ better sales.
5. I'm looking forward to _____.
6. These are really _____ numbers.

### ⊕ Bonus Resources

## make headway  진척을 이루다

A: We're **making headway** with the proposed project. We might sign the contract next month.
제안된 프로젝트가 진행되고 있습니다. 다음 달에 계약서 서명할 수도 있겠어요.

B: Finally! That's great news! 드디어! 아주 좋은 소식입니다!

원래 headway는 배의 전진을 뜻하는데, 비즈니스상 무언가 진척될 때 make headway 라는 표현을 흔히 사용한다. 일의 진전이 없는 상황에서는 not make headway라는 표현을 쓰면 된다.

**Grammar Points**

### Read the following and practice making sentences.

**1. The numbers indicate that ~**

> The numbers indicate that ~은 '이 수치는 ~을 나타내고 있습니다'를 뜻한다. 여기서 the numbers는 발표에서 이전에 언급한 수치, 계산, 또는 통계를 의미한다. 'that' 뒤에는 이 수치의 해석이나 의미가 이어진다.
>
> *The numbers indicate that sales are on the rise.* 이 수치는 매출이 증가하고 있음을 나타내고 있습니다.

**a)** The numbers indicate that _____.
　이 수치는 저희가 곧 목표에 도달할 것을 나타내고 있습니다.

**b)** The numbers indicate that _____.
　이 수치는 당신이 맞았다는 것을 나타내고 있습니다.

**c)** The numbers indicate that _____.
　이 수치는 이번 달 수익이 감소하였음을 나타내고 있습니다.

**2. We anticipate ~**

> 무언가를 예측할 때 유용하게 사용할 수 있는 표현인 We anticipate ~는, 간단하게 '우리는 ~을 예상합니다'로 번역된다. We are anticipating ~을 써도 무방하다.
>
> *We anticipate some trouble up ahead.* 앞으로 문제가 좀 있을 것을 예상합니다.

**a)** We anticipate _____. 경영진의 저항을 예상합니다.

**b)** We anticipate _____. 느린 회복을 예상합니다.

**c)** We anticipate _____. 두 달의 배송 지연을 예상합니다.

## Practice

**Making Sentences**

**Practice writing sentences. Then, read your sentences to your partner or group.**

1. This translates into ~

   - _____
   - _____
   - _____

2. I'd venture to say ~

   - _____
   - _____
   - _____

**Write**

**Write a short presentation script that discusses a particular expense.**

_____
_____
_____

**Real Presentation**

**Read the scenario and write down four key items on the flashcard below. Then, talk about some financial results for a product. When another member of your group presents, use the checklist below.**

Scenario

> You are in charge of electric tools at a manufacturing company. You're talking to the executive committee about the revenue from your new power tool, which is well over initial predictions. It was designed and manufactured in three months but is showing substantial profits. This month, an upgraded model will go on sale, and you think that you'll see strong sales for it as well. You anticipate over $65 million in revenue for both models this year based on pre-order numbers.

### Flashcard

| | |
|---|---|
| 1. | 2. |
| 3. | 4. |

| ✓ Presentation Checklist | Y | N |
|---|---|---|
| The presenter made eye contact with the audience. | | |
| The presenter used gestures and body language. | | |
| The presenter spoke clearly and confidently. | | |
| The presenter correctly used words/expressions from the lesson. | | |

 **Homework**

You are talking to a group of financiers for your company. Write a part of a presentation where you give them some positive news about your finances for the year. Then, shoot a video of yourself giving the presentation. Your presentation should be at least 2 minutes long. Watch your video and think about how you can improve your presentation.

___

**Warm Up Sample Answers**
1. (Yes, I / No, I don't) like discussing finances.
2. I talk about finances (sometimes / quite often). / I never talk about finances.
3. (Yes, it's / No, it's not) difficult to discuss poor financial performance.

**Comprehension Check Answers**
1. The numbers indicate that the company's operating expenses have been well-managed and within budget.
2. The speaker anticipates a 25% growth rate for the coming year.

**Vocabulary Answers**
1. a, 2. e, 3. b, 4. f, 5. c, 6. d

**Vocab Test Answers**
1. rolled out, 2. indicates, 3. forecast, 4. translate into, 5. the coming year, 6. healthy

**Grammar Points Answers**
1. a) we will reach our target/objective soon b) you were correct/right c) profits are down this month
2. a) resistance from their management b) a slow recovery c) a two-month delay in delivery

**Making Sentences Answers**
1. This translates into (more money for the workers / a better deal for us / higher targets).
2. I'd venture to say (that is quite possible / you'll feel better about it tomorrow / we did a good job).

**Write Sample Answer**
The numbers indicate that our housing expenses increased by 10% last year. This translates into a minor concern to be addressed.

**Real Presentation Sample Answer**
The numbers indicate that the revenue from our new power tool is well over our initial predictions. This translates into substantial profits for us this year. Not bad, considering it was designed and manufactured in three months.
With the upgraded model coming out this month, I'd venture to say we should see strong sales for this one as well.
The pre-order numbers support this. We anticipate over $65 million in revenue for both models this year.

**Homework Sample Answer**
The numbers indicate that sales improved significantly last quarter. This translates into higher profits as well. Not bad, considering we're in the middle of a recession.
With sales rising even higher this quarter, I'd venture to say we'll continue to make headway for the rest of the year.
Our accountants agree. We anticipate a net profit of 10% this year.

**Presentation Tip**

# Presenting Data More Effectively
데이터를 더욱 효과적으로 제시하기

① **Make numbers meaningful.** 숫자가 의미 있다는 것을 보여준다.

Whenever possible, try to use actual words instead of just numbers. For example, instead of saying "49% said they like our service," try something like, "Nearly half of the respondents like our service." The audience is more likely to remember the latter.

가능하면 단순히 숫자만 사용하는 대신 실제 단어를 사용해 본다. 예를 들어 '49%가 저희 서비스를 좋아한다고 했습니다'라고 말하는 대신 '거의 절반에 가까운 응답자가 저희 서비스를 좋아한다고 했습니다'라고 한다. 청중은 후자를 기억할 가능성이 더 높다.

② **Use round numbers.** 반올림으로 제시한다.

If a number on the slide is 207,080 or a similar figure, rather than saying the number as-is, you can say, "about 210 thousand." Documents should include exact numbers, but it is generally better to round the numbers when you're speaking.

슬라이드에 나온 숫자가 207,080 또는 유사한 숫자라면, 그대로 읽지 말고, '21만 정도'라고 하자. 문서에는 정확한 숫자가 포함되어야 하지만, 일반적으로 말할 때는 반올림하는 것이 좋다.

③ **Interpret the data.** 데이터를 해석한다.

Don't just throw out numbers at the audience. The whole point of a presentation is to let the audience know what the numbers actually mean. For example, suppose that you tell the audience, "Sales went up by 10% last year." You might add, "It's the highest year-to-year increase we've had in 10 years."

청중에게 숫자만 던지는 것은 삼가자. 프레젠테이션의 목표는 이 수치가 실제로 무엇을 의미하는지 알려주는 것이다. 예를 들어, '작년에 매출이 10% 늘었습니다'라고 한다고 치자. 이런 경우, '10년 만에 가장 높은 전년 대비 증가율입니다'라고 덧붙일 수 있다.

④ **Use the right graphics.** 적절한 도표를 사용한다.

Choose the right graphic for your data. Use a pie chart to show parts of a whole, like survey answers, where all pieces add up to 100%. Use bar charts to compare things, like sales of different products. Use line graphs to show changes over time, like yearly sales over ten years.

데이터에 맞는 도표를 선택하자. 설문조사 응답과 같은 전체 중 일부를 보여줄 때는 원그래프를 사용한다. 모든 답변의 백분율은 100%가 되어야 한다. 서로 다른 제품의 매출 등 두 가지 이상의 요소 간의 관계를 표시할 때는 막대그래프를 사용한다. 10년간의 연도별 판매와 같은 시간에 따른 변화를 보여주고 싶을 때는, 선 그래프를 사용한다.

# 9 Using Analogies

 **Learning Objectives**

- Learners can use an analogy to help the audience understand the message.
- Learners can build on the analogy to describe a process.
- Learners can engage the audience by making them part of the analogy.

 **Warm Up**

**Work with a partner or in a group. Discuss the following questions.**

1. Do you often use analogies during your presentations?
2. What do you think is the best way to use analogies?
3. Is it easy for you to use analogies in English?

## Sample Presentation Script

**Read the presentation aloud.**

Speaking of brands, let's talk about how they are made.

**Building a brand is much like constructing a skyscraper.** With every brand, you need the right strategies to put a picture of that skyscraper in the minds of consumers.

**Just as an architect carefully designs every element of a building, we too must craft our strategies with precision.** You might say we are all like architects in that sense. We don't just come up with a structure. We have to fill it in.

브랜드에 대해 이야기하자면, 브랜드가 어떻게 만들어지는지에 대해 얘기해 보죠.

**브랜드를 구축하는 것은 고층 건물을 짓는 것과 매우 유사합니다.** 모든 브랜드에서 고층 건물의 이미지를 소비자의 마음속에 심어줄 적절한 전략이 필요합니다.

**건축가가 건물의 모든 요소를 꼼꼼히 설계하는 것처럼, 저희도 전략을 세밀하게 세워야 합니다.** 그런 면에서 저희 모두가 마치 건축가와 같다고 말할 수 있습니다. 저희는 단순히 구조를 생각해 내는 것이 아닙니다. 그것을 채워 넣어야 합니다.

### ✓ Comprehension Check

**Answer the questions.**

1. According to the speaker, building a brand is like constructing what?
2. In addition to coming up with a structure, what else do we have to do?

# Vocabulary

**Match the words or expressions with the correct definitions.**

1. much like _____
2. skyscraper _____
3. element _____
4. craft _____
5. precision _____
6. come up with _____

a. 고층 건물
b. 정확성
c. ~와 매우 유사한
d. 만들다
e. ~을 생각해 내다
f. 요소

## ✓ Vocab Test

**Fill in the blanks with the correct words or expressions.**

much like / skyscrapers / elements / crafted / precision / come up with

1. What _____ should we include in this report?
2. John _____ a great marketing strategy.
3. Their team is _____ ours.
4. Mindy always chooses her words with _____.
5. There are a lot of _____ in the city.
6. We need to _____ some new ideas.

## ⊕ Bonus Resources

### worlds apart 극과 극으로 다른

A: Did you and Beth decide on the slogan for the product?
Beth랑 제품 슬로건을 정했나요?

B: Not yet. The problem is we are **worlds apart** in our ideas.
아직요. 문제는 저희 아이디어가 극과 극으로 다르다는 겁니다.

world는 '세계'를 의미하고, apart는 공간이나 거리, 시간 등으로 동떨어져 있는 것을 말하는데, worlds apart라고 하면 '세계들 사이의 차이'가 된다. 그만큼 두 사람 사이의 생각이 아주 다르다는 의미다.

# Grammar Points

**Read the following and practice making sentences.**

1. A is much like B.

> 간단하게 쓸 수 있는 A is much like B는 'A는 B와 매우 유사합니다'를 뜻한다. 어떤 두 가지 물체의 개념을 비교하는 데 아주 유용하다. 일반 명사도 사용하지만, 흔히 동명사를 쓰는 경우가 많다.
>
> *Preparing a presentation is much like planning a journey.*
> 프레젠테이션을 준비하는 것은 여행을 계획하는 것과 매우 유사합니다.

a) Writing a business report is much like _____.
   비즈니스 보고서를 쓰는 것은 논문 쓰는 것과 매우 유사합니다.

b) Going on a business trip to Paris is much like _____.
   파리로 출장 가는 것은 휴가 가는 것과 매우 유사합니다.

c) Attending a meeting is much like _____.
   회의에 참가하는 것은 미로를 탐색하는 것과 매우 유사합니다.

2. Just as ~, we too ~

> Just as ~, we too ~는 '~처럼, 우리도 ~하다'라는 뜻이다. 어떤 물체나 사람의 행위를 먼저 언급한 후, 특정 물체나 사람의 행동을 언급한 뒤, 그것을 '우리'의 행동과 비교할 때 사용하는 표현이다.
>
> *Just as doctors prescribe medicine for their patients, we too should provide customized solutions for our special customers.*
> 의사가 환자에게 약을 처방하는 것처럼, 저희도 특별한 고객에게 맞춤형 솔루션을 제공해야 합니다.

a) Just as people can choose a pen or a pencil, we too _____.
   사람들이 펜이나 연필을 선택할 수 있는 것처럼, 저희도 올바른 도구를 선택할 수 있습니다.

b) Just as a novelist writes a good novel, we too _____.
   소설가가 좋은 소설을 쓰는 것처럼, 저희도 잘 정리된 프로그램을 만들어야 합니다.

c) Just as a sports team hires good players, we too _____.
   스포츠팀이 좋은 선수를 고용하는 것처럼, 저희도 좋은 팀원을 고용하고 싶습니다.

 **Practice**

**Making Sentences**

**Practice writing sentences. Then, read your sentences to your partner or group.**

1. You might say ~

   - 
   - 
   - 

2. We don't just ~

   - 
   - 
   - 

**Write**

**Write a short presentation script that uses an analogy to talk about a company's product or service.**

## Real Presentation

**Read the scenario and write down four key items on the flashcard below. Then, use an analogy to discuss work that's important for your company. When another member of your group presents, use the checklist below.**

Scenario

> You are an executive at a construction firm. You're talking to some project managers at the company during an annual company retreat. You're using an analogy to talk about managing projects. You say that managing a project is like putting together a Lego set: you need the right pieces that ultimately fit together to become a whole. Just like Lego enthusiasts, you have to find the right people and gather the right materials. So you are all like Lego enthusiasts in that way, not just joining pieces together but building a finished product.

### Flashcard

| | |
|---|---|
| 1. | 2. |
| 3. | 4. |

| ✓ Presentation Checklist | Y | N |
|---|---|---|
| The presenter made eye contact with the audience. | | |
| The presenter used gestures and body language. | | |
| The presenter spoke clearly and confidently. | | |
| The presenter correctly used words/expressions from the lesson. | | |

 **Homework**

**You are talking to some peers at a trade association luncheon. Write a part of a presentation where you use an analogy to describe how certain products are developed. Then, shoot a video of yourself giving the presentation. Your presentation should be at least 2 minutes long. Watch your video and think about how you can improve your presentation.**

---

**Warm Up Sample Answers**
1. (Yes, I / No, I don't) often use analogies during my presentations.
2. I think the best way to use analogies is to (be as creative as you can / use real-life examples / use simple language).
3. (Yes, it's / No, it's not) easy for me to use analogies in English.

**Comprehension Check Answers**
1. Building a brand is like constructing a skyscraper.
2. We have to fill it in.

**Vocabulary Answers**
1. c, 2. a, 3. f, 4. d, 5. b, 6. e

**Vocab Test Answers**
1. elements, 2. crafted, 3. much like, 4. precision, 5. skyscrapers, 6. come up with

**Grammar Points Answers**
1. a) writing a thesis b) taking a vacation c) navigating a maze
2. a) can choose the right tools b) must/should create an organized program c) would like to hire good team members.

**Making Sentences Answers**
1. You might say (it was a hard negotiation / this is good news / that's a possibility).
2. We don't just (design it for fun / talk about it / go to lunch with a client).

**Write Sample Answer**
Creating a new training program is like writing a short play. With every new program, you need the right balance of rhythm and words.

**Real Presentation Sample Answer**
Speaking of projects, let's talk about managing them.
Managing a project is much like putting together a Lego set. With every project, you need the right pieces that ultimately fit together to become a whole.
Just as Lego enthusiasts find and gather the right pieces, we too must find the right people and gather the right materials for the project. You might say we are all like Lego enthusiasts in that way. We don't just join pieces together. We have to build a finished product.

**Homework Sample Answer**
Speaking of fountain pens, let's talk about the development process.
Developing a new fountain pen is much like writing a song. With every new pen, you need to know who your "audience" or end user will be.
Just as a songwriter decides whether a song will be an easy-listening song for older folks or a song to get young people dancing in the club, we too must decide whether the pen will be more classic-looking and mature or trendier and more youthful. The products that result will be very different, because the two concepts are worlds apart. You might say we are all like songwriters in that sense. We don't just design pens. We have to design items to match particular lifestyles.

### Presentation Tip

# Using Analogies Effectively
효과적으로 비유하기

It's not enough to think of an analogy. It should be relevant to your subject and specific to your audience.
단순히 비유를 생각해 낸다고 끝나는 것이 아니다. 주제와 관련이 있어야 하고 청중에게 맞추어져야 한다.

## ① Customize your analogy to your audience. 청중에 맞게 비유한다.

Even if the subject matter is the same, you shouldn't use the same analogy every time. Consider the makeup of the audience. Are the members a mix of younger and older customers? Or are they people in your industry? For the former, you should use an analogy that everyone can understand. For the latter, you can use a more industry-specific analogy.

주제가 동일할지라도 항상 같은 비유를 쓰는 것은 좋지 않다. 청중의 구성을 고려하자. 청중이 젊은 고객과 노년층이 섞여 있는가? 아니면 나와 같은 업계에 종사하는 사람들인가? 전자의 경우 모두가 이해할 수 있는 비유를 사용해야 한다. 후자의 경우, 업계에 맞는 비유를 사용할 수 있다.

## ② Add the right details to your analogy. 비유할 때 적절한 디테일을 포함한다.

You should be very clear with your analogy. Make sure that it can't be interpreted in a way that is not intended. Also, the analogy should not contradict your point. Provide enough detail so that the analogy is understood in the way you intended.

비유할 때는 매우 명확하게 해야 한다. 의도하지 않은 방향으로 해석되지 않도록 신경 써야 한다. 또한 요점과 모순되지 않아야 한다. 의도한 대로 이해되도록 충분한 디테일을 포함하자.

## ③ Use dynamic language. 역동적인 표현을 사용한다.

When making an analogy, use words that evoke strong images. Use good, descriptive words and strong adjectives. For example, let's say that you're talking about riding a bicycle. You might say something like, "At first, it's hard enough to keep balance on the bicycle. Later, as you get better, you don't worry about the bicycle anymore. You see the green trees and the clear river, feel the nice breeze on your face, and smell the crisp air."

비유할 때는 강한 이미지를 떠올리게 하는 단어를 사용한다. 구체적인 단어와 강렬한 형용사를 사용하자. 예를 들어 자전거를 타는 것에 대해 이야기한다고 치자. 다음과 같이 얘기해 볼 수 있다. '처음에는 자전거를 탈 때 균형을 유지하기가 어렵습니다. 나중에 더 능숙해지면 더 이상 자전거를 걱정하지 않게 되죠. 푸른 나무와 맑은 강이 보이고 얼굴에 산들바람을 느끼며 상쾌한 공기를 맡을 수 있습니다.'

# 10 Making a Proposal

### Learning Objectives

- Learners can make a presentation suggesting a partnership.
- Learners can suggest partnering up for mutual benefit.
- Learners can offer reasons why partnering up would be beneficial.

### Warm Up

**Work with a partner or in a group. Discuss the following questions.**

1. Have you ever made a presentation suggesting a partnership of some kind?
2. Do you think joint marketing campaigns or promotions with other companies are generally effective?
3. What would be an ideal duration for a joint marketing campaign or promotion?

**Sample Presentation Script**

**Read the presentation aloud.**

> **We are convinced that a partnership between our company and XYZ, Inc. could be mutually beneficial.**
>
> We both cater to young, stylish consumers looking to stand out from the crowd. Not only that, we also both sell our products from high-end department stores and online stores.
>
> **Together, we can enhance our brand image and maximize profits through product collaboration.** There are quite a lot of areas where we can try a joint promotion, product development, and even short-term co-branding.

당사와 XYZ, Inc. 간의 협업은 서로에게 이익이 될 것임을 확신합니다.

양사 모두 젊고 멋진 소비자들을 대상으로 하며, 군중에서 돋보이길 원하는 이들에게 제품을 제공하고 있습니다. 그뿐만 아니라, 양사 모두 고급 백화점과 온라인 매장에서 제품을 판매하고 있습니다.

함께하면, 저희는 브랜드 이미지를 강화하고 제품 협력을 통해 이익을 극대화할 수 있습니다. 공동 행사, 제품 개발, 그리고 단기적 브랜드 제휴까지, 시도할 수 있는 부분이 꽤 많습니다.

### ⊘ Comprehension Check

**Answer the questions.**

1. According to the speaker, what types of consumers do both companies cater to?
2. Where do they both sell their products from?

## Vocabulary

**Match the words or expressions with the correct definitions.**

1. convinced _____
2. mutually beneficial _____
3. cater to _____
4. stylish _____
5. high-end _____
6. collaboration _____

a. 멋진, 스타일리시한
b. 서로에게 이익이 되는
c. ~에 응하다, ~을 충족시키다
d. 협업
e. 고급의
f. 확신하는

### ✓ Vocab Test

**Fill in the blanks with the correct words or expressions.**

convinced / mutually beneficial / cater to / stylish / high-end / collaboration

1. This is _____, since both companies will save money.
2. Our products always look modern and _____.
3. The company makes _____ audio equipment, so customers expect excellent performance.
4. They are _____ that we're hiding something.
5. It was produced in _____ with another company.
6. We _____ older consumers.

### ⊕ Bonus Resources

### Many hands make light work. 백지장도 맞들면 낫다.

A: Do you need a hand with moving the desk?
그 책상 옮기는 데 도움 필요하세요?

B: That would be great. Thanks. **Many hands make light work**, right?
그러면 아주 좋죠. 고마워요. 백지장도 맞들면 낫네요, 그렇죠?

'Many hands make light work'는 14세기 영국 속담에서 유래된 표현으로, '많은 사람이 도와주면 일이 쉬워진다'는 의미다. 이는 우리나라 속담인 '백지장도 맞들면 낫다'와 유사한 표현이다.

 **Grammar Points**

### Read the following and practice making sentences.

1. **We are convinced that ~**

> We are convinced that ~은 '저희는 ~을 확신합니다'를 뜻한다. 원래 convince는 동사로 '설득하다'를 의미하는데, be convinced는 이미 설득이 된 상태인 셈이다. 더 캐주얼한 상황에서는 convinced 대신 sure를 써도 무방하다.
>
> 📧 *We are convinced that the event is too small.* 그 행사가 너무 작다는 것을 확신합니다.

a) We are convinced that _____. 이것은 아주 좋은 아이디어라는 것을 확신합니다.

b) We are convinced that _____. 신규 서비스가 성공할 것임을 확신합니다.

c) We are convinced that _____. 이사회가 제안서를 수락할 것을 확신합니다.

2. **Together, we can ~**

> '우리는 ~할 수 있다'를 뜻하는 we can에 '함께'를 말하는 together를 더해서 강조하는 것이다. 특히 together가 문장의 앞에 오는 만큼, '함께 어떤 일을 하는 것'에 집중한다. 조금 더 격식을 차리고 싶다면 can 대신 could를 사용할 수 있다.
>
> 📧 *Together, we can make this work.* 함께하면, 이 일을 성사시킬 수 있습니다.

a) Together, we can _____. 함께하면, 더 좋은 회사를 만들 수 있습니다.

b) Together, we can _____. 함께하면, 이 문제의 해결책을 찾을 수 있습니다.

c) Together, we can _____. 함께하면, CEO를 설득할 수 있습니다.

# Practice

**Making Sentences**

**Practice writing sentences. Then, read your sentences to your partner or group.**

1. Not only that, ~

   - _____
   - _____
   - _____

2. There are quite a lot of ~

   - _____
   - _____
   - _____

**Write**

**Write a short presentation script that proposes that you and others work together for a single purpose.**

_____
_____
_____

**Real Presentation**

**Read the scenario and write down four key items on the flashcard below. Then, talk to a small audience of executives about doing a joint promotion. When another member of your group presents, use the checklist below.**

Scenario

> You are an executive of a company producing chips and cookies. You're talking to some executives of another company that mostly produces chocolates and candy. You're proposing a joint promotion during the holiday season. You point out that both companies have snacks coming out with special Christmas packaging, and both supply all the major supermarkets in the area. The promotion would save marketing and advertising costs while increasing holiday revenue. There are additional benefits as well.

**Flashcard**

| 1. | 2. |
|---|---|
| 3. | 4. |

| ✓ Presentation Checklist | Y | N |
|---|---|---|
| The presenter made eye contact with the audience. | | |
| The presenter used gestures and body language. | | |
| The presenter spoke clearly and confidently. | | |
| The presenter correctly used words/expressions from the lesson. | | |

# Homework

**You are talking to important executives at another company. Write a part of a presentation where you suggest a possible joint venture to develop a product. Then, shoot a video of yourself giving the presentation. Your presentation should be at least 2 minutes long. Watch your video and think about how you can improve your presentation.**

---

**Warm Up Sample Answers**
1. (Yes, I have / No, I have never) made a presentation suggesting a partnership.
2. (Yes, I think / No, I don't think) they're generally effective.
3. I think (a few weeks / a few months / half a year or so) would be an ideal duration.

**Comprehension Check Answers**
1. They both cater to young, stylish consumers looking to stand out from the crowd.
2. They both sell from high-end department stores and online stores.

**Vocabulary Answers**
1. f, 2. b, 3. c, 4. a, 5. e, 6. d

**Vocab Test Answers**
1. mutually beneficial, 2. stylish, 3. high-end, 4. convinced, 5. collaboration, 6. cater to

**Grammar Points Answers**
1. a) this is a great idea b) the new service will succeed / be successful c) the board (of directors) will approve the proposal
2. a) build a better company b) find a solution to this problem c) convince the CEO

**Making Sentences Answers**
1. Not only that, (you can get another free sample / we have more in the back / I can go with you).
2. There are quite a lot of (problems at the site / interesting ideas here / people asking questions).

**Write Sample Answer**
Together, we can create the right design and engineering for our client's office building. There are quite a lot of areas where each team can contribute its unique set of expertise.

**Real Presentation Sample Answer**
We are convinced that a joint promotion during the holiday season could prove mutually beneficial.
We both have snacks coming out with special Christmas packaging. Not only that, we also both supply all the major supermarkets in the area.
Together, we can save marketing and advertising costs while increasing both our holiday revenue. There are quite a lot of other benefits that come with this type of joint promotion as well.

**Homework Sample Answer**
We are convinced that a joint venture between our two companies will be mutually beneficial.
We have both been developing mobile games for decades. Not only that, but we also have many employees who have experience working at other major game companies.
Together, we can bring a new game to the market much faster. There are quite a lot of areas where we can concentrate our core developers. Many hands make light work.

**Presentation Tip**

# Making a Partnership Proposal
협업 제안하기

When making a partnership proposal, don't focus on what you will gain. Focus instead on how the partnership will benefit the other company.
협업 제안할 때는 내가 무엇을 얻을 수 있는지에 초점을 두지 말자. 대신 협업이 상대 회사에 어떤 이점이 줄지에 집중하자.

### ① Research the company thoroughly. 상대 회사에 대해서 철저히 조사한다.

Do research on the company's history, key milestones, and executives and staff. In addition, read articles and case studies on the company, its press releases, and its social media pages. Become knowledgeable about the products and services it offers. You should do all this to get enough data to make a proposal as well as to be ready when talking directly with them.

상대 회사의 역사와 중대한 업적, 그리고 임원과 직원에 대해 조사한다. 더불어 회사에 관한 기사와 사례 연구, 회사의 보도자료와 SNS 페이지 등을 살펴본다. 회사가 제공하는 제품과 서비스에 대해 잘 알아둔다. 이 모든 과정을 통해 충분한 데이터를 확보하여 제안서를 작성하고, 직접 대화할 때 준비가 되어 있어야 한다.

### ② Create the right structure. 따라가기 쉬운 구성으로 만든다.

The structure of your presentation should be simple, short, and persuasive. Start by grabbing their attention with a question or a possible future scenario. State the problems or needs the potential partner might be facing. Then, describe how a partnership will provide a solution. Summarize your points at the end.

프레젠테이션의 구성은 간단하고 짧으면서도 설득력이 있어야 한다. 먼저 질문이나 가능한 미래 시나리오로 청중의 관심을 사로잡으며 시작하자. 잠재적인 파트너가 직면할 수 있는 문제나 니즈를 언급한다. 그런 다음, 협업이 어떻게 해결책이 될지를 설명한다. 마지막에는 요점을 요약한다.

### ③ Be straightforward. 간단명료하게 말한다.

Avoid using unnecessarily dramatic language. Keep your statements professional and simple. Go ahead and mention your own company's accomplishments. However, be careful not to sound too much like you are making a sales pitch. Remember, you're not talking to a potential customer. You're talking to a potential partner. Highlight how a partnership will be mutually beneficial.

불필요하게 과장된 표현은 피한다. 전문적이고 간단하게 유지하자. 내가 다니는 회사의 업적은 언급하되, 너무 홍보하는 것처럼 들리지 않도록 주의한다. 잠재적인 고객과 얘기하는 것이 아니라는 것을 기억하자. 잠재적인 파트너와 이야기하고 있다. 협업이 어떻게 상호 이익이 될 것인지를 강조한다.

# 11 Concluding a Presentation

## Learning Objectives

- Learners can finish a presentation in a structured way.
- Learners can end with a call to action or a memorable statement.
- Learners can engage the audience with expressions that evoke their emotions.

## Warm Up

**Work with a partner or in a group. Discuss the following questions.**

1. How easy is it for you to transition smoothly to the conclusion of a presentation?
2. Do you often try to end your presentation with a call to action?
3. Do you think asking people to ask themselves a question is effective?

**Sample Presentation Script**

**Read the presentation aloud.**

> **Before I go, I would like to ask you all to do one small thing when you drive home tonight. Just think about the question I brought up a few times during my talk.**
>
> Once again, that question is this: "Am I currently content with the quality of our product?"
>
> If the answer is "yes," that's great. That's a good feeling. You're all set.
>
> If the answer is "no," though, I would like you to know that our team is ready to assist you in making your product more flexible and better able to meet customer expectations.

제가 마치기 전에, 오늘 밤 집에 들어가시면서 한 가지 작은 부탁드리겠습니다. 오늘 프레젠테이션에서 제가 몇 번 언급한 질문에 대해 한번 생각해 보셨으면 합니다.

다시 말씀드리지만, 질문은 바로 이겁니다. '현재 제품 품질에 만족하고 있는가?'

답이 '예'라면 다행입니다. 기분이 좋으시겠어요. 모든 준비가 됐으니까요.

하지만 답이 '아니다'라면, 저희 팀이 고객 기대에 보다 더 유연하고 더 나은 제품을 만드는 데 도움을 드릴 준비가 되어 있다는 점을 알아주시기를 바랍니다.

### Comprehension Check

**Answer the questions.**

1. What is the question the speaker wants the audience to think about?
2. If the answer is "no," what does the speaker want the audience to know?

# Vocabulary

**Match the words or expressions with the correct definitions.**

1. bring up _____
2. once again _____
3. content _____
4. be all set _____
5. flexible _____
6. expectation _____

a. (화제를) 꺼내다, 제시하다
b. 준비되어 있다, 다 끝났다
c. 유연한
d. 다시 한번
e. 기대
f. 만족하는

### ✓ Vocab Test

**Fill in the blanks with the correct words or expressions.**

> bringing this up / once again / content / are all set / flexible / expectations

1. _____ , Max is going to make changes to the manual.
2. I'm _____ with my job.
3. I am _____ because it's important.
4. That didn't meet my _____ at all.
5. The teams _____ to start the project.
6. They're offering a _____ rental plan.

### ⊕ Bonus Resources

**have nothing to lose** 손해 볼 것이 없다

A: So, should I ask for a time extension? 그럼, 기간 연장을 요청할까요?
B: You **have nothing to lose**. If he says "no," nothing changes. If he says "yes," you get the extra time you want.
손해 볼 건 없잖아요. 거절하면, 달라지는 게 없죠. 수락하면 추가로 시간을 얻고요.

have nothing to lose는 '잃을 것이 아무것도 없다'는 뜻으로 사용된다. 현 상황에서 더 이상 나빠지지 않을 것이라는 의미를 말한다.

## Grammar Points

**Read the following and practice making sentences.**

**1. I would like to ask you all to ~**

> I would like to ask you all to ~는 '여러분 모두에게 ~하길 요청합니다'라는 뜻이다. 상황이나 맥락에 따라 요청이 될 수도 있고 지시로 느껴질 수 있으므로, 이 표현을 쓸 때 주의가 필요하다.
>
> 📖 *I would like to ask you all to try it for a few days*. 여러분 모두 며칠 동안 시도해 보시길 바랍니다.

a) I would like to ask you all to _____. 여러분 모두 양손을 들어 주시길 바랍니다.

b) I would like to ask you all to _____.
여러분 모두 그것에 대해 팀과 논의해 보셨으면 합니다.

c) I would like to ask you all to _____.
여러분 모두 여러분의 책 20쪽을 펼쳐 주시길 바랍니다.

**2. Just think about ~**

> 무언가에 대해 생각해 보라고 할 때, 간단하게 Just를 추가하여 think about ~을 사용하면 '한번 생각해 보세요'를 의미한다. 그 뒤에는 명사뿐만 아니라 what, when, where, why, who, how 등이 올 수 있다.
>
> 📖 *Just think about the situation in Singapore.* 싱가포르 상황을 한번 생각해 보세요.

a) Just think about _____. 저희가 왜 이것을 하는지에 대해 한번 생각해 보세요.

b) Just think about _____. 공장에 있는 모든 직원을 한번 생각해 보세요.

c) Just think about _____. CEO의 메모에 대해 한번 생각해 보세요.

 **Practice**

**Making Sentences**

**Practice writing sentences. Then, read your sentences to your partner or group.**

1. That's a good ~

- 
- 
- 

2. I would like you to know ~

- 
- 
- 

**Write**

**Write a short presentation script that asks the audience to do something at the end of a presentation.**

## Real Presentation

**Read the scenario and write down four key items on the flashcard below. Then, conclude your presentation with a call to imagine using the product you've been talking about. When another member of your group presents, use the checklist below.**

Scenario

> You're a sales manager for an electronics company. You've been talking to some potential customers for the new E-Slim Max. You're at the end of your presentation. To wrap up, you ask the audience to imagine using a lighter, faster laptop like yours and to think about all the benefits of owning one. Tell them to ask themselves whether they would be more productive if they got one. If the answer is "no," assume that they are doing well without it. If the answer is "yes," you want them to consider getting the new E-Slim Max.

### Flashcard

| | |
|---|---|
| 1. | 2. |
| 3. | 4. |

| ✓ Presentation Checklist | Y | N |
|---|---|---|
| The presenter made eye contact with the audience. | | |
| The presenter used gestures and body language. | | |
| The presenter spoke clearly and confidently. | | |
| The presenter correctly used words/expressions from the lesson. | | |

 **Homework**

**You are talking to some interested potential customers for your consulting service. Write a part of a presentation where you conclude by asking the audience to ponder a question. Then, shoot a video of yourself giving the presentation. Your presentation should be at least 2 minutes long. Watch your video and think about how you can improve your presentation.**

_____

_____

_____

**Warm Up Sample Answers**
1. It's (not / kind of / pretty) easy for me.
2. (Yes, I / No, I don't) often try to end with a call to action.
3. (Yes, I / No, I don't) think asking people to ask themselves a question is effective.

**Comprehension Check Answers**
1. The question is, "Am I currently content with the quality of our product?"
2. The speaker wants the audience to know that his/her team is ready to assist them in making their product more flexible.

**Vocabulary Answers**
1. a, 2. d, 3. f, 4. b, 5. c, 6. e

**Vocab Test Answers**
1. Once again, 2. content, 3. bringing this up, 4. expectations, 5. are all set, 6. flexible

**Grammar Points Answers**
1. a) raise both your hands b) talk to your teams about it c) open your books to page 20
2. a) why we are doing this b) all the employees in the factory/plant c) the memo from the CEO

**Making Sentences Answers**
1. That's a good (way to talk to people / situation to be in / piece of advice from your boss).
2. I would like you to know (what will happen / two things / the answer to this question).

**Write Sample Answer**
I would like to ask you all to take a moment to look at your phones. Just think about what it would be like to have a much smaller one in your hand.

**Real Presentation Sample Answer**
Before I go, I would like to ask you all to imagine using a lighter, faster laptop like ours. Just think about all the benefits of owning one.
Ask yourself: "If I got one, would I be more productive?"
If the answer is "no," that's fine. That's a nice situation to be in—it means you're doing well.
If the answer is "yes," though, I would like you to consider the new E-Slim Max.

**Homework Sample Answer**
Before I go, I would like to ask you all to ask yourselves this one thing once you get home tonight. Just think about the main question posed during my talk.
Once again, this is the question: "Are we effectively communicating with our team members?"
If the answer is "yes," that's fabulous. That's a good sign. You're doing just fine.
If the answer is "no," though, I would like you to know that you can contact us for a consultation on communication skills. You have nothing to lose.

**Presentation Tip**

# Three Powerful Ways to Conclude Your Presentation
프레젠테이션을 마무리하는 세 가지 효과적인 방법

There is no single right way to end your presentation. However, the following three methods are probably the most common.
프레젠테이션을 올바르게 끝내는 딱 하나의 방법은 없다. 그러나 다음 세 가지 방법은 아마도 가장 흔한 방식일 것이다.

## ① Summarize the main points. 주요 내용을 요약한다.

At the end, you might want to summarize the main ideas of your presentation so that the audience will remember them. Remember to keep the summary to just three main points.
끝나기 전에, 청중이 기억하도록 프레젠테이션의 주요 내용을 요약하는 것이 좋다. 세 가지 핵심 사항으로만 요약하는 것을 기억하자.

- *Let me briefly summarize the main points.* 주요 요점을 간단하게 요약해드리겠습니다.
  *I'd like to summarize what I talked about today.* 오늘 제가 이야기한 내용을 요약하겠습니다.
  *Before we finish, here are the main ideas we discussed.* 끝나기 전에, 저희가 논의한 주요 아이디어는 다음과 같습니다.

## ② Persuade them. 청중을 설득한다.

A lot of times, you have to persuade the audience to do something new or change the way they think.
청중에게 새로운 것을 하도록 설득하거나 그들의 사고방식을 바꾸어야 하는 경우가 많다.

- *I'm convinced that it's the best product for your team.* 이것은 당신 팀에게 가장 좋은 제품임을 확신합니다.
  *Why not give it a chance?* 기회를 한 번 주면 어떨까요?
  *You have nothing to lose by trying it out.* 당신이 이것을 사용해 본다고 해서 잃을 것은 없습니다.

## ③ Ask them to act. 청중에게 행동을 취할 것을 권한다.

This is especially important for sales presentations. You want to get the audience to take a specific action as soon as possible, such as trying out or purchasing your product or service.
이는 특히 세일즈 프레젠테이션에서 매우 중요하다. 청중이 제품이나 서비스를 가능한 한 빨리 사용해 보거나 구매하는 등 구체적인 행동을 하도록 하는 것이 좋다.

- *Let's start using Paragon 5!* Paragon 5를 쓰기 시작합시다!
  *Why wait? Act now!* 기다리실 필요가 있나요? 지금 하죠!
  *Find out more about Paragon 5.* Paragon 5에 대해 더 알아보세요.
  *Register for free at paragon.com.* paragon.com에서 무료로 등록하세요.

# 12 Q&A Sessions

 **Learning Objectives**

- Learners can open up the floor to questions during a presentation.
- Learners can answer each question succinctly.
- Learners can offer to contact a person later with an answer or additional information.

 **Warm Up**

**Work with a partner or in a group. Discuss the following questions.**
1. Do you enjoy Q&A sessions?
2. Are these sessions usually done individually or as a group?
3. What do you do when you don't know an answer to a question?

## Sample Presentation Script

**Read the presentation aloud.**

> **I'm here to help clarify any questions you may have.** So, if you have any, please go right ahead and ask me.
>
> Yes, what's your question?
> Ah, yes, we do offer that smaller model in three different colors. I have the brochures here with me, so right after this, please come see me.
>
> Yes? Great question! **I'll need to do some further research on that and get back to you.** Why don't you give me your business card later?
>
> Okay. Any more questions?

제가 여러분이 궁금하실 수 있는 것에 명확한 답을 드리겠습니다. 질문이 있다면 바로 말씀해 주세요.

네, 궁금한 게 있으신가요?
아, 네, 더 작은 모델은 세 가지 색상으로 제공하고 있습니다. 여기 책자를 가지고 있으니, 끝난 뒤에 바로 저한테 찾아와 주세요.

네? 아주 좋은 질문입니다! 그거에 대해 조금 더 알아보고 연락드려야 할 것 같습니다. 나중에 저에게 명함을 주시면 어떨까요?

좋습니다. 또 다른 질문 있나요?

### ✓ Comprehension Check

**Answer the questions.**

1. The company offers the smaller model in how many different colors?
2. What does the speaker ask the second person to do?

 **Vocabulary**

**Match the words or expressions with the correct definitions.**

1. clarify _____
2. go right ahead _____
3. brochure _____
4. right after _____
5. further _____
6. get back to _____

a. 바로 직후
b. 명확히 하다
c. ~에게 나중에 연락하다
d. 편하게 하세요
e. 추가로
f. 책자

### ✓ Vocab Test

**Fill in the blanks with the correct words or expressions.**

clarify / go right ahead / brochures / right after / further / get back to

1. _____ and say what you think.
2. I need to _____ you on that.
3. Could you _____ something for me?
4. Let's do _____ analysis before we tell the boss.
5. These are some _____ and pamphlets of our products.
6. We start back up _____ lunch.

### ⊕ Bonus Resources

**fire away** (말이나 질문을) 던지다

A: I need to interrupt you for a second and ask you a question.
실례지만 질문 하나만 하겠습니다.

B: Sure. **Fire away**. What's your question? 네. 말씀하세요. 뭐가 궁금하시나요?

fire away는 상대방에게 말이나 질문해도 된다고 할 때 쓴다. 명령처럼 들릴 듯하면 앞에 Please를 넣으면 된다. 원래 fire away는 '사격하기 시작하다', '발포하기 시작하다'를 의미한다.

# Grammar Points

**Read the following and practice making sentences.**

**1. I'm here to help ~**

> I'm here to help ~를 직역하면 '저는 ~을 돕기 위해 여기 왔습니다'지만, 더 정확하게는 '~하도록 제가 도와드리겠습니다'를 말한다. help 뒤에는 실제로 어떤 행동을 할 것인지를 나타내는 동사 원형을 사용하면 된다.
>
> *I'm here to help change the date.* 제가 날짜 변경 도와드리겠습니다.

a) I'm here to help _____. 액션 플랜을 만들 수 있게 제가 도와드리겠습니다.

b) I'm here to help _____. 프로젝트 일정을 완성할 수 있게 제가 도와드리겠습니다.

c) I'm here to help _____. 올해 전략 계획을 짤 수 있게 제가 도와드리겠습니다.

**2. I'll need to ~**

> I'll need to ~는 '저는 ~해야 할 것 같습니다'를 의미한다. need 대신 have를 쓰는 경우도 많다. 무언가를 해야 할 때 must라는 단어가 떠오를 수 있지만, 그 단어는 마치 의무적인 것처럼 느껴지기 때문에 need to를 사용하는 것이 좋다.
>
> *I'll need to check with the team first.* 먼저 팀과 확인해야 할 것 같습니다.

a) I'll need to _____. 그것에 대해 제 상사께 여쭤봐야 할 것 같습니다.

b) I'll need to _____. 오늘 회의는 일찍 마쳐야 할 것 같습니다.

c) I'll need to _____. 온라인으로 더 조사해야 할 것 같습니다.

 **Practice**

**Making Sentences**

**Practice writing sentences. Then, read your sentences to your partner or group.**

1. Please go right ahead and ~

   - 
   - 
   - 

2. Why don't you give me ~?

   - 
   - 
   - 

**Write**

**Write a short presentation script that tells a person asking a question that you'll need to get back to that person later.**

**Real Presentation**

**Read the scenario and write down four key items on the flashcard below. Then, answer some questions from an audience about the availability of some products. When another member of your group presents, use the checklist below.**

Scenario

> You are a salesperson for an office supply company. You've just finished presenting some of your key products to an audience. Now, you are conducting a Q&A session. You answer the first question by saying a particular product was discontinued last winter, after which you add that there are similar products that he or she may like. On the second question about another product, you say that you need to check if there are some left in stock, adding that if the person can wait after the talk while you call the warehouse, you can get them an answer quickly.

### Flashcard

| | |
|---|---|
| 1. | 2. |
| 3. | 4. |

| ✓ Presentation Checklist | Y | N |
|---|---|---|
| The presenter made eye contact with the audience. | | |
| The presenter used gestures and body language. | | |
| The presenter spoke clearly and confidently. | | |
| The presenter correctly used words/expressions from the lesson. | | |

## Homework

**You are talking to some business clients. Write a part of a presentation where you answer some questions about the services you've just talked about. Then, shoot a video of yourself giving the presentation. Your presentation should be at least 2 minutes long. Watch your video and think about how you can improve your presentation.**

---

**Warm Up Sample Answers**
1. (Yes, I / No, I don't) enjoy Q&A sessions.
2. They are usually done (individually / as a group). / It depends on the presentation.
3. I (try not to panic / tell the person I'll get back to him or her later).

**Comprehension Check Answers**
1. The company offers the smaller model in three different colors.
2. The speaker asks the second person to give him/her a business card.

**Vocabulary Answers**
1. b, 2. d, 3. f, 4. a, 5. e, 6. c

**Vocab Test Answers**
1. Go right ahead, 2. get back to, 3. clarify, 4. further, 5. brochures, 6. right after

**Grammar Points Answers**
1. a) create an action plan b) complete the project schedule c) plan this year's strategy
2. a) ask my boss about it/that b) end/finish the meeting early today c) (do/conduct) (more/further) research online

**Making Sentences Answers**
1. Please go right ahead and (ask me anything / have a seat / pick a color).
2. Why don't you give me (a minute to think about it / some options / a call later)?

**Write Sample Answer**
I'll need to ask my engineer about that. Why don't you leave your e-mail address, and I'll contact you in a few days?

**Real Presentation Sample Answer**
I'm here to address any questions you may have about the office supply products I've talked about. So, if you have any, please ask.
Yes, your question?
No, we discontinued that product last winter. We have similar products you might like though, so please come see me after this.
Yes? Good question. I'll need to see if we have some left in stock. If you can stay a few minutes after the talk, I'll call the warehouse and get you a quick answer.
Okay. Anyone else?

**Homework Sample Answer**
I'm here to answer any questions you may have about our services. So, if you have any, please go right ahead and fire away.
Yes, you have a question?
Ah, yes, we do offer one-on-one coaching during the weekends. I have some pamphlets with me, so please come see me after this.
Yes? Great question! I'll need to find out if we can do that seminar online and get back to you. Why don't you leave a business card with me, and I'll get you an answer ASAP?
Okay. Anyone else have any other questions?

**Presentation Tip**

# Conducting a Highly Effective Q&A Session
### Q&A를 매우 순조롭게 진행하기

You've probably already seen some good but generic advice about answering questions during your presentation. Here are a few effective but more unique methods you can try out at your next Q&A session.

프레젠테이션 중 질의응답하는 것에 대해 훌륭하면서도 일반적인 조언을 이미 받았을 것이다. 앞으로 Q&A에서 시도해 볼 수 있는 효과적이면서도 더 독특한 몇 가지 방법을 소개한다.

## ① Prepare some questions yourself. 질문을 사전에 준비한다.

Sometimes you open the floor to questions only to find that no one is willing to be the first to ask one. So, you might prepare some questions and corresponding answers and practice them beforehand. You can have pre-written cards with these questions with you when you start the session. This way, you can "break the ice" for the session, as well as set the tone for the types of questions you want to be asked.

때로는 질문받을 준비가 됐는데 아무도 먼저 질문하려고 하지 않은 경우가 있다. 따라서 사전에 질문과 그에 맞는 답변을 준비하여 연습하는 게 좋다. Q&A를 시작할 때, 미리 써 놓은 질문 카드를 가지고 Q&A를 시작할 수 있다. 그러면 Q&A에서 '서먹서먹한 분위기를 깨면서' 원하는 질문이 나오도록 분위기를 조성할 수 있다.

## ② Get the audience to write questions. 청중에게 질문을 쓰도록 한다.

You might pass out some blank cards in advance so that the audience can write questions as they think of them during your presentation. By getting questions on cards, you spare the audience from having to ask questions out loud, and this also gives you the advantage of reading the questions to the audience yourself.

프레젠테이션 중에 청중이 생각나는 질문을 적을 수 있도록 미리 백지 카드를 나눠줄 수 있다. 카드로 질문을 받으면, 청중이 질문을 큰 목소리로 질문하지 않아도 되므로 청중을 편안하게 할 수 있으며, 직접 청중에게 질문을 읽어 줄 수 있는 장점도 생긴다.

## ③ Get a moderator. 사회자를 구한다.

Obviously, this doesn't need to mean going out and hiring a professional moderator. Instead, this person can be someone from your team or a co-presenter. Working with a moderator, you will seem to have more authority. You will also have more time to think about a question before answering it.

물론 그렇다고 해서 전문 사회자를 고용해야 한다는 의미는 아니다. 대신, 이 사람은 나의 팀원일 수도 있고 공동 발표자일 수도 있다. 사회자와 함께하게 되면 권위를 더 갖춘 것처럼 보일 것이다. 또한 질문에 대한 답을 생각하는 시간을 더 벌 수 있다.

# MEMO